Louis Marshall

Louis Marshall
✦
1856–1929

A Life Devoted to Justice and Judaism

Herbert Alpert

iUniverse, Inc.
New York Bloomington

Louis Marshall
1856–1929

Copyright © 2008 by Herbert Alpert

All rights reserved. No part of this book may be used or reproduced by any means, graphic,electronic, or mechanical, including photocopying, recording, taping or by any information storage retrieval system without the written permission of the publisher except in the case of brief quotations embodied in critical articles and reviews.

iUniverse books may be ordered through booksellers or by contacting:

iUniverse
1663 Liberty Drive
Bloomington, IN 47403
www.iuniverse.com
1-800-Authors (1-800-288-4677)

Because of the dynamic nature of the Internet, any Web addresses or links contained in this book may have changed since publication and may no longer be valid.

The views expressed in this work are solely those of the author and do not necessarily reflect the views of the publisher, and the publisher hereby disclaims any responsibility for them.

ISBN: 978-0-595-48230-6 (pbk)
ISBN: 978-0-595-48882-7 (cloth)
ISBN: 978-0-595-60322-0 (ebk)

Printed in the United States of America

iUniverse Rev. 10/22/08

*This is dedicated to my loving wife, Ettarae.
Without her this work would not, could not,
have been accomplished
and
to our sons and daughters:
Mark, Susan, Carol and Robert,
and to their children.*

They are evidence to us that there is God.

Contents

Preface ix
The Cedar Street "Y" in Syracuse, N.Y. 1910–1945 1
A Providential Wind 4
To New York City 13
The Passport Question 17
Five Interesting Years 36
Florence 40
The Leo Frank Case and the Supreme Court 56
War and Ideals 67
Versailles 1919: The Jewish Aspect 93
Return to Blessed America 109
The Rosenbluth Case 119
Henry Ford's Belated Apology—Fini? 148
1922 and 1926 166
The Twenties—Toward The Jewish Agency 170
Toward the Jewish Agency—Continued 182
Zionists and Non-Zionists—Coming Together 1929 194
The Death of Louis Marshall 199
After Marshall's Death 206
Afterword 211
Bibliography and Other Sources 215
Acknowledgments 221
Index 225

Preface

When I was a child in Syracuse, New York I knew that the Jewish Community Center, the "Y", was once the family home of Jacob and Zilli Marshall and their six children, and that it was given to the Jewish community long ago by their son Louis. For some fifty years Louis Marshall was a shadow in my childhood memory. Then in 1985 I read a book that told of a negotiation in the early 1930s between the German Government and the Zionist Organization. It was hoped that it would enable German Jews to leave Germany, but the negotiation failed. The book made a passing reference to the American Jewish community leaders of the 1920s, and it included Marshall.

I assumed that it was not the man from Syracuse, but when I learned that indeed this national leader was from Syracuse, I looked for a biography of his life. I found two that told of his achievements: *Champion of Liberty* and *Defender of Human Rights*. Both had been out of print for years, but while looking for these books I found many references to Marshall in books and articles by historians and scholars. There was little about his wife, his children, and his personal life. I did discover that Mr. Marshall's personal and career documents were at the Jacob Rader Marcus Center at the American Jewish Archives in Cincinnati, Ohio. It is a large collection covering much of his law career, his activities on behalf of the Jewish people and his family. To examine the collection, one needed permission from grandson Jonathan Marshall or from his sole surviving child George. When I asked the Archives for permission, the archivist advised me that in all probability it would not be given by either of the Marshalls. He was right.

In the succeeding years I leisurely accumulated information from other sources. In 1988, my wife and I visited Israel. Before we left I asked my friend, Dr. Alan L. Berger, then the chairman of the Syracuse University Department of Judaic Studies, if it would be possible, or practical, to look for something about Louis Marshall in Israel. He arranged a meeting with well-known scholar Dr. Moshe Davis at Hebrew University in Jerusalem, but when we arrived in Jerusalem we were informed that Dr. Davis was ill. The meeting was cancelled, but his office arranged for Dr. Menahem Kaufman, who was an esteemed professor at Hebrew University, to meet with us at our hotel. When he arrived he was carrying a large file from the Zionist archives. That was a bit surprising because I had read that Marshall would not join the Zionist organization because he was not in favor of the creation of a Jewish nation. I did not know then that in later years Marshall changed his mind about Zionism. Professor Kaufman showed us that the file was filled with speeches, letters, records and other documents that told of Marshall's relationship with Chaim Weizmann and their joint efforts for Palestine. He said that to learn about Mr. Marshall one would have to read a hundred books. That was many years ago, and more than a hundred books ago. In my memory it was yesterday.

His remark was, of course, rhetorical, an exaggeration to make a point. At that time I had no intention of either finding these books, or writing about him. Actually, in terms of references to, and stories about Mr. Marshall, I have read or referred to somewhat more than that "hundred books."

When we left Israel in 1988, my wife and I flew to London, where George Marshall, the youngest of the Marshall children, lived with his wife. I had written to him, asking if we could visit him after we left Israel, and he agreed. We visited him in the drawing room of his Bellgravia home, and conversed for an hour. He helped to answer some of the questions that I had about the family, especially Louis' loving relationship with his wife Florence. He confirmed that, and also confirmed that since the Marshall family was relatively low income, it had to scrape for funds for Louis to attend Columbia Law College, and therefore it was beneficial for Louis to leave Columbia after one year.

Upon our return home from London, I wrote to George and asked for his permission to go through the collection of Louis Marshall's papers at the American Jewish Archives. Regretfully he refused.

Since any serious examination of Marshall's life was not possible without access to the Marshall papers at the American Jewish Archives, I set the project aside for several years. All in all from the start of my search to my next try was about ten years.

In 1997 I sent an e-mail to the American Jewish Archives in one last attempt to get permission to examine the Marshall Collection. The reply from the then archivist Dr. Abraham J. Peck said that the access restrictions had not been changed, but that he would pass on my request anyway. Three weeks later, I received a congratulatory letter from Dr. Peck with a copy of Jonathan Marshall's letter approving my request. Two months later I arrived in Cincinnati where I met the staff of the archives, as well was members of the faculty of Hebrew Union College. I began a thorough study of the Marshall Collection, and in the course of my visits there, I was granted a fellowship to do research, and present an oral and written report on an aspect of Marshall's life.

I soon realized that very few members of the legal profession, and almost no one outside of the scholarly field knew who he was, and that Marshall's life, his law career, his leadership of the American Jewish Community, and the complete story of Marshall's full life was not yet written.

The Cedar Street "Y" in Syracuse, N.Y. 1910–1945

Memory becomes history, either instantly or eventually or anytime in between. The events of childhood become nostalgia, sweetened, soured even and if not forgotten, history. From younger days, when things are remembered as good or bad, happy or sad, or both, it was the time when we lived at home, but we played at the YMHA. It began for me at the age of nine, in the era when recreation at home was limited for people of quite limited means. Radio was new and addictive, but confining for youngsters. When we said that we went to the "show" it meant the movies. Movies were great, but cost money, and were usually for weekends. Talking about the movies was as much fun as going.

By 1935 the neighborhood where the majority of lower income Jewish families lived had become fairly run-down. The YMHA was in that section of Syracuse on Cedar Street a few blocks from downtown. The "Y" was our country club. From the age of nine, the kids in our neighborhood went to the "Y" almost every day, except Friday, and not before sunset on Saturday. In every season except summer, from Monday to Thursday, right after supper, sneaks, shorts, a shirt, socks, a jock strap (if you owned one) were wrapped inside a rolled up towel. Usually two or more kids met on the street and walked the eight short blocks, making first a left turn for two blocks, then a right for four or five blocks, and finally a left turn onto Cedar and down half a block to the "Y." Depending on the season, it was dark, dusk, or daylight, but there was no hesitation about walking there, ever. On most nights there would be many kids, mostly boys, for gym, for club meetings, for ping pong or shooting pool.

It had been the home of a wealthy family, and had been remodeled to house club rooms and game rooms, with shower and locker rooms in the ancient basement. It was connected to an adjacent building that had a gymnasium that doubled as a dance hall and a theater for plays. In the foyer there was a large photograph of the man who had given his house to the community. The man had white hair, paunchy and an unsmiling face, as was typical of pictures of older people. We knew that his name was Louis Marshall, a rich Jewish lawyer who had lived in the house before moving to New York City years ago. There were several organizations in the community that bore his name: The Louis Marshall Lodge of B'nai Brith and a young men's club called the Marshall Society. I do not recall anyone who ever asked about him or why he was important.

Jacob and Zilli Marshall lived in Syracuse for more than fifty years. They had two sons and four daughters, living comfortably on Cedar Street for most of those years. Jacob had a successful hide and leather business which became a partnership when his younger son Benjamin entered into the business. Jacob was retired, and eighty years old when Zilli died at 84 in 1910. He moved to Philadelphia to live with one of his daughters and her husband.

At that time all of the children were married, Benjamin being the only one living in Syracuse. With the parents gone the children arranged to make their family home available to the Syracuse Jewish community, with provisos that the building would be used as a center for Jewish activities. The older son, Louis made the legal and communal arrangements, incorporating the "Zilli Marshall Memorial Society." Its charter said that the objects of the organization were to promote religious, educational, charitable and benevolent objects among the Jews of the city of Syracuse and the perpetuation of its history and traditions, and to that end to afford facilities to other organizations now or hereafter existing in the city of Syracuse. Louis spoke at the presentation ceremony in 1910:

> On behalf of my father, I now deliver to the Marshall Memorial Society, for the benefit of the Jewish community of Syracuse, a deed conveying the premises in which we are now gathered.... Regarding this home as a sacred shrine, my father felt that it would best tend to perpetuate the memory of our dear departed and to extend the sphere of her radiant influence, to dedicate it such works as would tend to preserve in the community with which she had so long been identified, that true spirit of Judaism which she so faithfully cherished ... She had, from its foundation, taken an active interest in the Council of Jewish Women. She was convinced that so long as the mothers and daughters of Israel devoted themselves to the study of the Bible, to the glorious history of our people and our faith, to the perpetuation of our traditions and the inculcation to the principles of our religion, the future would be secure ... She stimulated her own children to take an active part in all movements that made for the betterment of mankind, and especially for the elevation of their brethren in faith.

Marshall who wrote poetry all of his life recited a poem dedicated to his mother:

> Full fifty years within these hallowed walls
> Here piety a godly altar reared,
> Unswerving Faith attended unafeared,
> And Righteousness with mercy mild instilled,
> The course of life and conduct safely steered;
> A simple Jewish home, with blessings filled.

With this gesture, the center of activities for many present and future members of the Syracuse Jewish community was created. This was the foundation for a YMHA in the city for people with limited means, a blessing for those who had emigrated to the U.S., and were intent on success. "The Cedar Street Y" was the Marshall family home from the second half of the nineteenth century until it was given to the Jewish community of Syracuse in 1910.

The YMHA faced many financial and social problems almost from its beginning, particularly during World War I when funds were needed to alleviate the suffering of the Jews in Eastern Europe. From then on, for twenty-five years, the Center was the place, along with synagogues, for much of Jewish communal life. When World War II came there were many changes as a result of the loss of young people who were called into military service as well as the aging of facilities. The "Y" began its decline. By 1945 it was no longer used, and communal activities took place at various synagogues.

From the Marshall family home, through the Syracuse YMHA to an appreciation of a great American-Jewish human being, for me it has been a long, rewarding odyssey

A Providential Wind

Louis Marshall was born on Sunday, December 14, 1856 in Syracuse, N.Y.

On Tuesday December 16, 1856 *The Syracuse Daily Standard* reported:

DAMAGE BY THE WIND

A violent hailstorm passed over this city on Sunday evening accompanied by a high wind which blew off the steeple of the Jewish Synagogue on Mulberry St. and the west balustrade from the roof of the First M.E. Zion Church. The damage to the M.E. Church was not very serious, but the beautiful spire of the Synagogue was entirely demolished, and a brood of doves which made the steeple their meeting place were killed. The wind also made free with various sign boards about town, but we hear of no serious damage except that mentioned above.

Louis Marshall's youngest son, George, was 83 when he mentioned this incident in a letter to the writer written in 1987: "It is my understanding, that on the night of December 14, 1856, when my father Louis Marshall was born, a high wind blew off the steeple of the Society of Concord Synagogue. This was next door to my grandparents' house, where my father was born."

Jacob and Zilli Marshall lived on the third floor of the house next door to the synagogue, and if the synagogue's steeple had fallen to the north, instead of to the south, Zilli Marshall and her newborn son might not have survived. That elegant steeple, evidence of a nod by the synagogue to the church architecture in the United States, was never to be replaced although the congregation used the building until 1911.

In the early nineteenth century, the Jewish population in America numbered approximately 6,000. Between 1820 and 1860, a surge of immigrants increased that number to 150,000. Many came from sections of southern Germany where a young Jewish man faced a very limited economic future. Often he was not allowed to establish a business or even have a family unless there was a place available due to a death or departure of a person or a family. To succeed he would have to leave his town, and Bavarian cities were to be avoided. With transportation to the New World available and relatively inexpensive, a young man could migrate to the United States, go to communities in the eastern United States where Germans had settled, and would offer assistance.

Jacob Marschall was one those young men. Southern Germany was rife with revolution and, as elsewhere in Central Europe; it offered few opportunities for Jews. In some small towns, young Jews were even encouraged to leave and given funds to do so by the community. Poor, energetic and Jewish, nineteen-year-old Jacob left Neidenstein, Bavaria in 1849.

Many years later his son Louis Marshall received a letter from a man who questioned him about having "such a distinctly Christian appelation (sic) as Marshall." He replied: "one of my favorite jokes is that when my father (Jacob Marschall) came to this country in 1849, after being on a sailing vessel for nearly fifty days, during all of which time he was seasick, he crossed the "c" out of his name."[1]

Jacob landed in the U.S on September 1, 1849 with only a five franc piece, the equivalent of ninety-five cents, and no means of assistance. He tried peddling goods but came down with typhoid fever; and while ill his goods were stolen.

A job as a track-hand on the construction of the Northern Central Railroad got Jacob as far as Canandaigua in west central New York State. After the construction contractor ran off without paying his workers, Jacob found work on the Erie Canal, the important gateway to the west. Eventually he came to Syracuse, a bustling community in the center of New York State and an important port on the Erie Canal. There were many German immigrants as well as a small Jewish immigrant community. Here he could practice his Judaism without hindrance. He became the proprietor of a small fruit and grocery store. Within a few years he started a business selling hides and leather and operated it until his retirement.

In 1849, when he arrived in America, he could not have dreamed that his first child, a son born seven years later, would be mourned throughout the United States and Europe when he died eighty years hence.

In 1853, Jacob met Zilli Strauss, a recent émigré from Wurttembourg, Germany. They were married in 1855 and settled in the section of Syracuse where other Jewish families lived.

Years later, on April 14, 1926, Louis Marshall wrote a letter to Senator David A. Reed, who had made a statement that appeared to belittle the misfortunes of stranded immigrants. In the letter, Marshall said, "This is the one hundredth anniversary of my mother's birth. She came here in a sailing vessel in 1853. The journey to Halifax took sixty-three days. The ship was brought into port by mutineers. She finally succeeded in reaching Syracuse, N.Y., with her brother and sister, after going through indescribable experiences. It is not improper for me to say that my mother became the best American that I have ever known and all that I will ever know and all that I have ever accomplished in life has been due to her influence."[2]

They lived in a flat that was on the top floor of a three-story house next door to the synagogue, Knesset Shalom, which was then an Orthodox congregation but would change to Reform Judaism in the next decade. The Marshalls remained active members of the synagogue while continuing to observe the Orthodox Jewish traditions.

Like many of their fellow immigrants, the family struggled, yet succeeded. When Jacob and Zilli spoke of their origins, they displayed no longing for the old country. "My parents ... experiences in Germany," Louis Marshall would later recall, "were of the most bitter kind, such as were little calculated to inspire love or tender recollections[3] ... we have taken great pride in our American citizenship, and have sought to perpetuate American ideals."[4]

After Louis came five more children; Benjamin, Marie, Bertha, Clara, and Ida, the youngest, born in 1870. In the Syracuse 1860 census Jacob's occupation was "fruit dealer", though by then he was in the leather and hide business, and he declared the value of his assets as "Value—Real (property) $900, Personal $800." Two children were listed "Lewis (sic) 3, Benjamin 1."

Zilli Marshall was self-educated with a taste for great literature. When Louis was very young, she would have him follow her from room to room, reading aloud in German as she did her housework. She taught him to memorize passages from Schiller, Scott and Hugo in German. In later years Marshall wrote, "I spoke German before I knew a word of English, and so long as my mother lived I never spoke to her otherwise than in German. From my earliest days she inspired me with a love of German literature, and especially its poetry. She had a marvelous memory, could recite almost every one of Schiller's poems by heart, and could repeat a German translation of Scott's Ivanhoe. She encouraged me to write essays and looking back seventy two years I can say without any qualification that she was the greatest influence upon my life."[5]

"I worshipped [at the Society of Concord] from my boyhood until I left Syracuse, and in the basement of which I attended religious school. My uncle had a shoe shop ... and it used to be my habit to come there early in the morning before I went to school, to read the *Syracuse Daily Courier* aloud to him and his workmen."[6]

When he was eight years old, Marshall worked in his father's store, doing odd jobs as well as keeping the books. In school, he became "certified" for admission to the "Academic Class" and when he entered Syracuse High School he was admitted to the debating club.

When Marshall was thirteen, he wrote a letter to George Brown, who had been his friend in school and had moved away. The letter's opening remarks, written in a florid handwriting that did not survive his adolescence, exhibit his precocious ability to communicate eloquently:

> "Dear Friend!
> The object of writing this letter is to give you a discription (sic) of something which you may not as yet have heard, viz; the street railroad." He describes the leveling and the paving of "the ground" and the laying of the tiles and rails on the city's streets. When completed, "the cart is drawn by horses, [and] is pretty large being about 15 ft long and 5 ft. wide, and commonly painted yellow ... if anyone wants to get on the car while it is in motion, he may just signify his intention to the conductor, who rings the bell and the car stops. The fare is commonly 6 cts ... The street railroads are of great use to schoolboys, who have to go a great distance ... habitually riding them costs a great deal of money during the year." This depiction of the beginning of the era of streetcar public transportation in a small city concludes: ... "the car, jogging, threw me forward upon the floor, and thereby sprained my ankle. I remain your good friend, Louis Marshall."[7]

His vocabulary and ability to describe an ordinary event in vivid detail foreshadow his future career. Marshall at age 13 had already decided to be a lawyer.

Marshall and Joseph Stolz were first cousins and friends maintaining a close relationship throughout their lives. Stolz, the son of David Stolz and Regina Strauss Stolz, Zilli Marshall's sister, was the Rabbi of a large Reform Temple in Chicago for more than forty years. The following is from *"Memories of Joseph Stolz"* written February 23, 1933:

> My mother was quite a favorite of Louis, and I have heard her tell that, during the Civil War, she made him a soldier's suit with brass buttons in which he loved to parade, which also might account for his militant spirit.
>
> We had German and Hebrew School every day but Friday, including Saturday and Sunday, and twice daily in vacation. Louis Marshall and Nathan Jacobson were the star-pupils. Being an ungraded school, they served as volunteer assistants to look over our figures and dictation in German spelling.
>
> When I was about twelve years old ... and Louis having graduated from High School and being a law student in a private office, my father prevailed

upon him to become the Hebrew and German teacher of the three of us and of his three sisters. In the summertime we sat under the trees in our back yard receiving dictation in German of Greek and Roman mythology and biblical history, and droning out the Hebrew alphabet in a sing-song original with us.

As I recall it, we studied with Louis about six months, until my Bar Mizva. Louis wrote my Bar Mizva speech in German upon the text Ps. 119.9 'wherewithal shall a young man keep his way pure? By taking heed according to thy word' which I delivered in the Schul, in the morning, and repeated at the family dinner at home, as well as the grace after meals (Benshen).

I also remember Louis' Bar Mizva. He recited in the temple the whole catechism in German, by heart; and I recall how my mother objected that in times like these his parents allowed him to swear before the open ark that he would never violate the Sabbath day.

Since then I have thought what a distinction it was to have been instructed by so distinguished a man in Israel. Louis gave me a present of Scott's *Ivanhoe* and *Quentin Durward*, and my father gave him Schlosser's *Welt-geschichte*, which he said helped him in the debates in which he loved to indulge, [and] gave him the material to take either side of a question.

Louis loved outdoor sports and I remember how after services on Saturday morning we all went to Jacobson and Whelan's yard on Cedar St., near Orange, and indulged very heartily in games of baseball or cricket. This was the only day in the week we had free.

Louis indulged in athletic games with much zest, always eager to be on the winning side; but his greatest pleasure was to be in debates and to get the decision in this intellectual competition.

I was very often present as a listener and younger onlooker at the debates of the 'Progress Club' [on] Sunday in the basement of the temple. Usually the leaders of the opposite sides were Louis and Nathan Jacobson. This not only gave them facility in debating, but prepared them pre-eminently for the practice of the profession of the law … acquiring readiness of speech and learning to think quickly while on their feet.

Uncle Jacob Marshall was engaged in buying hides, wool, etc. He went on the road Monday mornings and usually came home Fridays, attending services on Saturday. He usually unpacked the week's purchases in the barn back of their house on Sunday mornings. Louis and Benjamin were usually of great assistance to their father, learning the practical, getting practical business experience etc.. Especially during the long vacation in the summer did they have the hard work of packing wool in the sacks. Very young did Louis keep books for his father, and thus did he gain the practical business experience which stood him in good stead, later in life.

His father thought that Louis could do almost anything, and he recommended him, when still in high school, to keep the books and minutes of the Congregation, Society of Concord, in German. He did this for several years, and thus had his training for the Secretaryship of Temple Emanuel and got his taste for Congregational life early.

I left Syracuse for Cincinnati to attend the Hebrew Union College, August 30, 1878, accompanied by my father. Louis I think had just come back from Columbia College, N.Y., a full-fledged lawyer, and took much interest in my venture to Cincinnati, writing a letter in my behalf to Jacob Ezekiel, Secretary of the Board of Governors. He also gave me some spending money each year as I left for Cincinnati after my summer vacation.

My father came to America in 1857 from Austria. I often heard him say that he was the only one in the family that subscribed for a newspaper. Louis read the morning newspaper, the *Democratic Daily Courier*, on his way to or from school, aloud to the shoemakers in (uncle) Jacob Stolz's shoeshop, and thus got his first interest in the politics of his country and the welfare of his native land to which he contributed so much as a constitutional lawyer; a friend of the immigrant, the poor, the oppressed, a lover of liberty; a Jew; a lover not only of our American institutions, but of the very soil of America, and all that grows upon it, the very trees of the forests.

Because he so passionately loved our country, N.Y. State, and especially Syracuse, did he, for 18 years, affectionately preside over the destinies of the Forestry College of the Syracuse University, which he was instrumental in founding and bringing to Syracuse.[8]

In Syracuse High School Marshall was a member of the debating club, and at graduation in June 1874 he delivered an oration "The Genius of the English Language". Marshall and his friend Nathan Jacobson were the first Jewish boys to graduate from the school.

Two years of apprenticeship [in a law office] gave him enough resources to allow him to spend a period of study in Columbia College Law School in New York City.[9]

On March 9, 1929, Marshall received a letter from Harold R. Medina of the Alumni Association of Columbia Law School. In response he wrote:

> I really do not know whether I am considered as an alumnus of the Law School of Columbia University or not. If I am, then it is very peculiar that it has not been until I have arrived at the mature age of seventy-two that I should receive a letter which is addressed to me as a "Dear Fellow Alumnus." I attended the Law School from September, 1876 to June, 1877. During that time I took not only the courses of the junior and senior years, but also every special course of lecture held at the school and participated in the argument ... of law submitted weekly either before the school or the Dwight Club, or wrote an opinion or a brief upon the question submitted. I never received a degree because two years actual attendance was required. I know nothing about the rules of the Association and am therefore unable to express an opinion as to whether or not this enables me to ascend to the cerulean heights of membership.

He was acclaimed by Columbia Professor Dwight as a "genius."[10]

He returned to Syracuse, and studied law in the office of Ruger, Wallace and Jenney one of the leading law firms in the city. When he was admitted to the bar in 1878, the firm added Marshall's name. Mr. Ruger would eventually be elected the Chief Judge of the New York State Court of Appeals. One of the partners became Dean of Syracuse University Law School; the others left for other cities. The firm continued as Jenney and Marshall and when William S. Jenney, son of the firm's partner, graduated from Princeton Law School he joined in the firm. He studied under Marshall for almost five years.

Jenney wrote to Samuel Untermyer after Marshall's death in 1929:

> In those days the Bar of Syracuse was accustomed to work at their offices in the evening as well as in the day time. Almost without exception Mr. Marshall worked from nine in the morning until midnight, going home for his lunch and dinner. He became so familiar with the leading New York cases ... in which the firm was engaged that, with respect to the ordinary ... negligence, I have often heard him dictate a brief, citing cases and quoting from opinions without leaving his desk or looking at a law book ... I doubt if any lawyer of this or any other time had in his head the knowledge

of cases, of both New York State and the United States Supreme Court, that Mr. Marshall did.

> While living at Syracuse he had little outside interests except his profession. Perhaps the most remarkable case I recall his conducting was the defense of a Catholic priest before a Church Tribunal, which he not only briefed but argued orally in Latin.[11]

On December 2, 1927 Marshall wrote to William Fox, the founder of Fox Films:

> When I attended the public schools of Syracuse, and I can assure you that ordinarily the relations between the Jews and non-Jews were most friendly, the Bible was read every morning by the teachers in charge of the various grades. Ordinarily the readings were from the New Testament, and usually I enjoyed them, although there were times when they were not what they should have been. The Catholic boys and girls withdrew when the Bible reading began, and I always honored them and their parents for this action and later regretted that I did not withdraw. On Good Fridays, however, the readings always related to the crucifixion and the teachers seemed to have the habit of intoning their reading, and especially when the word 'Jew' was mentioned in such a manner as to convey the idea not only of contempt but also of hatred.
>
> This was always followed during the recess and for several days after by the most hostile demeanor on the part of the Christian boys and girls of the school, some of whom resorted to physical violence and most of them to the calling of names and the making of scurrilous remarks.[12]

Notes

1 Reznikoff V1 Pg 6
2 Ibid Pg 235
3 Ibid Pg 6
4 Ibid Pg 7
5 Ibid Pg 5
6 Ibid Pg 7
7 AJA-MC Letter to George brown May 19, 1870
8 AJA-MC Memories of Joseph Stolz
9 Reznikoff Vl Pg xi of the introduction by Oscar Handlin. The name, Columbia Law College, would become Columbia law School.
10 Reznikoff V1 Pg 8
11 Ibid Pgs 8-9
12 AJA-MC Letter to William Fox

To New York City

In 1894 Louis Marshall was invited by his classmate at Columbia Law College, Samuel Untermyer, to join his law firm in New York City as a partner. Marshall accepted, and soon became part of a New York City group of successful Jews who had either emigrated from Germany or were the offspring of those who had come to America earlier.

In late 1894, Marshall and Untermyer went to the opera, where Untermyer introduced Marshall to his cousin Florence Lowenstein. Florence was twenty-two, Marshall was thirty-eight. A romance apparently blossomed, because within a brief period, Louis asked if he might call on her. She wrote to him:

"My Dear Mr. Marshall,

Owing to a feeling of deference due to my uncle's wishes, I cannot accept your very kind and courteous invitation. Please do not consider that I lack in appreciation of your generosity, but believe me to be honestly grateful. You know that I am always pleased to see you. Hence, whenever you feel inclined to call, be at all times assured of a hearty welcome, from

Yours very sincerely,
Florence Lowenstein

February 28, 1895"

It was the era of instant delivery. On that same day he replied:

"My Dear Miss Lowenstein,

Although your declination of my invitation has caused me pain, yet I cannot fail to admire the high sense of duty, which has activated it. Availing myself of the welcome which you have accorded to me, I must ask you not to deem me too persistent, if I request you to receive me on Saturday evening. I have much to say to you.

Very truly yours,
Louis Marshall

February 28, 1895"

Apparently he did have "much to say", because one week later they were engaged. Her letter to him on that day began: "My Dear Kind Louis". Formal letters were a thing of the past, and they were married on May 6, 1895. Florence was a contented partner of her prestigious Louis and a devoted mother to their four children: James, Ruth, Robert and George. In the twenty years of their marriage, they continually stressed their love for each other.

In his careers, Marshall was sometimes characterized as stern, stubborn, unswerving, intractable, and self centered, even cold. But, in the twenty years of their marriage, he often traveled and in their daily letters, he often wrote that he was her lover. The letters are beautiful; their ardor never left them. When she died of cancer at age 42, he was grief stricken, and was afflicted with insomnia. He would write to their children about her, notably on birthdays or anniversaries, or the annual observance of her death. He never remarried.

Florence's family history in America began when her grandfather Benedict Lowenstein and his two brothers immigrated to the United States in 1848 from the southern part of Germany. They landed in New Orleans, Louisiana, and started in a business common to many immigrants of the era; selling goods from a pushcart or wagon. They worked their way to Memphis, Tennessee, where they opened a dry-goods store that would eventually become Lowenstein's Department Store.

Benedict became the cotton buyer for the business. He often traveled to New York City, there he made the acquaintance of young Sophia Mendelson.

Her father Nathan Mendelson had also come from Germany to the United States, settling in Lynchburg, Virginia, where he met and married Adelhide Untermyer. They moved to New York City, where Sophia was born.

Adelhide's relatives in Virginia were southerners. Her father Isidor Untermyer owned land, grew tobacco and prospered. At the outbreak of the Civil War, he joined the Confederate Army, serving as a lieutenant. When he returned home after the war ended, he found his plantation despoiled and much of his property gone. He died soon after. Without opportunities to support or educate their children in Virginia, the Untermyers moved to New York City to be with relatives Nathan and Adelhide Mendelson.

In New York Benedict Lowenstein met their daughter Sophia. He had become a solid citizen of the United States, apparently untouched by the ravages of the Civil War. He and Sophia married in 1866, had a son and five daughters, with the youngest born after Benedict died at age 47 in 1879. Sophia died five years later, at 37. The orphaned family was kept together by their bachelor uncle Bernard Lowenstein and a housekeeper and the families from Virginia who provided family warmth and support.

Due to the attention and wherewithal of uncle Bernard, the parentless Lowenstein children grew up in a comfortable environment. Florence was educated at Hunter Normal College.

From their beginning Florence and Louis were active members of Manhattan's prestigious Temple Emanu-El, and Marshall would quickly become a member of its board. With his great interest in Jewish affairs, he gained a prominent foothold in the Jewish community. Eventually, Marshall would become president of the Temple, a position that enabled him to nurture sound friendships with key figures in the New York City Jewish social scene. All were bound by a deep concern for the well being of their fellow Jews.

By 1901 Marshall and his friends, the majority being members of Temple Emanu-El, had developed a deep interest in the Jewish Theological Seminary. Banker and philanthropist Jacob Schiff spearheaded this movement. The Seminary, founded in the late 1800s to cultivate rabbis for the Conservative Jewish movement, had not gained enough public support to continue. Schiff had bought land on Upper Broadway in Manhattan to build a library and made the land available to the Seminary. This small group of benefactors, mainly Reform Jews, used that as a springboard to reorganize the Seminary. Marshall and his close friend Cyrus Adler were the active leaders of the rejuvenated school. Solomon Schechter was a well-regarded rabbinic scholar and professor at Cambridge University and University College in England. Adler and Judge Mayer Sulzberger knew Schechter and invited him to come from England to be the dean of the Seminary. On March 1, 1904 Schechter was given a contract which stated that he was to receive an annual salary of $6,500 for the first year and increases of $500 for each of the next two years. For his family's protection he was given a life insurance policy for $10,000. He attracted a distinguished faculty composed of scholars and rabbis and he was instrumental in founding the United Synagogue of America in 1913. He served for thirteen successful years, until he died in 1915. Jacob Schiff suggested that Mrs. Mathilde Schechter be given more than the $10,000 insurance. Schiff and Marshall exchanged letters that suggested varying increases of the insurance proceeds. Finally, they agreed on and paid his family $100,000. Solomon Schechter would become an icon for future generations of Jews.

With increasing vision and drive these men, Jacob Schiff, Cyrus Adler, Marshall and others of their station founded the American Jewish Committee in 1906. An executive committee member from its inception, Marshall would represent the AJC throughout his life in all of its major activities.

Note

AJA-MC

The Passport Question

In 1902, as Marshall approached his middle years he could take satisfaction in his life. He had married Florence Lowenstein, a fine young woman sixteen years his junior and they had a daughter and three sons all between six years of age and newborn. He was established in his career as an attorney in New York City after successfully practicing in Syracuse, New York for sixteen years. He was known in Albany, New York and in Washington D.C. as a fine business lawyer, an expert on the U.S. Constitution, and a defender of individual rights.

He was active in Jewish circles and a loyal member of Reform Congregation Emanu-El, and supporter of all movements in Judaism. He and his friends had recognized the need of the Orthodox Jewish immigrants from Europe who would not follow Reform Judaism. The Jewish Theological Seminary was a seminary begun in 1887 to educate and graduate rabbis for a fledgling Conservative movement. After almost fifteen years of limited success it was languishing and its survival was in question. In 1901-02 a group of concerned Jews led by Jacob Schiff, Cyrus Adler, Marshall and others reorganized and rejuvenated the seminary with their money and their dedication. It was an important step in the progress of the American Jewish community. The next step for this group would be the formation of the American Jewish Committee.

By the year 1906, his passions for justice and Judaism were the motivation of Louis Marshall's life.

In 1908 Marshall would face the most challenging contest of his life to date. As an individual and in concert with other leaders in a matter of United States national integrity and moral significance, galvanized by his passions for American Law and Judaism, he assumed a pivotal role in confronting an international issue that would advance his progress as a leader of American Jewry and a champion of human rights.

In1832 the venerable Russian Empire and the young United States of America entered into a treaty intended to inspire trade between the two nations. It was also an enlightened pact that guaranteed the right of Russians and Americans to travel freely within each other's countries. From 1865 to 1880 there were sporadic cases in which Russia would not readily honor passports of American Jews wishing to visit or conduct business on her soil. In this she remained constant and unyielding. For more than thirty years the United States would protest Russia's unjust policy. There were complaints from members of Congress, and protests by State Departments in eight United States Administrations, but the State Departments did not consider these incidents serious enough to move the Congress to suggest discontinuing the Treaty. The U.S. Government protests were ignored as Russia remained constant and unyielding. However, by 1906 there were popular movements by sympathetic Americans other than Jews advocating annulment of the Treaty.

Even though Russia and the U.S. had enjoyed amicable relations for the better part of a century, the problems with the 1832 treaty became an increasingly contentious issue. Not content with blocking American passports, Russia insisted that foreign Jews traveling on Russian soil in the nineteenth and twentieth centuries were subject to the same discriminatory laws that applied to Russian Jews.

Why had it come to this in 1911?

Seeds of dissent were planted in Eastern Europe in the late eighteenth century when Catherine II (the Great) of Russia seized a portion of Poland and found herself saddled with a large concentration of Jews.[1]

Russia imposed crippling restraints on the lives of its Jews. They could settle only in restricted, often barren regions. They could work only in a few occupations. Some prospered as merchants, middlemen, and moneylenders. Most suffered from limited economic opportunity and unbridled religious discrimination. All lived under the constant threat of outbreaks of organized anti-Semitic violence, the pogroms.

The Treaty of 1832 had functioned well enough since inception as a means of bolstering commerce between Russia and the United States, but it also dictated the interactions of people and in this it was a source of great injustice. When Russia engaged in harsh treatment of naturalized Americans citizens who returned for business or to visit family, it violated the spirit, if not the principle of the treaty.

In 1879 a man, one T. Rosenstraus went back to Russia to start a sewing machine company. After arranging to purchase property, he was denied legal title to the land and complained to United States authorities. A resolution was subsequently introduced to Congress. It read, in part:

> Whereas the Russian Government has discriminated against one T. Rosenstraus, a naturalized citizen of the United Sates, by prohibiting him from holding real estate after his purchasing some, because of his being an Israelite ... if existing treaties ... be found, as is alleged, to discriminate ... as to any

classes of our citizens, the President is requested to take immediate action, to have the treaties so amended as to remedy this grievance.[2]

The House of Representatives passed the resolution on June 10, 1879. No action was taken.

Then, a sudden and deadly event in 1881 spelled upheaval for Russia and disaster for her Jews. Russian revolutionaries had assassinated Czar Alexander II; some were thought to be Jews. Fevered suspicion whipped mobs of Russians into an anti-Semitic frenzy as pogroms raged throughout the country. In Kiev, for example, few Jewish homes were left unharmed

These assaults did not go unnoticed in the United States. Representative Samuel Cox identified 167 places where riots, burning, pillaging, and murder took a ruinous toll. Russian government officials stood accused of complying with and even implementing the pogroms. Desperate Jews fled Russia in droves, most seeking refuge in the United States where they became citizens.

As with all émigrés from Russia, the Czar's Government was adamant about one thing: those who had not gained permission from Russia to become citizens of their newly adopted countries were subject to Russian law. Despite objections by the United States, the 1832 treaty maintained that Russia could treat American Jews on her soil in the same way that she dealt with Russian Jews. Representative Dungan from Ohio asked for a joint resolution by Congress to sever diplomatic relations with Russia. It was not supported.

Instances of discrimination against American Jewish citizens by Russia continued. In 1882 Congressman Samuel Cox presented several resolutions in Congress imploring the U.S. Government to "exercise its influence with the Government of Russia to stay the spirit of persecution as directed against the Jews, and protect the citizens of the United States resident in Russia."[3]

In 1883, 1884, 1896, and 1892 Congressional resolutions protested Russian treatment of Jews who were former Russian subjects and who had become U.S. citizens. They complained because they were subject to the same discriminatory laws as were applied to Russian Jews, or they were threatened with expulsion. A number of diplomatic protests proved ineffective.

Violent attacks against the Jews of Russia began to wane by 1891, but abusive incidents continued to encourage immigration to the United States.

Within Russia the "Jewish Problem" persisted, but repression extended beyond the world of the Jews. Imprisoned Russians lived under despicable conditions, subjected to hunger, icy weather, illness, overcrowding, as well as an excessively brutal police force.⁴ Good will between America and Czarist Russia was diminishing.

American journalist George Kennan wrote and spoke passionately about life in Russia during these times. From 1885 to 1890 he traveled there to interview people and to investigate the conditions under which Russians lived. Published in the popular *Century Magazine* and other periodicals, his findings exposed the tyranny in the Czarist state. Kennan's books about exiles to Siberia drew attention to the situation, sparking anger in the U.S. and other countries. Empowered, Kennan lectured, and organized groups to protest,⁵ but his efforts met with limited success.

In February 1893, Pierre Botkine, secretary of the Russian legation in Washington spoke up, and quoted in *Century Magazine*:

> Which was the first of the nations to extend to you a brotherly hand and to bring you moral support from abroad, in the hour of trial during your civil war? I need not remind you that it was Russia; the story of the arrival of our fleet at the port of New York in that period is yet fresh in the memory of the appreciative American people.⁶

Pogroms in Russia decreased in the early 1890s; life for her Jews did not improve. For the most part Jewish Russians existed on the edge of peril, their lives defined by poor living conditions and meager possibilities. As the century turned, pogroms exploded across the land with renewed ferocity.

Infamous Easter Holiday sermons of 1903 inflamed the public at large as incendiary news reportage kindled mob anger. Outbursts of burning, raping, plundering, and killing rained upon the Jews of Kishinev, capital of Bessarabia. Czarist officials took no action.⁷ In a moment of supreme irony, Russia's ambassador to the United States blamed the Jews themselves for arousing anti-Semitism among the peasants in and around Kishinev. American friends offered to send aid. Russian authorities refused. The Jews of Kishinev, they said, were not suffering.⁸ Fervent outcries shook the Western World as outrage spread beyond America to Jew and non-Jew alike. Protest meetings were held. William Randolph Hearst's newspapers criticized Russia, urging the Secretary of State to voice objection. Condemnations of the Kishinev horrors went via diplomatic channels to the Czar and a number of Russians were eventually brought to trial. Just two were convicted and sentenced to jail for five and seven years. Twenty-two others received even lighter sentences. Further legal actions ended in acquittals or dismissals.

In 1904 Russia had more important concerns than the treaty with America. She was at odds with Japan over eastern territories in Asia. The Japanese feared Russian influence in Asia, and Russia eyed expansion into Siberia. Russia with more white people than any other nation on earth, urged the white world to join forces against the so-called yellow peril: the "half-civilized country" of Japan. [9]

If Russia were to overcome Japan, heathen Korea and barbaric Manchuria would be ripe for conversion to the Russian Orthodox Faith. However, if Japan were to defeat Russia, all Asia would be lost to Christianity.

Without warning Japan broke off diplomatic relations with Russia. Japanese warships attacked the Russian navy at Port Arthur, China. A number of American newspapers praised the "clever and plucky Japanese," who had caught mighty Russia napping.[10] Russia, irate and humiliated, fumed. (Almost thirty-eight years later, in 1941, when Japan attacked the United States at Pearl Harbor in a similar manner, America had no praise for the "plucky Japanese.")

War plunged Russia into turmoil. Public protestations stormed across the land over the high casualties and the blunt fact that Mother Russia was losing the war. Americans openly scorned Czarism and the shabby way the country treated its dissidents and its Jewish minority. In America there was little sympathy for Russia and her defeat in the war with Japan.

President Theodore Roosevelt arranged for the peace treaty signing in September 1905 in Portsmouth, New Hampshire. In 1905 there was a failed attempt at revolution against the Czar's Government. Perhaps in retaliation there was renewed anti-Semitism and fierce pogroms, most notably in the city of Kishinev. Jewish immigration to the United States increased.

Roosevelt did not ignore the problem of the Passport Question, but at this point Russia had no interest in changing any part of a treaty mutually agreed upon in 1832.

In 1906 a group of Jewish men who called themselves "The Wanderers" and had been meeting socially for discussions, decided to establish an organization that would address Jewish problems in America and elsewhere. It was not a new idea but to these men the time had come for a national organization. At that time the Jewish population in America was composed largely of those who had embarked on a new life in a strange country. It was not unheard of for Jews to run from persecution or from poverty, or endure eviction for two millennia, and for these same reasons they came to America. But there was one significant difference between their native countries and America. It was probably the only country in modern history that did not have laws applicable to Jews. They were left to themselves in a place where they could live as they wanted, but with the primary obstacles of language and learning. And there was a significant difference in religious life. Poverty was not limited to the European places where they were born and raised, but there were opportunities to rise above the financial burdens. Many were poor, and needed help in many walks of life.

The American Jewish Committee would provide some of that help. Most of the founders were adherents of Reform Judaism, but it would never restrict its help to any Jew, most of whom were Orthodox Jewish immigrants from Eastern Europe.

Initially fifteen men who were well established in their business careers and family lives, and would devote their talents and funds to help the immigrants to the United States, met to get organized. The group included banker and philanthropist Jacob Schiff, scholar Cyrus Adler who had a prestigious position with National Museum in Washington, Oscar Straus once a United States minister to Turkey, Louis Marshall, and Judge Mayer Sulzberger. There were discussions as to form and procedure, and on February 3, 1906 thirty-four Jewish Americans gathered to begin the formation of a national organization, The American Jewish Committee. On November 11, 1906 it held its first meeting in New York City. Judge Sulzberger was the President, and the others were either officers or members of the executive committee.

In the first year the A.J.C. became involved in some Jewish matters, and set a policy of addressing things without publicity or fanfare whenever possible. That would be its credo for many years.

In 1907 the Committee visited The Passport Question. By then, it was a cause championed by some members of Congress for several decades. Recently some popular movements from Jewish and sympathetic non-Jewish Americans advocated annulment of the Treaty.

America had been taking exception to the passport and related issues since 1881 to no avail, and in1907 it was time to act. In some cases Russian officials simply refused visas to naturalized Jewish Americans. Other times, Americans who were given visas were subject to arrest in Russia for breaking Russian law. Russia still maintained that Jews in the Czar's realm, including Americans, were subject to Czarist restrictions. Jews from other countries could not enjoy rights that were not available to Russian Jews.

Secretary of State Elihu Root, possibly hoping to resolve the difficulties, turned the Passport Question into a crisis when the State department issued a circular:

> RUSSIA
> Notice to American Citizens Formerly Subjects of Russia who
> Contemplate Returning to that Country
>
> A Russian subject who becomes a citizen of another country without consent of the Russian Government commits an offense against Russian law, for which he is liable to arrest and punishment, if he returns without previously obtaining the permission of the Russian Government.
>
> This Government dissents from this provision of Russian law, but an American citizen formerly a subject of Russia who returns to that country places himself within the jurisdiction of Russian law and cannot expect immunity from its operations.
>
> Jews, whether they were formerly Russian subjects or not, are not admitted to Russia unless they obtain special permission in advance from the Russian Government, and this Department will not issue passports to former Russian subjects or to Jews who intend going to Russian territory, unless it has assurance that the Russian Government will consent to their admission.
>
> No one is admitted to Russia without a passport, which must be viseed, or indorsed, by a Russian diplomatic or consular representative.
>
> Elihu Root

Department of State, Washington, May 28, 1907 [11]

It would be six months before anyone knew about the document and the disgraceful policy that it endorsed. The purpose of the circular was crystal clear. All American Jews would be hindered in obtaining passports to Russia. In Jewish circles there was astonishment and dismay. Prominent members of the Jewish Community reacted swiftly with open disapproval.

The American Jewish Committee wrote a letter of objection to Root on February 1, 1908:

> Sir, in a circular letter, dated May 28, 1907, issued by the Department of State over your signature, appears the following paragraph:
>
> "Jews, whether they were formerly Russian subjects or not are not admitted to Russia, unless the obtain special permission in advance from the Russian Government, and this Department will not issue passports to former Russian subjects, or to Jews who intend going into Russian Territory, unless it

has assurance that the Russian Government will consent to their admission."

The meaning of this announcement cannot be misunderstood. It segregates from the mass of American citizens those of the Jewish Faith, whether naturalized or native-born ... if they harbor the intention of visiting Russia. Under the plain implication of this regulation ... an American citizen applying to the State Department, for a passport, who is suspected of being a Jew, is for the first time in our history obliged to disclose his faith, and must, if he be a Jew, satisfy the Department that he does not intend to avail himself of the privilege of going to Russia, secured to him ... under the treaty solemnized between the United States and Russia in 1832.

Now, however, there seems to have occurred a reversal of time-honored policy ... to apply an unconstitutional religious test to upwards of a million of our own citizens, not only naturalized but native-born you are respectfully requested to reconsider the subject and to cause the circular letter to be withdrawn.

> Very respectfully yours,
> Louis Marshall
> Edward Lauterbach [12]

Five days later the State Department announced that the circular had been cleansed of objectionable word and restated:

Under Russian law a Russian subject who becomes a citizen of another country without the consent of the Russian Government is deemed to have committed an offense for which he is liable for arrest and punishment if he returns without previously obtaining the permission of the Russian Government.

This Government dissents from this provision of Russian law, but an American citizen formerly a subject of Russia who returns to that country places himself within the jurisdiction of Russian law, and cannot expect immunity from its operations.

> No one is admitted to Russia unless his passport has been viseed, or endorsed, by a Russian diplomatic or consular representative.[13]
>
> Elihu Root

The problem of the State Department circular was resolved, but did not begin to resolve the problem of issuing visas to American Jews without discrimination. Russia would neither comply nor discuss the matter.

Secretary Root sent this new circular to Marshall and Lauterbach. They replied:

> These (statutes) proclaim to all the world, the American doctrine of the right of expatriation; the right of all naturalized citizens of the United States, while in foreign countries, to receive from our Government the same protection which is accorded to native-born citizens.[14]

In 1908 Mayer Sulzberger, a prominent judge and highly respected lawyer in Philadelphia and president of the American Jewish Committee, wrote to President Theodore Roosevelt, about the many years of difficulty with Russia over its violations of the Treaty of 1832, and harassment of American Jews wanting to go to Russia. Sulzberger noted that an American Jew could receive a visa without any trouble from the Russian Consul by booking passage on a Russian ship. Apparently traveling in a Russian conveyance held more sway with the Russians.

Sulzberger offered a definitive suggestion for dealing with the treaty of 1832, as well as with another Russo-American treaty, that was devoid of controversy. "Our Government, we fondly believe, is the greatest on earth with respect to freedom, equity and justice …" he wrote. "Our prayer is that due notice be given to Russia of the intended termination of these two treaties."[15] The American administration was quite willing to discuss it, but Russia's foreign office was not.

In the presidential election in 1908, Republicans, Democrats and Independents issued similar statements on "rights while traveling":

> It is the unquestioned duty of the Government to procure for all our citizens, without distinction, the rights of travel and sojourn, in friendly countries, and we declare ourselves in favor of all proper efforts tending to that end.

Republican candidate William Howard Taft affirmed his fervent support of American citizens, the integrity of their passports, and their right to travel freely. Taft won the election and in his inaugural address he stated that:

> We shall make every effort to prevent humiliating and degrading prohibition against any of our citizens wishing temporarily to sojourn to foreign countries because of race or religion.

Over the next year and a half it became clear to the American Jewish Committee that President Taft did not consider "every effort" to include cancellation of the treaty with Russia—especially since American business interests might suffer.

Wasting no time, the American Jewish Committee provided a history of the Passport Question to Ambassador to Russia W.W. Rockhill. It was ineffective.

However, President Taft did look further into the passport question. In May 1910 he called a special conference with AJC President Sulzberger, Jacob Schiff, Cyrus Adler and Ambassador Rockhill. Alert as ever, AJC members sent a memorandum to the President urging that …

> … as a preliminary step our Government should insist upon the transfer of the negotiations from St. Petersburg to Washington and that failure either in accomplishing this or achieving desired results the reform should be followed by denunciation of the treaties. There are reasons … which warrant the conclusion that as soon as Russia realizes that our Government is in earnest … that its efforts are not merely for public consumption, Russia's attitude will change. Even Russia needs the support of a world-opinion.[16]

Despite meetings with the President, there was no progress. Traditionally, the American Jewish Committee did not publicize Jewish problems. In the past quiet negotiation had usually succeeded. The problem with Russia was different. The Executive Committee of the AJC realized that one effective option remained open to them: an open appeal to the people of the United States.

December 24, 1910. Louis Marshall wrote to Jacob Schiff: "Negotiations have been in progress for thirty years and will continue for thirty years longer, with the same results, unless our negotiators are brought to a realizing sense that they cannot fool all of the people all of the time. We have during the entire existence of the American Jewish Committee pursued the policy of silence with regard to the passport question. We can point to no triumphs as a result of this policy."

When Marshall was invited to speak at the twenty-second council of the Union of American Hebrew Congregations at the Astor Hotel in Manhattan, he asked Jacob Schiff for advice as to whether he ought to speak on the passport question: "I am not anxious to act as the voice of the Committee, but the time has in my judgment come when somebody's voice must be heard."[17]

January 19, 1911. The Union of American Hebrew Congregations held its council. At the closing session, Marshall delivered an address that he called "The American Passport."

The next day he wrote to Sulzberger: "Until last Friday I was in serious doubt as to whether or not I would prepare a paper on the subject of the passport, there being such a contrariety of opinion as to the advisability of making a public statement. On Friday evening I prepared my paper ... and finally decided that it would be best to read the paper, having absolute assurance that there would be no discussion and that all of the lodge orators and rabbis would be muzzled with 'triple brass.' This pledge was kept."[18]

Here is the heart of Marshall's powerful appeal:

> The character of a nation is the reflex of the character of its citizens. If they are virtuous, virile, and self-respecting, the nation will of necessity possess the same qualities. If they have no pride in the honor and dignity of their citizenship it inevitably follows that the national sense of honor is lacking, or falls below the ideal standard which should prevail.... Rome became a world power when with conscious pride, its sons gloried in the declaration, "civis Romanus sum" [I am a citizen of Rome]. It fell when the members of the State ceased to respond to that magic phrase. American citizenship has hitherto been regarded as a priceless treasure ... It has meant to them life, liberty, and the pursuit of happiness ... a badge of honor and distinction ... and the richest guerdon of all their hopes and aspirations ... And yet there rests a stain on the honor of our Nation and on the integrity of American citizenship; for the passport issued by the State Department of the United States, bearing the great seal of our country, and which vouches for the citizenship of him to whom it is issued, is dishonored, rejected, and arbitrarily disregarded by the Russian Government whenever the citizen by whom it is presented happens to be a Jew ... For more than thirty years this has been the declared policy of the Russian Government.... It is not the Jew who is insulted; it is the American people. And the finding of a proper remedy against this degradation is not a Jewish, but an American question. Ever since 1832, Russia has been under treaty obligation to accord to all of our citizens, without distinction, the liberty to sojourn and reside in all parts of her territory and to guarantee to them security and protection. There is no exception, express or implied ... no distinction of race or color, creed or sex. No discrimination is contemplated or permitted.

All Russians are to be admitted here. If Russia should declare that no citizens of the United States residing west of the Mississippi, or south of the Ohio, should receive the benefits of this treaty... should announce that it would not honor the passport of the United States when held by an Episcopalian or a Presbyterian, a Methodist, or a Roman Catholic, our country would not look upon this breach of treaty obligation as a mere insult to the Episcopalians or the Presbyterians ... but would justly treat it as a blow inflicted upon every man who holds dear the American Dream. Russia has persisted in the practice of requiring its consuls to interrogate American citizens as to their race and religious faith, and upon ascertainment thereof to deny to Jews authentification of passports ... for use in Russia. The Russian Government has thus broken its compact, flouted its obligations, and ignored a series of continued protests voiced by every President of the United States since the administration of President Hayes. As a crowning insult, it has recently issued a special edict offering to an American Ambassador the privilege of entering its territory, "notwithstanding that he was one of the Jewish persuasion". By a special act of grace, an accredited representative of the Government of the United States was tendered absolution for the crime of being a Jew. For more than thirty years this condition, described in many of our diplomatic dispatches to Russia as intolerable, has nevertheless been tolerated. The painfully slow methods of diplomacy have failed. We stand at the door of Russia, hat in hand, pleading with it that it shall recognize and perform its contract. With sardonic smile Russia answers: 'Not yet.' ... Imagine the patience of a creditor who for thirty years waits upon his debtor and pleads with him at his home for the payment of his debt. Does this mean that we should go to war with Russia? The mission of America, as well as of Israel, is peace. It is within the power of a country situated as ours is, to isolate Russia and to terminate all treaty relations with a Government which fails to recognize the solemnity and sanctity of its treaty obligations, and that is exactly what should be done without further delay. it may be argued that the suspension of commercial relations between the two countries may hurt our trade.... However extensive our trade with Russia might be, we could well afford to jeopardize it rather than to have it said that our country rates the dollar higher than it does the man, that it esteems the volume of its trade more than its national dignity. but let us assume that Russia has, from any motive whatsoever, extended to us offices of friendship. Have we not fully requited all of its kindnesses? Was it not through the intervention of President Roosevelt that Russia was extricated from one of the bloodiest and most disastrous wars known to history? The account between the two countries has been fully balanced so far as political favors are concerned. But there still remains a long account against Russia of broken promises, of violated obligations ... of dishonor inflicted upon our country and its citizens, and unless the virtue of manhood has deserted this Republic, its citizens will no longer patiently witness the mockery of diplomatic procedure, but will insist on a complete abrogation of every treaty now existing between the United States and Russia.

As gripping as it was impassioned, the speech earned Marshall "a rising vote of thanks." A resolution demanding the termination of the treaty with Russia was immediately proposed, passed, and prepared for presentation to President Taft, the State Department, and Congress. No longer would the Jewish community tiptoe around the issue and to the delicate endeavors of diplomacy.

On the next day *The New York Times* published an editorial reflecting upon the sad record of related violations and failed diplomacy, *The Times* wrote: We do not know what answer, if any, the Russian Foreign Office could make to Mr. Louis Marshall's most forcible presentation of the injustice, and in the international sense, the illegality of Russia's long-continued and persistent refusal to recognize passports issued by our State Department to Jewish Citizens of this Republic. The simple statement of the facts show how difficult it would be to make any answer at all. It would seem that if Russia values her friendly relations with us, she must pay some heed to these protests. They represent the General American feeling; they are based upon justice, upon law, upon a contractual agreement. It is the impulse of every one who considers the matter to say that there is no sense to the policy Russia pursues; it is an even stronger objection to say, which is perfectly true, that it is in plain violation of her treaty with us.

January 27, 1911. Even as the UAHC Resolution was presented to President Taft, New York City Congressman Herbert Parsons implored him to support it. The President refused. Within days Taft invited a group of Jewish leaders, including Marshall and Schiff, to an informal luncheon and conference at the White House. During that session the President reminded his guests of business with Russia, amounting to $100 million a year, constituting a considerable portion of America's foreign trade. Did he have the right, he asked, to imperil such substantial American business in Russia?

Marshall spoke up. "These are negligible matters, Mr. President," he said, "compared with the great ... question of the dignity of American citizenship." Taft would not alter his position, and Jacob Schiff became so incensed that he would not even shake the President's hand when the conference ended.

February 16, 1911. The House of Representatives Committee on Foreign Affairs initiated hearings on the Parsons resolution. As Parsons and other Congressmen begged for termination of the treaty, questions and answers from members and witnesses followed. Witness Louis Marshall began with this moving statement:

> First of all I wish to express my sincere thanks and appreciation to Mr. Parsons for what he has done in this matter. It is a fine exhibition of American citizenship and I am sure that the members of the committee, when they come to consider the question in its entirety, the history of it, and what it means—not to the Jews, but to the entire American people—will be rejoiced at the fact that Mr. Parsons has had the patriotism to present this resolution for their consideration.
>
> I am a Jew by religion. I am one of 2,000,000 Jews who live in this country, but I would not raise my voice for an instant in the halls of Congress for the purpose of asking any special favors to the Jewish people. My only reason for coming here is because I am an American citizen, and because I glory in that citizenship I desire that there shall be no taint or stain inflicted upon its integrity.
>
> Mr. Parsons has well said that this is not a Jewish question, it is an American question. I should deplore the day when there should ever arise a Jewish, a Catholic, or a Protestant question in the United States. We can never suffer any questions here concerning individual rights but such as relate to the entire American people. It is inconceivable that the United States of America should have entered into a contract with another nation upon the theory that it was giving everything and receiving nothing: that it was giving to Russian citizens the right to travel and sojourn in the United States territory, whereas American citizens were to have that right.... with respect to a certain portion of the American people, but not as to all; that the right was to be conferred upon those who were of one faith, but not upon those who were of other faiths. It is impossible to believe that an exception was written into that treaty... there is not one Member of the Senate who would not stand aghast at the suggestion, nor would there be a single Member of the House whose blood would not boil with indignation at the very thought.

I was born in this country, my wife was born here, her mother was born here; my children were born in this country. My parents and my wife's father were born in Germany… none of us, so far as I have any trace, has ever placed a foot on Russian soil. If my children should tomorrow, for purposes of business or any other legitimate object, desire tomorrow to visit Russia they would go to the State Department of the United States and there receive a passport bearing the great seal of the United States, certifying to their citizenship and to their equality before the law of the United States. Yet they would be warned that '… you must secure vise to this passport from the Russian ambassador or from some Russian consul' The first question that would be asked of them would be, 'What is your religion?' If they should answer, as I hope they and their descendants may for generations to come, 'I am a Jew by religion,' they would be told: 'You cannot enter Russia … you cannot enter the door of Russia.' For 30 years these negotiations have been going on, and we have not advanced one step. Administration follows administration in he thorny paths of diplomacy … The only remedy lies in the abrogation of the treaty.

The Committee adjourned and met again six days later. Congressman Henry Goldfogle reviewed the history of the treaty resolutions and its effects, as introduced or supported by him from 1902 to 1909. The effect was memorable and Congress swore to terminate the treaty at once, unless Russia complied. President Taft again attempted to negotiate with Russia, unsuccessfully. He was praised for acting "honestly and energetically" in his efforts to comply with the Committee's resolution, but the President would not support nullification of the treaty.

December 4, 1911. After a year of various proclamations demanding termination of the treaty, William Sulzer, popular Congressman from New York, introduced a successful joint resolution to that effect.

Over 70 resolutions from different Jewish groups in Massachusetts were presented a week later by Senator Henry Cabot Lodge.[19] More came in from Wisconsin, Virginia, Connecticut, Minnesota, and Rhode Island. Even Christian groups rallied to the cause since Protestant ministers and Catholic priests were also subject to Russian restrictions. It seemed the powerful in Russia—from the Czar Nicholas and the Czarina Alexandra, to Russian Church leaders—were governing under the influence of charismatic priest Gregory Rasputin. The Russian rulers did not take kindly to any that might try to convert their people to other faiths.

There were public protest meetings in several American states that culminated in a large gathering at New York City's Carnegie Hall on December 11,

1911. It was estimated that there were more than five-thousand people shouting support and applauding the prominent speakers that included politicians, merchants, diplomats and clergy of all persuasions. An editorial in the next day's *New York Times* said it all:

DEMAND BREAK WITH RUSSIA

> A great meeting was held in Carnegie Hall last night to protest against the discriminations of the Russian Government in recognizing passports issued to American citizens.... Carnegie Hall seating about 4,500 persons, was filled to its last square foot of space long before the meeting began ... Dozens of prominent men came across States to join in this protest which was not made on behalf of Jewish citizens, or on behalf of some of the Catholic clergy, or on behalf of the Protestant clergy, but it was many times declared, on behalf of American citizens.... against a condition which has existed since 1832, and against which this country has vainly protested for forty years.[20]

On stage were the Speaker for the House of Representatives Champ Clark, New Jersey Governor , newspaper tycoon and politician William Randolph Hearst, and numerous speakers from all three political parties. Thunderous cheers from the excited crowd greeted each one.

Few cheers, however, were raised for Andrew D. White, a former ambassador to Russia. White claimed that cancellation was not the first step to take. "Russia [might] say, 'well, let them go, we can live without a treaty as long as they can ... at any rate we will hear no more of the question of Jewish rights or of the rights of Protestants, of Catholic American Clergymen, or indeed of American rights ...'"

"Russia is a proud nation," White went on. "May it not be better for all concerned that we hold the abrogation of the treaty for at least a short time? I plead ... as a first step for a recourse to the Hague Tribunal." The ensuing demonstration was brief and hostile.

Senator James A. O'Gorman's remarks were punctuated by handclapping. "For forty years," O'Gorman exclaimed, "our government has made unavailing protest against Russia's attitude ... holders of our passports have been degraded and humiliated and the dignity of the nation has been offended ... We do not resent this indignity to our aggrieved citizens because they are Jews, but because they are Americans."[21]

The celebrated newspaper publisher and politician William Randolph Hearst spoke up and demanded action. "The principle involved is not a question of Judaism," he said. "It is a question of justice. It is not a question of religion. It is a question of right. It is not merely an outrage upon the individual. It is an insult to the American nation." [22]

Governor of New Jersey received a hearty ovation, amid calls for "our next president." "He straightened his tall form, smiled broadly, gently waved the cries down." Wilson started by reciting history of the dispute and a possible loss of commerce with Russia. Then he spoke of the Jews: "They are not Jews in America," he said. "They are American citizens. By our action for them shall be tested our sincerity, our genuineness, the reality of principle among us." [23]

Other notable speakers included representatives of nineteen state legislatures. "In my opinion," said Congressman Sulzer, "this resolution is as sure of becoming law as the sun is sure to rise tomorrow morning. Then Russia will ask us for a new treaty." Sulzer's role at this point was a key one: he would propose the resolution in the House of Representatives.[24]

Many public figures sent telegrams of support, deploring their inability to attend the Carnegie Hall meeting. Louis Marshall was known to be quite active in the creation of the rally and he was there. It was by all accounts an exhilarating event.

Congressman William S. Bennett summed it up succinctly: "My proposition is this; if we all can't get into Russia, let us all stay out."

The House of Representatives debated for a week and charged Russia with violating the 1832 treaty. The resulting resolution was blunt: terminate the treaty! It passed 301-1. The sole dissenting Congressman claimed such a course would damage U.S. business and do the Jews no good. Nonetheless, President Taft was instructed to put Russia on notice, and to declare that the treaty be ended. Some felt it wiser to state the charge to the President in more diplomatic terms. The response to that was an emphatic negative.

Jacob Schiff's elation was evidenced by the following letter: "This is like a dream ... and I little thought, when I said to the President last February ... 'this question will not down, Mr. President ... we shall now go to the American people,' that the latter could be so easily aroused and that action on their part would be so prompt and so effectual. Louis Marshall has outdone himself all through, and to him, more than to anybody else, is due what has been accomplished." [25]

The United States Senate passed the resolution unanimously. Yet the State Department still felt that economic interests should not be endangered because a few Jews were denied entry visas to Russia each year. Taft tried to get the Russian Foreign Office to join him in a statement saying a new treaty was being negotiated to replace the one soon ending. The angry Russian foreign minister, M. Sazonov, could not understand why America would risk the loss of trade because of "a few

Jews." Sazonov said he was "willing to consider an arrangement by which all Jews might be transferred from his country to the United States."[26]

President Taft viewed the House Resolution as offensive, harshly worded. He wanted what he considered a "quiet and formal notice of termination."[27] He gave notice of revocation of the treaty effective per the terms of the agreement of the Treaty of 1832, one year from December 31, 1912. In fact, the Senate did pass a more tactfully worded note, which the House endorsed, but it meant nothing to Russian officials. Cartoons in the Russian press characterized Uncle Sam as a Jew while Russian papers charged that Jewish bankers had "become the real lords of America."[28]

A euphoric Louis Marshall wrote to his cousin Benjamin Stolz in Syracuse: "I feel as though I had won the greatest lawsuit in which I have ever been engaged or will be engaged, in bringing about the abrogation of the Russian treaty ... It is a lesson to all the world by showing the regard in which Jewish citizens are held by our country ..."

The triumph was that the point was made. In terminating the treaty, the United States told Russia and other European powers that the sanctity of American citizenship was more important than trade, and that America would not continue, after thirty years of failed diplomatic attempts, to tolerate ill treatment to her citizens

For the Jews in Russia, there was no lessening of abusive treatment. American goods were subject to Russian tariff increases, re-igniting the Passport Question. Congressmen who had supported the treaty's end were besieged with anxious letters and complaints as other nations sought to replace the U.S. in commerce with Russia.

Still, it was a great and unique victory over unjustified discrimination of any Americans by any national power. The stellar role of the American Jewish Committee would resonate for the future, and in fact be an important leader within two years when a War would grip the World.

In January of 1912 Marshall wrote to another cousin, Rabbi Joseph Stolz, in Chicago: "The little snowball which began to roll from the mountaintop finally became a tremendous avalanche, which swept everything before it. Whatever I have done in this matter has been a labor of love and the attainment of one of the ambitions of my boyhood ... in that God has enabled me to aid in the solution of at least one of the Jewish problems. It is a source of sorrow to me that my mother did not live to witness the accomplishment of this result, for which she greatly yearned."[29]

Notes

1 Bailey Pg 121
2 AJYB 1909-1910 Pgs 21-22
3 AJYB 1909-1910 Pgs 21-22
4 Bailey Pg 129
5 Bailey Pgs 127-128
6 Bailey Pgs 133-134
7 Bailey Pg 179
8 Bailey Pg 180
9 Ibid
10 Bailey Pg 186
11 AJYB 1911-1912 Pg 23
12 Ibid Pgs 23-24
13 AJYB Pg 25
14 AJYB Pg 26
15 AJYB Pg 32
16 AJYB Pg 51
17 Reznikoff V1 Pgs 58-59
18 Reznikoff V1 Pg 59 f/n
19 Bailey Pg 217
20 *New York Times* December 7, 1911 Ibid
21 Ibid
22 Ibid
23 Ibid
24 Ibid
25 Schiff V2 Pg 151
26 Bailey Pg 220
27 Ibid
28 Bailey Pg 221
29 Reznikoff V1 Pg 103

Five Interesting Years

Marshall's role in terminating the 1832 Treaty with Czarist Russia in 1912 did not deter him from participating in other matters. He maintained his great interest in the care and feeding of the environment, encouraging his family to love and respect it as he did. In 1910 Marshall became a Syracuse University Trustee; he told Chancellor James R. Day of his interest in having an agricultural and forestry school at the University. By 1911 Marshall's efforts resulted in a New York State bill to fund the project; Governor Dix approved an appropriation of $250,000. Marshall was appointed as President of the new college's board and proceeded to campaign for funds for a number of years.

He had worked closely with several members of Congress, especially Congressman William Sulzer of New York. Democrat Sulzer and Republican Marshall maintained that relationship. Sulzer, in his ninth term in Congress, was the chairman of the House Foreign Affairs Committee, and had introduced the resolution to abrogate the treaty with Russia. In 1913 Sulzer was the newly-elected Governor of New York State, and Marshall requested, and then had to press Sulzer to approve an appropriation bill of $250,000 for construction of a building for the New York State College of Forestry.

A year earlier, in 1912, the New York State Democrats held their convention in Syracuse, N.Y. The Democratic Party was led by the "Tammany Hall" political machine, and William Sulzer was nominated as their candidate for Governor. With the support of the powerful Democratic Party machine, he was elected Governor of New York. It was expected that Sulzer would kowtow to the political wishes of the machine but he would not. He took office in January 1913 and by mid-September he was on trial. Of the charges against him, the most serious was for using campaign funds for his personal use. "A High Court of Impeachment" by the New York State Legislature was held. His arrogance and unwillingness to compromise had lost Sulzer the support of voters, political groups, and a number of newspapers that had supported him. Sulzer called on Louis Marshall to head his defense team and Marshall agreed, though he told his wife that he was not enthusiastic about the outcome The chief defense argument was that the alleged misuse of the money had taken place before Sulzer was elected, were not committed during his term as Governor, and could not be considered as violations of his office, and the charges were not relevant. The trial did not go well; Sulzer did not even testify in his own defense. Sulzer was found guilty; the only New York State governor to be removed from office. He practiced law for some years, and occasionally spoke to Marshall. He died in 1941 at seventy-eight.

In 1910 and 1911 Marshall was a willing, and active, candidate for a seat on the United States Supreme Court. There were two openings in that period, and several prominent citizens who were friends of President Taft urged him to appoint Marshall. He was known as an outstanding Constitutional lawyer who was highly qualified to be a justice on the Court, as well as an outstanding citizen in the United States. It was the only office that Marshall ever wanted; the only time in his life that he sought an appointed or elected post. He was not appointed.

The events of 1914 would have a deep effect on the lives of the Louis and Florence Marshall family. Florence kept a diary for many years. Significant events included:

> Thur. Feb. 26. In the evening Louis spoke at the tenth anniversary celebration of Emanuel Brotherhood at Temple Emanu-El. Pres. Wm. H. Taft was the principal, for whom there was afterwards a reception at Delmonico's. Fri. Feb. 27: Pa [Jacob Marshall] died at about 11 A.M. at Bertha's house in Philadelphia. Louis left 2 P.M. for Philadelphia. Sat. Feb 28: I arrived in Philadelphia at noon. In the evening there were services at Bertha's house, Dr. Landman reading the [service]. Louis and I remained overnight at Clara's. Sun. Mar.1: We all left Philadelphia at 7:45 a.m. in the Penn. & D.L. R.R. arriving in Syracuse 5:45 p.m. We went to the Onondaga hotel, where we all had dinner, afterwards going to the Marshall Memorial Home [Marshall Family home that was given to Syracuse Jewish Community] Mon. Mar. 2: Pa's funeral took place at the Marshall Memorial Home at 2 p.m., Dr. Gutman & Dr. Coblenz officiating. We all had dinner at Ida's.

Jacob Marshall, esteemed citizen of Syracuse, was buried beside his wife Zilli in the Temple Society of Concord section of Woodlawn Cemetery

In November 1914, Marshall's unbreakable relationship to Syracuse, the Jewish Community and American Judaism were illustrated in a special event.

Florence's entry in her diary was:

> Nov. 26, 1914: Louis delivered an address at the dedication of the Jewish Social Institute in Syracuse. *[NOTE: The dedication was for a new building, an annex to the Marshall Memorial Building on Cedar St. Four hundred people*

attended. It was reported in the Syracuse Post Standard, November 27, 1914. Marshall and Syracuse University Chancellor James Day delivered addresses.]

HEBREWS OPEN INSTITUTE WITH MUCH CEREMONY
Dedication of the New Building Epoch in Community
HALL FILLED TO CAPACITY

The dedication last night of the Jewish Social Institute Building on Cedar Street marked a new epoch in the life of the Jewish community in Syracuse. More than 500 men and women filled the Nathan Jacobson Memorial gymnasium to its capacity and heard the career of the new institute mapped out in speeches by Louis Marshall of New York, Chancellor Day of Syracuse University.

The address of Mr. Marshall was remarkable in many respects. His parents Jacob and Zillah [sic] Marshall gave the Young Men's Hebrew Association and the Council of Jewish Women their family homestead, where Louis Marshall spent his boyhood, for their headquarters....

'Now that the building is complete,' (he) said, 'what was a mere ideal only a short time ago is now an actuality. But the real work is only begun. Bricks and mortar of themselves are nothing unless there is a soul within'....

Mr. Marshall's sermon, as he chose to call it, conveyed two distinct messages. The first was a plea for organized study of the Bible and Hebrew literature ...

'Within the last twenty-five years ... it has become fashionable among our own people to sneer at the Bible and at those who study it. Yet, if all the literature of the world, all the product of the printing presses for the last 200 years, yes 2000 years, were wiped out, leaving nothing but the Bible, mankind would still have food for thought and deep consideration.'

The second message concerned what Marshall termed Jewish solidarity. He spoke critically of the book, *The Melting Pot,* written by Marshall's friend Israel Zangwill.

'Keep out of the melting pot,' he warned. 'Keep unto yourselves that which made Israel of old a priest—people ... He [Zangwill] would pour the gold, the silver, the zinc, copper, lead and iron all into one pot and melt them. When he got through, he would have a mixture, but no virtues. It would be too cheap for jewelry, it could not replace silver, it would be too brittle to replace iron and not docile enough for copper.'

Mr. Marshall made a plea for the elimination of the artificial barriers which are dividing the Jewish communities of America into sections, one of which thinks it is better than the other.

'You are all descended from the same nobility ... and there is no aristocracy but the aristocracy of character.'

Mr. Marshall is one of a committee of influential Jews having charge of a campaign for funds for aid of the Jews in Poland, East Prussia, Galicia, Roumania, and other countries in the eastern theater of war, and he made a plea for assistance for them."

It was a successful and satisfying achievement for the Syracuse Jewish Community, building on the foundation that had been laid by the Jacob and Zilli Marshall family.

Note

AJA-MC

Florence

In the summer of 1914, the Marshall family moved to their summer home in the Adirondack Mountains of New York State on Lower Saranac Lake in a section known as Knollwood. It was in an area known for its "great camps" that were owned by a number of affluent families from New York City. They had done so every year since the house was built in 1900; Florence and the children lived there for three months, very comfortably, frequently hosting visiting friends and relatives.

Louis stayed in New York during the week and would take the train on the long overnight trip north, arrive Saturday morning and the family would be reunited. During the week he wrote almost daily, and his letters and poems were expressions of his love and joy for their time together, and he voiced his unhappiness when he had to return to New York City. On Sunday night he would make the overnight return trip to the city. His favorite time was the three full weeks that he was there in July with Florence and the children.

On August 14, 1914, he wrote his daily letter;

My darling Florence,

How strange it seems to be away from my dear ones after these delightful weeks in paradise. There have been so many red letter days in my existence—an oasis where peace has reigned, while all the world has been on war. Here everything is turmoil and excitement. The air is thick with rumors of murder, battle, and destruction. It is announced that England has declared war against Germany. I hate to believe it. Prophesy however is useless in this bedlam. The entire civilized world seems to have gone mad, and nothing can be judged by normal standards of conduct.

[He then talked about various friends, and family activities, and then returned to his reaction to the war in Europe that had recently begun].

I am entirely dazed. The imagination stands aghast at these nightmare conditions. The only hope now is that it cannot last long. The contending parties will be so utterly exhausted physically and financially that they must stop willy nilly.

Fortunate are we to live in this blessed land. I doubt whether our children actually appreciate how good God has been to them and to us. If we lived abroad James would now be drafted into the army.

And now my dear sweetheart, my chat must come to a close. May God's blessing rest upon you, and may our beloved Knollwood ever be a haven of peace and a sanctuary of love for us and our dear ones.

Your own devoted lover,
Louis [1]

It was the 19th year of their marriage.

Florence became ill in 1915, but its severity and the prognosis, were not mentioned in their letters. When Louis traveled, their letters spoke mainly of the family and emphasized their undying care for each other. On June 7, 1915 Florence wrote to Louis from their home on East 72nd Street in New York City. He was probably in Albany.

My Darling Louis,

As I was busy shopping this morning and much occupied in the house this afternoon there is nothing new to report. *I feel so very tired tonight* [author's italics] that I am going to bed now, and I know you will pardon me if my letter is not a lengthy one....

You have in your (sweet) sympathy been such a comfort to me, my sweetheart, during these awful days. I do not know if I could have remained as calm without YOU near me, with that sense of security and that feeling of love.

Goodnight, my lover, with a thousand embraces from

Your own
Florence[2]

It was a more subdued tone than in past letters, and the somewhat scattered fluidity of her handwriting when compared to her usual clear script was possibly a sign of what was to come. In July when she was at their summer home, Louis wrote to her from Albany:

My darling Florence,

I am much pleased to know that you have summoned up courage to take a walk and hope that when I join you on Saturday you will be able to take one of our usual strolls through the woods.

I hope that James will soon be with us. I am missing him exceedingly though I rejoice at the opportunities that this trip has afforded him with love and embraces to all of you I am

Your lover and admirer
Louis[3]

On August 21, 1915 Florence wrote:

My darling Louis,

I am much pleased to know by your letter that you are taking a sufficient amount of exercise, which is particularly necessary for you now while the work is so arduous.

Today started cloudy here and this afternoon it is raining, so I've decided to remain in bed, a comfortable place under the circumstances ...

I certainly think that the dignified unostentatious way in which the Frank funeral was conducted was preferable to a public funeral. [This refers to Leo Frank, who was lynched on August 15, 1915 in Georgia. There were 20 people at the funeral in Brooklyn, in accordance with the family's wishes]

I was also surprised to see that Judge Mack [Julian Mack, Marshall's friend, a member of the American Jewish Committee, and a Zionist] had presided in Chicago in a movement for forming Jews into "a nation of their own". It is astonishing that he should lend his name to such a thing at this particular time, when one considers the conditions in this country, which may be on a war basis at any time.

Do you think that if you and Mr. Brandeis met that it would be possible to avert a disruption in Judaism, which is bound to come if there is both a Conference & a Congress. [There was serious disagreement between the American Jewish Committee, the Zionist Organization, and other organizations about the structure of the American Jewish community's response and actions for European Jews when the World War would end].

Much love to you and James, in which the youngsters join.

Your own devoted
Florence[4]

For the rest of that summer of 1915 her letters were cheerful, with no mention of illness. Yet there was concern, as evidenced by a letter in January 1916 to Louis from his boyhood friend in Syracuse, Dr. Henry Elsner:

My Dear Louis:

I wish you would continue to keep me posted with regard to Florence. I can see no reason why with the care, which she gets, and the scientific treatment of her physicians she should not make a prompt recovery if her trouble is localized only to the intestinal tract and her symptoms are due to consecutive toxemia.

When we go to New York I shall certainly see you.

Love to all from all.

Sincerely as always,
Henry L. Elsner[5]

On April 17, 1916 Louis wrote from Albany:

My darling Florence,

Your telegram indicating that you had a good night and were feeling comfortable made me very happy. I hope the day has been a good one for you. The weather has been perfect, the air being full of you.... I left the train at half past seven, took breakfast at a kosher restaurant ... where I indulged with matzos broken into coffee....

The news from Washington is most serious. I think that there was nothing else for us to do but to issue an ultimatum to Germany. Had [President] Wilson been less of a jellyfish six months ago we would not have reached this pass. [He refers to March 25, 1916 when a German submarine torpedoed and sank a packet boat with passengers, with some loss of life, despite the promise from a high German official in September 1915 that Germany would not sink passenger ships without warning]. It is still possible that Germany will yield, or at least open the door for an understanding which will save its face … unless Germany again becomes the aggressor, there will be no alternative (to war). It is horrible to contemplate, but then the whole world has gone mad. But all this means little. The important thing for me is that my beloved sweetheart shall soon be on the road to convalescence and that the happiness of my dear home may again be restored by the lovely presence of its guiding spirit's full strength, vigor and loveliness. With ten thousand kisses and embraces, I am

Your eternal love[6]

On May 6, 1916, their twenty-first anniversary; Louis wrote a tribute:

My darling Florence,

This is to certify that you are not only my creditor for the sweetness and light which you have brought into my life, and for the immeasurable happiness that you have brought me, but also for a silver fox set, to be chosen by you whenever and wherever you desire, in honor of this great and glorious anniversary.

With my most ardent expression of love and devotion, of adoration, and gratitude, I am

Eternally yours,
Louis[7]

A card was enclosed with it:

To the Sweetest, the Loveliest and the Best of all the Earth, on this the Most Blessed of Days, from Her Devoted Husband and Lover.

May 6, 1916.[8]

Sometime later in that month, Florence expressed her last wishes to Louis; he wrote them exactly as she requested;

> My Wishes
> Dr. Magnes to speak (if available)[9]
> very briefly and to read my
> favorite psalms the 23rd and 90th
> No fuss, everything simple and
> natural. A simple floral
> full of pink roses (my favorites)
> sent by Louis and my family
> Nothing extravagant.
> In regard to wearing mourning,
> although I believe it cannot in-
> dicate one's feelings yet I have
> always felt that it shows a certain
> mark of respect. Therefore I would
> suggest that my boys wear black
> neckties and black gloves, for a
> time. Ruth to wear black coat
> and hat, but I would like her
> dresses and waists to be some-
> what relieved by white later.
>
> If this enormous house is to be
> kept going, there should be a
> housekeeper or trained nurse
> housekeeper. I should think the
> latter preferable, to relieve Louis
> of all anxiety concerning the
> children's health.
> Patience with the children.
> I would like to have those
> whom I have assisted to con-
> tinue to be helped, Mrs. (illegible)

for the shopping, Miss (illegible)
for hosiery and underwear,
Joyce and Kathryn Gopri
should she ever require assistance
also G. Dillinan.

The children are to be loving and
helpful to each other and to have
in mind what would have pleased me.

Their special care to be directed
to their beloved father, who could
need loving hands to help him.

(Gifts)
James Ruby and diamond
engagement ring. Pin of
diamonds and peach with
turquoise in center

Robert Ring with two diamonds
and a pearl

George Ring with two diamonds
and a ruby

Ruth Pearl necklace
Diamond necklace
Diamond heart
Laces [?] are to be divided between Ruth and boys
My confirmation watch
Enamel watch chain
To Louis My Bible, which contains
no thoughts more beauti-
ful than his, no actions
more noble.

The above are <u>suggestions</u> for what I would like the children to have and to guard and treasure and to hand down only to those of their children who are worthy to wear what I loved so much for the sake of the givers. I would particularly ask James to be careful about my engagement ring, perhaps the dearest of all the jewelry.

(to relatives of Florence and Louis)

Addie Gold key and purse.
Blanche Platinum and diamond watch
    bracelet.
Elsie Diamond bar pin.
Beatrice Diamond and pearl chain
    & diamond platinum
Selma Small diamond handle and diamond slide on black cord.
Edna Diamond & crystal pin.

Each nephew and niece of my family to receive $2000.

Bureau of Education (Girls department)	$ 500
Emanuel Sisterhood	$ 2000
Lakeview Home	$ 2000
? Chapter of ? Settlement	$ 2000
Young Women's Hebrew Association	$ 500
Committee on Delinquent Girls	$ 1000

> I would like some books presented
> to the Seminary Library, costing
> $ 500 to $ 1000
>
> A gift from my effects to Bertha, Clara, Ida
>   Leopold and Ida Marshall
> [sisters of Florence and Louis]
>
> The above are suggestions only, which I
> would like to have executed, if Louis
> agrees, or he should make suggestions
> as his better judgment dictates.[10]

She died on May 27, 1916. She was 43. Louis was 59. James was 20, Ruth 17, Robert 15, George 12.

There were announcements in the press in New York and Syracuse and tributes from the organizations in which she had been an active officer or director, including Temple Emanu-El Sisterhood, the National Council of Jewish Women, Hunter College Alumnae, and the Jewish Protectory and Aid Society.

Louis created a trust in memory of Florence and asked several of his friends to serve as trustees of the fund that he would endow. On June 27, 1916, in a letter to them, he wrote that he was establishing "The Florence Marshall Memorial School for Girls," with a trust fund of $150,000 to provide an income to further the religious education of the Jewish Girls of New York City:

> For some time past I have been impressed by the fact, that although the Jews of America have been generous in caring for the poor, the sick, the aged, the orphan, and the abnormal, they have given comparatively little attention to the religious ... and the education of their children. It has recently been authoritatively shown that not to exceed 25 percent of children of school age of Jewish parentage residing in New York City are receiving any systemized training whatsoever ... in this direction. The percentage of the girls who are afforded the opportunity for such instruction being considerably less than that of the boys. As one who believes in the essential importance of such education, who has become more and more filled with admiration for the exalted ethical content of Judaism and its ennobling influence, and who above all regards on the part of the future mothers of Israel, I consider present conditions deplorable. Here in America ... the synagogue has been virtually abandoned by the younger generation, and nothing of the preservation of our faith to be in large measure dependent on familiarity with its

precepts, and of love for its traditions, religious nature has taken its place. In consequence the ideals, which made Judaism triumphant even when the Jew was most despised, are for the moment passing, as it were, under a cloud....

I firmly believe that the preservation of our noble spiritual prestige is indispensable to civilization and to the perpetuation of the most perfect conceptions of justice, of righteousness, of purity and of human brotherhood that the world has known. The relation of woman to our modern life is such that ... her secular training in our public schools is precisely the same as that of her brother ... all employments are open to her ... she is rapidly supplanting man as a teacher in the field of primary education ... her influence in society is enlarging in every direction.... Are the Jewish mothers of tomorrow to be devoid of that training of their emotions which will best qualify them to perform the sacred duties which are inevitably to devolve on them? Are they to know nothing of the religion of their ancestors of their marvelous history ... of their lofty traditions? Mrs. Marshall and I often discussed this subject and reached the ... conclusion that no present-day problem in Jewish communal life is so urgent ... for immediate solution as that which relates to the education of our girls. I have decided to establish ... 'The Florence Marshall Memorial Fund' which shall so far as its income permits stimulate and further the education of the Jewish girls of New York. I am devoting ... the sum of $150,000, fully recognizing its inadequacy and greatly deploring my inability to increase the amount.

It is evident that this can but be a beginning—an effort to grapple seriously and in a practical way with a task of vast dimensions and of transcendent importance ... It is to be hoped that this, the greatest and the richest community in all Jewry, which has the means, and I believe the spirit of the determination to act....

Very truly yours,
Louis Marshall[11]

Soon afterward Louis went to their summer home. Afflicted with insomnia, he increased his workload and expanded his activities.

Louis composed many poems about family, life, love, religion and the environment, often in a florid style, usually in rhyme. In June, he went alone to their summer home. There, he wrote of his love and his loss.

> "The forest glades where we were wont to stray
> In joyous ecstasy through blissful years,
> Whose every leaf the thought of thee endears,
> Are steeped in gloom where poignant sorrows prey,
> No healing balm can e'er my pain allay.
> As preordained, each flower reappears
> That thou didst love,—but thou hast passed away,
> And for thy sweetness there abide but tears.
> Oft in this grove where now the pine-trees moan,
> Our Temple—we in reverent mood would stand
> Clasped in each others arms and our eyes shone
> In thankfulness for God's great gift, and scanned
> Our aged selves still wand'ring hand in hand—
> But thou art gone, and I am left alone.
>
> Knollwood, June 22, 1916"[12]

Louis would observe the traditional year of mourning, and he expected the children to do the same. After six months, his son James, expressed his feelings and frustrations in a letter to his father:

> You have always taught us to solve our problems and to rely on ourselves as far as is possible ...
>
> What I have been leading up to is the question of mourning. For more than six months I have refrained from discussing the question because I did not have the courage or the brutality to hurt you while the wound was yet so fresh ...
>
> Pop, I have not a moping nature nor one that can weep for long, for I see the pleasant, hopeful side of things too easily and enter into them with much more will and fire. Please do not condemn me for it. Mother took pleasure in it, and it was because of these reactions that I could afford her much comfort during her illness.
>
> Philosophically and psychologically I can see no reason for maintaining a year of exile from those harmless pleasures one has been accustomed to

enjoy. They serve my purpose as reliefs from the nervous strain of work, they are just as important during the year after death as at any other time.

As to your friends I know that some of them may be shock [ed], though fewer I expect than you think, when they find that I am not doing what they took for granted your son would do. But, I cannot guide my life by what they may think ... As it is I dislike being known and treated as Louis Marshall's son. I want to be known as James Marshall ... and I dislike the way that people take it for granted that I am doing and am always going to do just what they would expect a son of Louis Marshall to do.

One of the chief reasons why I have shied at going to Law School was that everyone expected it of me and said, 'Of course you are going to follow in your father's footsteps.' But, I do not want to follow in even you [r] footsteps ...

Pop, I believe that one should do what he thinks is 'right,' or at least that which will bring him in the near future closer to what he believes to be 'right'. There is at least something heroic in a man's plunging forward recklessly to reach his Lorelei, animate, inanimate, or ideal.

Had I spoken six months ago, I would have been a reckless fool. Were I to keep silent for six months longer, I would be the miserable coward....

I am not chosing [sic] the easy road, dear Pop, nor the cruel and treacherous paths—I intend to go to the opera, to decent plays, to small dances, and I hope that you will understand that I do it not without heartache and misgiving for the pain it will cause you, and not without a feeling of devout tenderness, love and happiness for having had the Mother that I did have, and for possessing the sweet memory that I do.

Pardon me once more, Pop, for writing this ... But please remember that I am doing what I think is right, trying to live as near my ideals as possible, which I confidently believe is what you and Mother have always desired.

Your never more loving son,
Jim[13]

Louis answered five days later:

> ... the abstention of a mourner from worldly amusements, for a time, is not a mortification of the flesh, or a penance, or a superstition. It is at most a form of self denial ... I do not know whether any of your remarks relate to the Kaddish—I hope they do not—for it is absolutely devoid of the slightest implication of superstition. It has always appealed to me as a fine spiritual manifestation ...
>
> Seven months have now passed since Mother left us. In four months the traditional year of mourning will be over ... if you really think that it is of sufficient importance to you to go to the opera, or to the theatre or to dances before those four months should have elapsed, much as I would wish it otherwise, your decision must govern ... With greater love than ever, I am
>
> Your affectionate father[14]

What James did about the period of mourning is not recorded. He did go into law, did become a part of his father's firm, and went on to a fine career in New York City as a lawyer and active supporter of public education. In his later years, James' reminiscences about his parents included:

> They were very devoted all their lives ... all of her life—she died age of forty-three, 1916. She was a fine hostess, but above all she was devoted to Father. I can remember standing with her at Knollwood when the boat went out and took him towards the station for New York, and it didn't seem as though I existed. All she was doing was to watch that boat with him departing, and he was equally devoted to her.[15]

Notes

1 AJA-MC
2 Ibid
3 Ibid
4 Ibid
5 Ibid
6 Ibid
7 Ibid
8 Ibid
9 Rabbi Judah L. Magnes the husband of Florence's sister Beatrice, and Marshall's close friend
10 Ibid
11 Ibid
12 Ibid
13 Ibid
14 Ibid
15 Oral History—American Jewish Committee

Florence Lowenstein Marshall
circa 1911

Florence with the children. Circa 1910 at Knollwood
Top—left to right. James, Ruth. Bottom—George, Robert

Jacob and Zilli Marshall at Knollwood 1904

The Leo Frank Case and the Supreme Court

In the middle years of the twentieth century's second decade the Louis and Florence Marshall family was not out of the ordinary. There was a middle-aged father, a younger, youthful wife, and three teen-age children plus one who would soon reach his teens. Louis Marshall was, as always, on a path crowded with challenges.

Louis' father Jacob passed on in 1914. After his wife Zilli died in 1910, he had retired from the business that he had built in Syracuse, and moved to Philadelphia to live in the comfortable home of one of his daughters.

Along with his law career, Louis was the president or chairman of the American Jewish Committee, the New York State College of Forestry, the Jewish Theological Seminary, the American Jewish Relief Committee, and would soon be president of Congregation Temple Emanu-El. In addition, with the outbreak of World War, he was a leading figure in the creation of the Joint Distribution Committee and other organizations that were formed to give support to the Jewish people in Europe who were suffering greatly from the shortages caused by the war, and who were victimized by the populaces of their countries.

But any satisfaction or joy that could be his was diluted and diminished by the lengthy illness from the disease that caused the death of Florence in 1916.

He was, of course, aware and sympathetic for Leo and Lucile Frank, a young Jewish couple in Atlanta, Georgia, who were engulfed by a tragedy.

It began in 1913 when Leo Frank was accused of the murder of a young girl. His arrest, trial, conviction and appeals became known as "The Leo Frank Case." An outbreak of anti-Semitism enveloped Atlanta Jewry in this well-known American community. As events unfolded the case attracted the attention of many people and the press of the United States. It was a horrendous crime, brutally executed, and when a Jew was considered to be one of the suspects, it inflamed the local populace.

Louis Marshall followed the events closely as they progressed, though he did not participate professionally until 1914. However, on September 9, 1913, a few weeks after Frank's conviction, he wrote a confidential letter to Judge Irving Lehman of the Supreme Court of New York State:

> I wish to call your attention to one of the greatest miscarriages of justice that has ever occurred in this country. It is in the case of Leo M. Frank ... My attention has been called to this matter as the President of the American Jewish Committee. Obviously it would be most unfortunate if anything were done in this case from the standpoint of the Jews. Whatever action is done must be done as a matter of justice, and any action that is taken should emanate from non-Jewish sources ... [1]

Marshall implored Judge Lehman to use his influence on Frank's behalf with a friend who was close to the owner of the Hearst paper in Atlanta, *The Georgian*. Marshall hoped that the paper's public support might forge a "wholesome public opinion, which will free this unfortunate young man from the terrible judgment which rests against him."[2]

The letter concludes: "I cannot ... too strongly urge upon you my absolute conviction that this case is almost a second Dreyfus case ... and that it would be impossible to imagine a case which would appeal stronger to one's sympathies as a man and ... as a citizen than this one."[3]

The American Jewish Committee feeling that local Georgians would react negatively to criticism and interference from outsiders, particularly Northern Jews, maintained its general policy of non-confrontation in the case.

Frank was born in 1884 in Texas to an ordinary working class Jewish family. The family moved to Brooklyn, New York, when he was four years old. In 1907, twenty-three year old Leo moved to Atlanta to work as superintendent of his uncle's pencil factory. He met and married Atlanta native Lucile Selig, and they became respected members of the Jewish community.

On the afternoon of April 26, 1913 Mary Phagan, a thirteen-year-old employee of the pencil factory, was murdered in the factory. The night watchman found her the next morning in the basement of the factory, her body battered and bloody. The previous day, when the crime was committed, was a Georgia State holiday so the factory was closed, but Frank, as the factory manager, was in the building on that day. The Atlanta police investigating officers found no hard evidence to implicate him. Nonetheless, when they interviewed the factory employees, who had not worked the holiday, several young women employees cast allegations of impropriety against Frank, saying that he invaded their dressing room in the factory on three occasions when they were in various stages of undress. They emphasized only the intrusions. According to other workers who were there, Frank quickly realized his mistake and left the room. The suggestion of sexual perversion aroused suspicion.

Jim Conley, a sweeper in the pencil factory, was questioned by the police and after changing his story several times, admitted that he and Frank were in the building and that Frank told him that he had "hurt" the girl and ordered him to carry her body into the basement of the building. Conley said that he did as he was told.[4] The police knew Conley. He had been jailed several times and was considered to be a liar, yet the police investigators chose to believe his story.

As to the accusations of the factory women, the investigating officers paid scant attention to other factory workers who extolled Frank's good character.

An inquest was held and Frank was charged with the crime. Before the trial there were biased police announcements and lurid newspaper reportage that agitated public sentiment against "the Jew from the North." Though there was little evidence against Frank, when he came to trial, the biased prosecutors, police provincialism and unreliable witnesses filled the court with lies, bigotry, and fear. The trial was held in Atlanta's City Hall while outside on the streets there was a mob, howling threats and anti-Semitic slurs. All of the threats and slurs could be heard by the jury and the judge. The press from the North was subjected to equal venom.

The prosecution was led by Hugh M. Dorsey, a very able attorney, and the Solicitor General of Fulton County, Georgia. The lead attorney for the defense was Luther Z. Rosser, who was a highly regarded, successful Georgian.

The other lead lawyers for the defense were Reuben Arnold and the only Jewish lawyer, Herbert Haas. There were also four lawyers who handled research and administrative work, and, when the occasions rose, handled motions for a new trial and appeals. "These men were about to conduct as inept a defense of an innocent man as was ever offered in an American courtroom. As brilliant and professional as they were Arnold and Rosser simply refused to believe witnesses would lie and a jury believe. In their defense, it is only fair to say no three American lawyers ever believed a mob could invade a courtroom, but invade the mob did …"[5]

Dorsey's careful conduct of the case was exemplified by his preparation and coaching of his most effective witness, the factory sweeper Jim Conley. Conley testified that Frank told him to dispose of the girl's body and he made blatant implications that Frank was a sexual pervert. These statements from Conley, who admitted to being a party to the crime, could not be overcome by the defense.

The trial began on July 28, 1913, ending less than four weeks later.

On August 22, 1913 the jury was about to retire to determine the outcome. Judge Roan showed the prosecution and defense attorneys three warning letters from the editors of Atlanta's three papers, each commenting on what would happen if the jury acquitted Frank. The Judge responded, "I think we know. The defendant would be lynched," adding "I fear for your lives" to Frank's attorneys. He suggested that Frank and his attorneys not be in the courtroom when the jury returned. The prosecutor agreed. If the Frank was acquitted, or the jury could not reach a verdict, a riot or a lynching was possible. He urged that Frank and his attorneys not be in the courtroom when the jury returned. That would be a clear violation of the defendant's Constitutional rights. Frank's attorney said,

"I don't think Frank will waive that right."

"Don't advise him he is waiving it," snapped the Judge. The judge charged the jury, and they retired to deliberate.

Frank left the courtroom, not knowing that he would not be in court when the Jury delivered the verdict, since the defense attorneys finally did agree to accede to the judge's admonition. There was a roar of approval from the crowd in the streets, when the guilty verdict was announced, but Leo Frank could not hear the verdict or the crowd. His family physician ran through those streets to the jail. He said, "Leo, the jury has found you guilty." Frank had not expected to be convicted.[6]

The grim outcome was only for Frank. Conley was convicted for his part as an accessory to the murder, and was sentenced to one year on the chain gang. Frank would be sentenced to die by hanging.

The outraged defense attorneys published a protest in the Atlanta newspapers: "The trial ... which resulted in Mr. Frank's conviction was a farce and not in any way a trial ... The time ought to come when this man will get a fair trial ... The final judgment of the American people is a fair one ..."[7] The defense filed a motion for a new trial, aware that the chances of that or a successful appeal were remote. The judge denied the motion, and scheduled Frank for final sentencing. At that time Frank was given an opportunity to speak. He pleaded his cause:

> In your honor's presence, and in the presence of the Supreme Judge who at this very moment is casting the light of His omnipotent and omnipresent eye upon me from His throne on high, I assert I am innocent of little Mary Phagan's death and have no knowledge of how it occurred. Your Honor, an astounding and outrageous state of affairs obtained previous to and during my trial. On the streets rumor and gossip carried vile, vicious and damning stories concerning me and my life. These stories were absolutely false and they did me great harm. From a public in this state of mind the jury that

tried me was chosen. Not alone were these stories circulated on the street but ... these vile insinuations crept into my very trial in the courtroom. The virus of these damning insinuations entered the minds of the twelve men and stole away their judicial frame of mind and their courage Your Honor, in this presence and before God, I earnestly ask that God in His mercy deal lightly with those who ... have erred against me, and will deal with them according to His divine judgment. If the State and the law will that my life be taken as a blood—atonement for the poor little child who was killed by another, then it remains for me only to die with whatever fortitude my manhood will allow. But I am innocent of this crime, and the future will prove it. I am now ready for your honor's sentence.[8]

With the trial concluded, Tom Watson, owner of the local newspaper, *The Jeffersonian,* joined the angry chorus against Frank, and in fact became one of the leaders of that chorus. As a candidate of the Populist Party Watson was elected to Congress in 1890, and defeated in a bid for re-election in 1892. In 1896 William Jennings Bryan was nominated by the Democratic Party as their candidate for president. The Populist Party nominated Bryan as well and Watson for Vice-President, but the Democrats choice for vice-president was Arthur Sewall. Therefore presidential candidate William Jennings Bryan had running mates on separate tickets. Watson then put forth liberal views advocating for example "Negroes for seats on the State Executive Committee of the Populist Party", and receiving cheers from residents of the Lower East Side. In 1904 the Populist Party nominated him for president; he gave his acceptance speech in New York City at a mass meeting, and he received much support from the "naturalized citizens" of the area. His defeats in 1896 and 1904 led to his realization that he could not advocate equality for the Negroes and succeed in the South. He overcame bitterness, eventually embraced white supremacy, denounced the Catholic Church, and became a powerful figure on the Atlanta political scene. Leo Frank's conviction played right into Watson's ambitions. While Watson had relatively little to say during Frank's trial, he "found in anti-Semitism the tidal wave he needed to ride back to personal power" [9]—and to regain his position in politics. Watson championed the white supremacy and the anti-Catholicism that was effective throughout the former Confederate states. As for the Jews, Watson seized that moment. "He was directly responsible for fomenting the only European-type pogrom against a Jewish community in the history of the United States."[10]

Beginning with his weekly *Jeffersonian* in March of 1914 until the sad ending of the Frank case in 1915—and for five years after until his election to the United

States Senate—Tom Watson hammered away at one theme: "Our little girl ... has been pursued to a hideous death and bloody grave by this filthy perverted Jew of New York." [11]

Watson continued chastising the Jews of Georgia and other states for years for defending Frank. "Tom Watson made an entire Jewish community feel insecure for the first time in America. The Jews of Atlanta lived with this insecurity and fear for an entire generation." [12]

The long legal road of Leo Frank's case went through the one jury trial and five appeals to the Georgia Courts. He was sentenced to death three times. With the State appeals process exhausted, the Frank Case was to be brought to the United States Supreme Court.

In 1914, one of Frank's attorneys asked Marshall to present Frank's petition to the Supreme Court. Marshall agreed.

He wrote to Albert D. Lasker, the prominent advertising executive who supported Frank from the beginning and assumed much of the legal expense: "Frank has not had a fair trial and therefore due process should mean not merely a right to be heard before a court, but it must be before a court that is not paralyzed by mob domination."[13]

At one point Marshall commented to a friend, "There is a strange fatality which surrounds the Frank case so that everything goes by contraries." To Justice Irving Lehman, he said: "What really convicted Frank was the suggestion that he was a Jewish capitalist engaged in abnormal sexual practices."[14] Perhaps true, but as events unfolded, that belief was overcome by bigots and bigotry.

Marshall went before Justice Lamar of the Supreme Court asking for an application for "a writ of error." Marshall attributed the error to the Supreme Court of Georgia on grounds that a significant Federal question was involved. It was denied because the Georgia Court had already decided the case. Applications to the other justices and the full Supreme Court were denied. Then Marshall filed a petition to Justice Lamar for a writ of habeas corpus (a judicial order that challenges the legality of his imprisonment and orders that the prisoner be brought to court). A hearing before the Supreme Court was scheduled for February 25, 1915.

Marshall received a letter from Atlanta Rabbi David Marx dated December 28, 1914. He wrote that he had "just heard of the signal victory which you have won ... I risk language for appreciation and make the effort to express to you my profound gratitude for making a rift in the clouds ... I thank God for this day and for having given you the heart and the mind to champion this just cause and roll away the disgrace which rests upon this State and the Country which we love and which we hope to ever have reason to cherish."[15]

On February 15, 1915, Marshall wrote to another Frank family friend, Rabbi Henry Cohen of Galveston, Texas. He said that there were still problems: "One of the most serious difficulties ... lies in the fact ... that the court would be very loath to render a decision which would result in the unconditional discharge of Frank, solely because of his absence from the court room at the time of the rendition of the verdict ... (the court) would not be inclined to look with favor upon a proposition which, after all, would mean, that a man who has been found guilty of a heinous crime by a jury, is to go scot free because of a technicality."[16]

On February 25, 1915, Marshall argued before the Supreme Court. He said that Frank had not been in the courtroom when the verdict was returned and therefore he had not received due process. "Frank was detained illegally since he had been deprived of rights guaranteed him by the Federal constitution," he concluded.[17] On April 19, 1915, by a vote of seven to two, the Court ruled against Marshall's petition. They held that the State of Georgia had a corrective process by which it considered Frank's rights, that he had received a fair trial, and that further Georgia State appeals were denied.

There could be no more Supreme Court pleas. The two dissenting Justices were Oliver Wendell Holmes and Charles Evan Hughes. Holmes' dissenting opinion contained the important statement: "Mob law does not become due process of law by securing the assent of a terrorized jury. Supposed the alleged facts (re: mob law) to be true ... if they were before the Georgia Supreme Court, it sanctioned a situation upon which the courts of the United States should act, and if for any reason they were not before the (Georgia) Supreme Court, it is our duty to act upon them now and to declare lynch law as little valid when practiced by a regularly drawn jury as when administered by one elected by a mob intent on death."[18] "It is inconceivable," Marshall wrote to Frank, "that with two judges of the Supreme Court of Georgia dissenting on the main appeal, and two justices of the United States Supreme Court dissenting on the Constitutional questions, executive clemency will be denied. The uniform practice of all governors has been to grant commutation wherever there has been a dissent in a court of appeals from the judgment affirming a conviction."[19]

Leo Frank was to be executed on June 22, 1915. His lawyers petitioned the Georgia State Prison Commissioners to commute his sentence to life imprisonment.[20]

Georgia Governor John M. Slaton was nearing the end of his term in 1915 and could not run for reelection. On June 10, 1915 the prison commissioners denied clemency for Frank, but Judge Patterson, one of the commissioners, flatly asserted that Frank was innocent. When Slaton was elected in 1913, he had Tom Watson's support, and now Watson pressured him to let Frank hang. Slaton's sense of fairness compelled him to study capital cases. He examined the records of Frank's case and announced that on June 12 he would begin hearings to consider commutation of Frank's sentence. His term as governor would end in14 days on June 26. If he were to commute Frank's sentence, his successor would likely attempt to reverse the commutation. Slaton reviewed all aspects of the trial, especially doubts voiced by the judge at the jury trial. Judge Roan had declared orally from the bench that he was not certain of the defendant's guilt; with all the thought he gave on the case, he was not convinced as to his guilt or innocence.

After long consideration of the facts and the emotions, Slaton concluded: "There is a territory beyond a reasonable doubt and absolute certainty, for which the law provides in allowing life imprisonment instead of execution. This case has been marked by doubt. The trial Judge doubted. Two Judges of the Supreme Court of Georgia doubted … in my judgment, by granting a commutation in this case, I am sustaining the jury, the judge, and the appellate tribunals, and at the same time am discharging that duty which is placed on me by the Constitution of the State." Governor Slaton issued the commutation order as of June 21, 1915.[21]

On that day, Louis Marshall wrote two letters. The first was to his wife: "I feel tremendously relieved, now that Frank's life has been saved. I began to fear the worst. The Governor is entitled to everlasting credit for his courage."[22] The second was written to Governor Slaton:

> As one who is convinced … that Leo M. Frank is an innocent man I wish to express my sincere admiration for the courage and spirit of justice which you have manifested in saving him from an ignominious death. You have saved the honor of your State. You have vindicated justice. You have earned the eternal gratitude of the good people of Georgia and the admiration of every lover of justice in America. May God's blessing rest upon you.[23]

Slaton was vilified by many Georgians and their newspapers. His political career was in ruins. Frank was imprisoned in a state farm in Milledgeville, Georgia, and within the month a convicted murderer attacked him while he slept. He cut Frank's throat and would have killed him had Frank not resisted a second stabbing and received prompt medical attention from a kind prisoner who had been a doctor.

On the morning of August 16, 1915, Frank's wife Lucile visited him. She found him healing from his wound and that he was adjusting to life in prison. She returned home to Atlanta. On that day he wrote the following letter to Dr. Benjamin Wildauer, Atlanta:

> I had promised myself this pleasure long since, but circumstances and Creen (his attacker) arose to defeat my purpose. Thank God, I am now on the road to recovery. It will be some time, however, before I get back to normal, in my neck. I am getting stronger every day, and eat and sleep well. Under the tender care of my dear Lucile, I am getting my health and strength back again. How do you view the recent changes, unrest and present situation in Atlanta? I get the *Journal* daily but it is hard for me to glean anything therefrom. I know you are posted on the inside. [24]
>
> Kindly give my greetings to Messrs. Schoen, Gershon, Borderer, Lichtenstein, Jacobs and all our other mutual friends. With warm regards to you and your good wife in which dear Lucile joins me, I am,
>
> Cordially yours,
Leo M. Frank

At 10 o'clock that night, a group calling itself an "Advance Guard of the Knights of Mary Phagan" left the town of Marietta, Georgia, in eight cars, bound for the prison at Milledgeville. The group, spawned by the mobs that had condemned Frank, stopped to confer outside the prison farm. They cut the prison telephone wires, and drove on to the prison.

The prison guards were unwilling to deter the armed party, wanting no part of a shooting war. Frank, in his nightshirt, was dragged from his cell, packed into the rear seat of a car, and driven off.

That caravan of evil arrived in Marietta at seven o'clock the next morning. Frank was marched through a grove to a large oak tree. He was asked if he had anything to say. "No," he answered. "We want to know whether you are guilty or innocent of the murder of Mary Phagan."

He purportedly said: "I think more of my wife and mother than I do of my own life." Then he asked, "Would you return my wedding ring?" One of the men took the wedding ring from Frank's finger as they got on with their business. Two of the lynchers looped a rope over a high branch, hoisted him on the top of a table and kicked it out from under him.

By eight o'clock of that morning about a thousand of the people of Marietta, Georgia crowded around the grove to view Frank's final agony.[25]

On August 17, *The New York Times* reported:

> Louis Marshall who argued the Frank case before the United States Supreme Court said today that Tom Watson, Editor of *The Jeffersonian* and at one time candidate for President of the Populist ticket, was responsible for the lynching of Leo M. Frank. The State of Georgia ought to regard Tom Watson as a principal in the murder of this innocent man who was taken from the sanctuary of the law and rushed to his death at the hands of a mob of assassins.

When the crime for the lynching was brought before a grand jury in Atlanta it took no action.

Sixty-nine years later, former Atlanta resident Alonzo Mann returned to the city where he lived as a young boy. He told authorities that in 1913 he had worked at the pencil factory as an office boy. On the day of Mary Phagan's murder he had seen Jim Conley carrying the girl's body. Conley threatened the 14-year-old boy to either keep quiet or he and his family would be killed. Mann, now 85 years old, said that he had been troubled by what he saw and by Frank's death and by the silence he had kept all those years.

Although Marshall was not successful in Frank's case, his argument in Frank's defense was used eight years later in a similar case, *Moore v. Dempsey*. Five black men were tried in Arkansas for hiring a lawyer to protect their rights against white landlords. The accused were the survivors of an attack by a mob that killed several of their group. They were told that they would be tried for whatever their alleged crime was and then would be hung. There was a 45-minute trial. The five were tried and found guilty after five minutes of deliberation. Somehow they were able to mount an appeal that eventually went before the U.S. Supreme Court. Justice Oliver Wendell Holmes spoke for the majority, citing his dissent in the Frank case. He cited Marshall's argument and ruled that the accused had been deprived of due process of the law. This time the majority ruled that a mob-dominated trial is no trial at all. It reversed the verdict.

In 1923 Walter White, the executive director of the NAACP wrote to Marshall to thank him for the habeas corpus proceedings that had saved the five lives.[26]

Notes

1 Reznikoff V1 Pg 295
2 Ibid Pg 295
3 Ibid Pg 295
4 Golden Pg 81
5 Ibid Pg 92
6 Ibid Pg 197
7 Ibid Pg 199
8 Ibid Pg 242
9 Ibid Pg 219
10 Ibid Pg 219
11 Ibid Pg 220
12 Ibid Pg 224
13 Golden Pg 246. On the same page Golden wrote, "No one in American Jewish life occupied the position Louis Marshall did from 1905 to 1930. No Jew, in fact, has ever achieved his prominence as a constitutional lawyer, with a worldwide reputation, nor has anyone since achieved Marshall's personal influence in the American Jewish community".
14 Ibid Pg 247
15 AJA-MC
16 Ibid
17 Golden Pg 247
18 Ibid Pg 249
19 Ibid Pg 251
20 Ibid Pg 252
21 Ibid Pg 271
22 AJA-MC
23 Reznikoff V1 Pg 313
24 AJA-LF
25 Golden Pg 293
26 Ibid Pg 250

War and Ideals

The era of the "giants" of the Jewish community in America rose to an energetic peak in the nineteenth century with the emergence of men and women who shared their success and their concern for their fellow Jews. Most had emigrated from Europe, looking for a better place than where they were born and raised, and providing personal freedom and better economic conditions. By the end of the nineteenth century they had achieved prominent communal, social and career positions. They and those who were born in America assumed the responsibilities of leadership.

Louis Marshall and Cyrus Adler are prime examples of these native born Americans who mixed with those who had come from Europe. Marshall often spoke of his parents love for America and hatred of Europe. They had come from the area of Central Europe that would eventually be a part of Germany and were quite aware of life's difficulties for the Jewish people in Europe. Cyrus Adler was born in Van Buren, Arkansas at the start of the Civil War. His parents moved north, and when his father died in 1867, his mother went to Philadelphia to live with her relatives, the Sulzberger family. Adler was a scholar from his earliest days, and in 1893 he was appointed to the prestigious post of Librarian of the Smithsonian Institute, a position that he held for many years. Ever the observant Jew, as a Jewish leader, he was one with the "giants" who built and supported the pillars of the expanding Jewish community.

Near the turn of the century Marshall and Adler began their friendship and would share many experiences. They did not forget their humble beginnings, and unhesitatingly accepted responsibilities to help their co-religionists in America and in Europe.

In 1918 when Marshall was selected to be one of the leaders of the Jewish American delegation to the Peace Conference in Paris he convinced Adler to go with him as a representative of the American Jewish Committee.

There were many others who had achieved financial and social prominence, were prominent American citizens, well regarded in all aspects of American life, and were considerate of the needs of their fellow Jews. They were proud of Jewish history and the Jewish contributions to the countries and the peoples of the old country. There was more to be accomplished.

In 1900, the future of the Jewish Theological Seminary was in doubt. It had been founded in 1887 by Rabbi Sabato Morais to provide education for men who would graduate as rabbis for the budding Conservative movement. Rabbi Morais died in 1897 and subsequently the seminary languished. Jacob Schiff, Cyrus Adler, Marshall, and others reorganized and revived it.

In 1906 they created the American Jewish Committee. In 1908, the members of the American Jewish Committee led protests against Russian violations of the 1832 Treaty between Russia and the United States. It took four years for the Jews and supporters from the non-Jewish community to convince the Congress and the reluctant American administration to abrogate the treaty. For the Jewish people of America, a small number in a large nation, that was an important victory.

American Jewry was well informed about the pogroms, persecutions, and economic deprivations that afflicted European Jews, and in the early years of the 20th century there was no relief.

In 1913, Marshall stuck his foot in the dark pool of European Jewish existence. He wrote to President Wilson, asking for support and financial aid for the Jews who were denied economic and civil rights in the countries of Eastern Europe where they had lived for many, many years. He pointed out that these issues were discussed at the Congress of Berlin in 1878. Out of that came the Treaty of Berlin, wherein Roumania became an independent country and the participating nations made provisions for protection of minorities. The Roumanian Government accepted the terms, but found ways to deny citizenship and attendant rights to Roumanian Jews. They refused to allow Jews to own rural land because they were classified as "aliens" and therefore not entitled to full citizenship. A collective protest from the signatories of the treaty, who were made aware of the violations, might have helped. There were none, and through the years the discrimination and persecution continued.

Although the United States was not a signatory to the 1878 Berlin Treaty, it became an interested party when the treatment of the Jewish people of Roumania resulted in a large increase in the number of Roumanian Jews immigrating to the United States. That flood of émigrés caused concern in America, and now that the United States had a definite interest in the ill treatment of Roumanian Jews, Secretary of State John M. Hay sent a strong protest to the Roumanian Government in

1902. After almost 24 years of Roumanian treaty violations some attention was paid. Mr. Hay wrote:

> Starting from the arbitrary and controvertible premises that the native Jews of Roumania domiciled there for centuries are 'aliens not subject to foreign protection,' the ability of the Jew to earn even the scanty means of existence that suffice for a frugal race has been constricted by degrees until nearly every opportunity to win a livelihood is denied; and the helpless poverty of the Jews has constrained an exodus of such opportunities as to cause general concern. The political disabilities of the Jews of Roumania, their exclusions from the Public service and the learned professions, the limitations of their civil rights, and the imposition upon them of exceptional taxes … are not so directly in point for my present purpose as the public acts which attack the inherent rights of trade. The Jews are prohibited from owning land, or even cultivating it as common labourers. Many branches of petty trade and manual production are closed to them in the overcrowded cities where they are forced to dwell. Even as ordinary artisans … they may only find employment in the proportion of one "unproductive alien" to two "Roumanians" under one employer. In short, by the cumulative effect of successive restrictions, the Jews of Roumania have become reduced to a state of wretched misery.

The British Government, a signatory to the Treaty of 1878, sent a note in reply to Secretary Hay:

> His Majesty's Government joins with the United States Government in deploring the depressed conditions of the Roumanian Jews and in regarding with apprehension the results of their enforced emigration.
>
> His majesty's Government will place themselves in communication with the other Powers to a joint representation to the Roumanian Government on this subject.[1]

There was no "representation" made to Roumania by any of the "other Powers" that were party to the treaty despite Secretary Hay's protest. Roumania's violations of the 1878 agreement continued when Marshall wrote to President Wilson in 1913.

Roumania was not the only practitioner of persecution. In Poland, authorities inflicted economic, religious, educational, and economic deprivations on its Jews before the World War, and it would continue to do so throughout the period when the Allies were supporting its bid for independence from Russia.

June 28, 1914 is a date to be memorialized in the Western World as the end of the comparatively innocent era of princely dominations and small wars. On that day an Austrian archduke and his duchess, symbols of a European empire were shot to death on a street in Bosnia. Within a few months the empires of Europe were firming up alliances, preparing for a brief conflict. Thus began the descent from the era of the "small wars" to the era of mass slaughter.

In 1912 Louis Marshall was elected as the second president of the American Jewish Committee succeeding Mayer Sulzberger. He would be involved in the preservation and safety of victims of the war that inflamed Europe.

Before the onset of the war in 1914 Marshall had been concerned about the Polish Jews who had suffered economic privation and political and physical persecution for decades. Poland, even when it was part of Russia, had installed especially harsh laws and restrictions on its Jewish residents. Efforts to improve their lot working through government agencies were not successful. In December 1915, representing of the American Jewish Committee, Marshall wrote to Pope Benedict XV. The original draft of his letter referred specifically to Polish persecution, but on the advice of his colleagues Marshall rewrote it, "making it general in its phraseology." "Yet," he wrote to Jacob Schiff, "nobody who has any knowledge of conditions can have the slightest doubt as to what we have in mind." He wrote:

> The petitioners, who are citizens of the United States of America and adherents of the Jewish faith, have learned with increasing horror of the unspeakable cruelties and hardships visited upon their co-religionists in various belligerent lands since the outbreak of the present worldwide conflict. Far beyond the sufferings which this calamity has inflicted upon those of other faiths, and in addition to the ravages and destruction occasioned by the clash of the contending armies to all who come within the sphere of their hostilities, the Jews have been marked for special persecution, and have been subject to oppressive measures not borne by their compatriots of other creeds. Passion and prejudice have been fomented against our unhappy brethren ... until their lot has ceased to be endurable. In some of the lands where they have long resided their very neighbors are bent upon their annihilation, practicing against them the most refined cruelty, and in many instances by means of an economic boycott condemning them to literal starvation.

> ... It is our sincere prayer that the occasion may be deemed a fitting one for resort to the authority vested in the Sovereign of the great Roman Hierarchy ... to admonish their flocks to hold in abhorrence these acts of persecution, of prejudice and of cruelty, which have overwhelmed our unfortunate breth-

ren. We confidently express the hope that timely action may be taken by the Vatican, to the end the sufferings ... by an act of that humanity to which Your Holiness is so passionately devoted, and that the cruel intolerance and unjust prejudice which have been aroused against them may forever vanish before this glorious exercise of Your Supreme Moral and Spiritual Power [2].

The reply, dated February 15, 1916, included:

 The Supreme Pontiff has with interest taken notice of the letter ... which you have been pleased to address to him in the name of the three million Jewish citizens of the United States of America in order to communicate to him generally the treatment to which your coreligionists complain that they have been exposed in various regions ... and you have requested him to interpose the weight of his supreme moral and spiritual power, in order that these sufferings may be terminated by an act of that humanity to which the Holy Father is so passionately devoted.... As the head of the Catholic Church (he) considers all men as brethren and teaches them to love one another, he will not cease to inculcate the observance among individuals as among nations of the principles of natural right, and to reprove every violation of them. This right should be observed and respected in relation to the Children of Israel as it should be as to all men.

Moreover, in his paternal heart, pained by the spectacle of the existing horrible war, the Supreme Pontiff feels ... more deeply than ever the necessity that all men shall recollect that they are brothers and that their salvation lies in the return to the law of love. He also desires to interest to this noble end all who, especially by reason of the sacred attributes of their pastoral ministrations, are able to bring efficient aid to this important result.

... His Holiness rejoices in the unity which in civil matters exists in the United States of America among the members of different faiths and which contributes so powerfully to the peaceful prosperity of your great country ...[3]

(Signed) Cardinal Gasparri.

Marshall reported the petition and the Pope's response to the members of the American Jewish Committee.

This petition called forth a reply from the Holy See which is a virtual encyclical against anti-Jewish prejudices, and has been followed by directions to the Catholic clergy of Poland admonishing them to use their best endeavors to put an end to the persecution which has prevailed. [4]

As the war dragged on, despite predictions that it would end quickly, Jews in many communities in Eastern Europe needed food and resources, and protection from all of the combatants. The American Jewish Committee (AJC) under Marshall's leadership wasted no time joining with the American Zionist Organization, the Orthodox Organizations, Labor Unions, and more. After protracted discussions and compromises they formed the Joint Distribution Committee to aid the war sufferers, with Marshall as one of the key active members.
Marshall issued a report to the AJC membership on September 1, 1914:

> A meeting of the Executive Committee of the American Jewish Committee was held yesterday at which communications were received from various parts of the world concerning the condition of the Jews in consequence of the late Balkan war and of the present general war raging in Europe.
>
> It was decided to appropriate $2,500 for the benefit of the Jewish orphans at Sofia, Bulgaria, who had lost their parents during (an earlier) war.
>
> Cablegrams were received from the Hon. Henry Morganthau, the American Ambassador at Constantinople ... indicating that the Palestinian Jews were confronting a serious crisis in consequence of the discontinuance of contributions... from their brethren in the several European lands that are now at war with each other.
>
> It was reported that the destruction of a number of flourishing colonies was threatened, unless financial assistance was at once forthcoming. The sum of $50,000 was stated to be immediately required ... and that a responsible committee had been formed ... for the establishment of a free loan society and for the support of families, (whose) bread-winners had been called into the army, (and) were in a destitute condition. The committee appropriated the sum of $25,000 ... Mr. Jacob H. Schiff adding $12,500 to this sum, and it being understood that the Zionist organizations would undertake to secure the remaining $12,500 needed to carry on this relief work.
>
> The committee then considered the effect of the war upon the Jews of Russia, Germany, Austria, the Balkan states, and other parts of the world ... In order to cope with the serious problems which in all probability must soon

be dealt with, a sub-committee was appointed to gather authentic information with regard to the situation ... and to make recommendations as to ways and means by which necessary and adequate assistance might at the proper time be rendered to all sufferers, without discrimination. The committee proposes to call upon other organizations to cooperate with it to aid in the formulation and carrying out of plans for the accomplishment of results commensurate with the immensity of the problem.[5]

In October, Marshall issued a call to all of the participating Jewish organizations:

> The stupendous conflict which is now raging on the European continent is a calamity, the extent of which transcends imagination. While all mankind is directly or indirectly involved in the consequences, the burden of suffering and of destitution rests with especial weight upon our brethren in Eastern Europe. The embattled armies are spreading havoc and desolation within the Jewish Pale of Settlement in Russia, and the Jews of Galicia and East Prussia dwell in the very heart of the war zone. Fully one-half of all the Jews of the world live in the regions where active hostilities are in progress. The Jews of Palestine, who have largely depended on Europe for assistance, have been literally cut off from their sources of supply.
>
> In this exigency, it is evident that the Jews of America must again come to the rescue. They must assume the duty of giving relief commensurate with the existing needs. They must be prepared to make sacrifices, and to proceed systematically in collecting and distributing a fund which will, so far as possible, alleviate this extraordinary distress. There is probably no parallel in history to the present status of the Jews. Unity of action is essential. There should be no division in counsel or in sentiment. All differences should be laid aside and forgotten. Nothing counts now but harmonious and effective action.
>
> You are invited to send three delegates to a conference, to be held by the various national Jewish organizations at Temple Emanu-El on Sunday, October 25, 1914 to consider the organization of a general committee and the formulation of plans to accomplish the largest measure of relief, and to deal adequately with the various phases of the problems presented.[6]

In November 1914 Jacob Schiff received a letter from W.A. Warschansky who was a member of a Jewish committee in Petrograd, Russia:

... I scarcely need to repeat, how great the need for help is, practically the whole of Russian Poland having been devastated by the hostile armies. It would take hundreds of millions ... to [re]store even part of their former prosperity to the population. In a great number of towns Jewish Committee [s] have been formed, working in unison with the non-Jewish institutions, since they all join in the common aim of assisting the poor victims, irrespective of their creed. Thanks to the Russian organization and to the Committee of the Grandduches [sic] Tatiana Nikolayevna ... the attitude towards the Jewish refugees from Poland has considerably improved lately.

As regards Jewish society, I may say they are doing their utmost ... but, as you will well understand, the means at their disposal are quite inadequate. I beg to suggest that the money collected by you be transmitted to the Asov-Don-Bank, Petrograd for account of the Jewish Committee for the aid of the victims of the War ...

I further wish to draw your attention to another matter. Owing to the war the immigrants in the United States have no possibility of remitting money to their relatives and friends in Russia (they) are thus deprived of the only support that kept them from starvation. Would it be possible for you to arrange with some institution in New York to receive the money from the immigrants and to remit it to the Jewish Colonization Association ... Petrograd?

I thank you in advance for everything you will do in favour of our suffering fellow-brethren.... [7]

By October 24, 1914 the American Jewish Committee had established the American Jewish Relief Committee (AJRC) and Orthodox leaders formed the Central Relief Committee that joined with the AJRC. They formed the Joint Distribution Committee of the American Friends for Jewish War Sufferers (*JDC*) that would solicit and collect funds for distribution to the victims of the war. In 1915 the Peoples relief Committee, representing labor, was added.[8]

The Zionists had formed the Provisional Executive Committee for Zionist Affairs on August 31, 1914, and it also stood ready to support the Jews in the countries in Eastern Europe. Its chairman was the prominent attorney Louis D. Brandeis who, in 1916,[9] was a friend of President Wilson, and the first Jew to become a justice to the United States Supreme Court.[10] Brandeis felt that the relationship would be helpful in supporting the growing prominence of the Zionist organization.

The organizations of the JDC collected funds that were sent to Europe through the available normal channels until the United States entered the war in 1917. Then, the U.S. State Department gave permission to establish an agency in Holland to distribute the funds.[11]

The organizations devoted their joint efforts to marshaling and distributing funds, but they could not agree on what their course would be when the war ended. The Jewish people of Europe were but one of several minorities in the nations of the defunct European empires. Who would represent their interests in peace negotiations? In the end it would be the Jewish delegations that would speak up for the rights of these minorities when the war ended and the time came for concluding a peace treaty.

The delegation of American Jews to a peace treaty conference would consist of members of the Joint Distribution Committee. It would not be easy to decide on the goals of the delegation, because there were widely different goals from the two leading proponents. The Zionists, and some others, wanted an American Jewish Congress elected by the Jews of America, to accomplish the realization of the ultimate dream, the creation of a Jewish Nation. The American Jewish Committee and others thought that was unrealistic, and were completely against it. The meetings boiled into discussions that were divisive, bitter and, at times, personally insulting.

The idea of a Jewish nation in the form of a political entity was contrary to the traditional beliefs of many of the leaders of the AJC. Their members had worked since the beginning of the twentieth century to improve the lives of the Jewish people of America. They had taken numerous private and public positions on behalf of Jews and Judaism in America and in Europe. Many of their founding members had become leaders and leading financial supporters of Jews in America, and had solicited and contributed a major share of the funds raised by the JDC. Their achievements and philanthropy had unselfishly supported the Jews in America.

The influx of Jews from Eastern Europe in the early years of the century gradually reduced the influence of the AJC. The immigrants became the Jewish majority, they had their leaders, but while their influence had grown, their wealth was much less than that of their predecessors.

On August 30, 1916 Marshall wrote a letter to his British friend Israel Zangwill, in reply to a letter of condolence for Florence's death in May 1916. Zangwill was the celebrated English author, playwright, and poet. Born to a poor Russian emigrant family in London in 1863, he was seriously concerned about the Jewish people and the Jewish religion, and Jewish life in the Diaspora. He and Marshall had several mutual friends including Jacob Schiff and the late Rabbi Solomon Schechter. Marshall wrote, sans oratorical niceties, on what was happening in the Jewish community:

> I thank you most sincerely for your very kind letter of sympathy. You, who knew Mrs. Marshall, can appreciate the poignancy of my grief and the extent of the loss, which I have sustained. She held you and Mrs. Zangwill in high esteem, and took the greatest delight in reading every line of your writings that came to her notice.
>
> You are entirely right in the thought that, in order to forget myself, I have resorted to hard work, and especially in regard to Jewish affairs. While we have been quite successful in raising funds for the victims in the war zone, the members of American Jewry have literally had each other by the ears.
>
> A spirit of madness seems to have possessed the world. Although our people have foes in profusion, they are not content, but are bent upon creating chaos and schism in their own ranks. To my mind the problems with which we have to deal are of so delicate a nature, that the mob cannot grapple with them. Yet a number of self-seekers have indulged in flattery, chicanery and misrepresentations, to such an extent that the average Jew really believes that if a Jewish Congress is held and adopts resolutions demanding that their brethren in Russia and Roumania shall be emancipated, that result will at once be accomplished As you may well expect, the American Jewish Committee and other national organizations which are not easily influenced by such nonsense, declined to take part in the Congress. We called a conference … Peace negotiations between the Congress Organization and the Conference took place as the result of my insistence and we arrived at terms of settlement, which were adopted with practical unanimity by the two Executive Committees. The Zionists are now seeking to defeat the settlement … the Zionists and Nationalists have been playing politics and have convinced themselves that they might convert all of American Jewry to their cause either by playing politics or by the sword. They have therefore slandered and libeled Mr. (Jacob) Schiff, Dr. (Cyrus) Adler, Judge (Mayer) Sulzberger, and to some extent, me, and have sought to destroy the influence of the American Jewish Committee. If the referendum results in ratification of the settlement, then I trust that we may accomplish some useful results through concerted action and cooperation with Jewish organizations abroad …

This is a mere sketch of a very small part of the work in which I have been engaged during the past few months. I must ... tell you of the great pleasure which I have had in reading your new book "The War for the World." It is really a work of genius. It is marvelous how you foresaw ... much of what has occurred during the past two cruel years ... I am only now beginning to appreciate the statesmanship of many of your utterances.[12]

Resolving the disagreement between the AJC and the Zionist factions had not been addressed when the JDC was created. By 1918, with the end of the war looming, aid needed for the Jewish people who were victimized by the war had not diminished. The organizations would have to compromise their differences. Louis Brandeis and Louis Marshall, leaders of the two factions, had a meeting, and the organizations of the JDC did come to an agreement. Together they would form an American Jewish Congress that would function until the conclusion of negotiations and completion of peace treaties with the countries in Eastern Europe. Then the American Jewish Congress would dissolve.

The change in sentiments is likely attributable to the famous British Government Declaration on November 2, 1917, that came about primarily from the efforts of Chaim Weizmann, the world leader of Zionism, and the British-Jewish leader Herbert Samuel. David Balfour, Britain's Foreign Secretary, wrote a letter to Lord Rothschild:

Dear Lord Rothschild:

I have much pleasure in conveying to you, on behalf of his Majesty's Government, the following declaration of sympathy with Jewish Zionist aspirations which has been submitted to, and approved by, the Cabinet.

'His Majesty's Government view with favour the establishment in Palestine of a national home for the Jewish people, and will use their best endeavours to facilitate the achievement of this object, it being clearly understood that nothing shall be done which may prejudice the civil and religious rights of existing communities in Palestine, to the rights and political status enjoyed by Jews in any other country'.

I should be grateful if you would bring this declaration to the knowledge of the Zionist Federation.

Yours,
(signed) Arthur James Balfour

This historic announcement greatly affected the people and organizations that provided support for the Jewish people suffering from the ravages of the war. Marshall's oldest son, James, had joined the U.S. Army and was a lieutenant serving in France on November 11, 1918 when an armistice agreement between the Allies and Germany concluded the hostilities. In December Louis wrote to him:

> It is quite possible that I may be compelled to go abroad within the next month. The American Jewish Committee has insisted that I must go as its representative to present the Jewish problems to the Peace Conference, and at the meeting of the American Jewish Congress held during the present week I was elected as one of the delegation which it is sending to France for the same purpose. Were it not for the fact that most of the American delegates are more interested in Palestine than they are with the fate of six million Jews of Eastern Europe, I would not permit myself to be persuaded, especially since I regard with horror the three weeks of seasickness which the round trip would involve. I had practically made up my mind that I would never again cross the Atlantic. I have also had requests from Jewish organizations in England and France to be on hand for the purpose of conferring with them as to our program. My present impression therefore is that I would not be justified in saying no.
>
> As you are aware, I have always considered the American Jewish Congress a misfortune were it to be convened as long as the war was in progress. I was entirely indifferent whether it should be held or not after the cessation of hostilities. It was that issue which I fought out from the spring of 1915 and thereby engendered much temporary hatred and some permanent animosities. At all events even those who at first were insistent upon the holding of the congress at the earliest possible moment saw the error of their ways and united with me in postponing the actual holding of the congress, even though the delegates were elected in 1917, until now. The congress met at Philadelphia on Sunday and continued until Wednesday evening. With the exception of Monday evening and Tuesday I was there continuously and took a very active part in its deliberations. I succeeded in having the congress unanimously adopt the proposed bill of rights which I drafted for the American Jewish Committee and submitted to President Wilson some time ago. Whatever changes were made were such as I was willing to accept.

Before I took hold of the matter there were five committees that were struggling with the subject and made no headway. I called them all together and performed what everybody considers the miracle of bringing about unanimous action by the conjoint committees, followed by the unanimous adoption of the report, with great enthusiasm and without debate, by the congress itself. The resolution with regard to Palestine is much more moderate than one would have supposed possible some months ago. The Zionists are beginning to see that it will not be possible for them to establish a sovereign State. They are looking forward now to the possibility of growing into one in the course of time under an English protectorate. That is precisely the attitude which the American Jewish Committee has long since taken and which it announced in the resolution which it accepted in April last.

It is quite likely that Dr. Cyrus Adler and Mr. Oscar S. Straus will also accompany me, if I go, on behalf of the American Jewish Committee.

If Ruth [Marshall's daughter] and I go I would not like to leave Robert and George without some kind of supervision. Were it not for the unpleasant notoriety that Dr. Magnes has had I would have been very glad to have invited his family to take charge of the house … but I am quite sure that it would be highly unwise to extend such an invitation. Dr. Magnes was recently operated for a rupture which he sustained while working in the garden at Chappequa … he also had his appendix removed. I wish that he could have had a little sanity and a great deal of common sense introduced in lieu of the rudimentary organ of which he has been deprived. [Rabbi Magnes was his brother-in-law and a close friend. Prominent in the Jewish community, in the early years of the war he spoke out against the entry of the United States, and was looked upon as being pro-German. Marshall of course disagreed with him].

The Jewish War Relief campaign is about ending, and with much difficulty and some camouflage the five million dollars which New York was to contribute have been subscrived (sic). This makes the total amount raised in the United States during 1918 $15,000,000, or a total since I called this work into being of over $30,000,000, a most extraordinary and gratifying achievement. When we began the suggestion that we should raise $10,000,000 was considered quixotic.

In your letter No. 52 you refer jocularly to a boy who wrote home that he wants to make the world "safe from democracy." A short time ago, while I was making a speech, through a slip of the tongue I made precisely the same remark, and when I appreciated what I had done from the titter which arose I remarked that I meant just what I had said—for I was referring to the political party from which it was necessary to rescue the world. That is just what I feel about the Democratic Party. Unless we shake it out of the control of our government in 1920 we will be in a sad state. I am entirely serious in what I say and am not speaking as a partisan. The South is in the saddle and is running amuck. It is displaying no statesmanship, no patriotism, and an utter lack of wisdom.

I agree with what you have said on the great achievement of the American Army in France. There can be no doubt that when it came it turned the tide. It did not come a moment too soon. Had it arrived a year earlier Russia would not have become what it now is, a bewildered chaos, and millions of men would have been saved. Our boys undoubtedly restored to the British and French armies the dash which was needed to drive the fear of God into the German brutes. We must not, however, forget that, but for France and England, Europe and America would at this moment lie prostrate at the feet of the Kaiser and militarism would have been so entrenched that it could not have been overthrown for centuries.

While in Philadelphia I saw Aunt Bertha, who though extremely weak, is feeling much more comfortable than she did ... Uncle Abe is also much better, but of all the fussers I have ever met he stands pre-eminent. His entire life is made up of a series of trivialities of which he constitutes the principal one ...

Your affectionate (father)[13]

The letter conveys a good deal of Louis Marshall's persona. He told, without modesty, of his success in overcoming the difficulties in convincing the prominent and numerically superior factions of the Jewish community to agree on a delegation. He would lead it.

Marshall was a Republican, and although he did criticize President Wilson on occasion during the War, he wrote to Wilson several times about the conditions of the Jews in Poland and Roumania asking for his support.

After the War ended, in 1918 and 1919, as Polish leaders were striving to reestablish Poland as an independent nation, the Polish society's harsh treatment of the Polish Jews was ongoing. Despite some moderation in the persecutions for a brief period, the harassments and discrimination in Poland continued.

As the War was nearing its conclusion, the renowned pianist Ignace J. Paderewski, the leading Polish official, was the "Representative and Plenipotentiary of the Polish National Committee in the United States." He and Roman Dmowski would be the leaders of the Polish representatives at the post-war peace conference.

Roman Dmowski was the leader of the *Polish National Democratic Party* (the Endek), which had been a part of political life since the late nineteenth century. *The Endek* concentrated on economic problems, with the slogan "Don't Buy Jewish" leading an aggressive boycott of Jewish businesses in 1912, and as the boycott spread it received wider support. In that year's election of representatives to the Duma, the Imperial Russian legislature, the Jews did not support the Endek candidates; the party proclaimed a "Polish—Jewish war" thereby intensifying the anti-Jewish boycott.

Dmowski led his party and its constant support of the boycott and he was characterized as a cold, hard, nationalistic politician who saw the Jews of Poland as his country's greatest problem. When asked by an American official about Poland's position vis-à-vis its minorities, he replied, "Jews form at least ten percent of our population, and in my judgment this is at least eight percent too much".[14]

By 1918 Dmowski was chairman of the Polish National Committee. On August 12, 1918, he wrote to Mr. Paderewski in Paris:

> ... I beg to inform you that by unanimous decision of the Polish National Committee, the following statement has been already made in Paris:
>
> 'Our aim is to create an independent Polish State, composed of all Polish territories inclusive of those which give Poland access to the sea; a strong state which would be able to keep in check its western neighbors ... and would constitute a bulwark against their expansion in Central Europe and the Orient.
>
> We fully realize that it is only with the assistance of the great free nations [the Allies], in war against the Central Powers [Germany] that we shall be in a position to achieve the unification as well as to obtain the independence of Poland ... The Polish State must have a democratic constitution. It must govern along principles of liberty and justice, coordinated with principles

of order ... No privileged classes should exist in new Poland: Polish citizens without distinction as to origin, race or creed must all stand equal before the law.

In September, 1918, Marshall wrote a letter to Paderewski about the prevailing conditions in Poland. He suggested that a conference of the Polish leaders, and Marshall and his associates, could be convened to formulate a declaration of principles so far as they affect the Polish Jews. The conference did not take place. However, in time Marshall did meet with Dmowski.

Mr. Dmowski's aforementioned letter that said that the "(Poland) must govern along principles of liberty and justice, etc ..." was certainly a change from all of his past positions.

Marshall and Dmowski agreed to meet in New York City on October 6, 1918. Marshall called on him at his apartments at the Plaza Hotel, and was greeted cordially. Marshall reported much of the conversation in a report to his AJC colleagues. What follows are excerpts from his narrative:

Dmowski immediately said that he regarded it important for the Jews to cooperate with the Poles in their aspirations for a restoration of their national existence.

> "I wish to be entirely frank and to explain my attitude and that of the Poles toward the Jews of Poland. My father conducted fisheries and had close business relationships with the Jews of our country. At his funeral there were probably more Jews present than non-Jews, and I looked upon them as friends ... For centuries there was no anti-Jewish prejudice in Poland ..."

Marshall interrupted,

> "the Polish nobility had evinced continued hostility and brutality toward the Jews of Poland ... the Church had from time to time evinced enmity, and I (am) familiar with Jewish history in Poland."

Dmowski replied,

> "... it was true that the nobility was brutal, but the brutality toward the Jews was of the same type as that which it practiced upon the Polish peasants. There never was a pogrom in Poland."

Marshall again interrupted,

"there (have) been Polish pogroms since 1914 and (you), as the leader of the National Democratic Party (have been charged) as having advocated pogroms in the newspaper, *Dwa Grosz.*"

Dmowski said that the charge was in error; then he said,

"I must confess that personally I have been hostile to the Jews and have as a leader of a political party deliberately engaged in a struggle with them, and am responsible for the economic boycott to which they have been subjected ... I will give you the reasons for my action. About 1908 a large number of Lithuanian Jews, who could no longer endure the treatment accorded to them by Russia, came to Poland. Strangely enough they persisted ... in speaking the Russian language obtrusively ... also began a movement whereby the Jews were induced to employ Jewish doctors and Jewish lawyers instead of Polish physicians and lawyers. Consequently they began what I call a boycott.... Jews voted for Jews in elections to the Duma ... There was economic competition between them ... (as well as) other reasons which led to a clash between the Poles and the Jews ... another reason for the growing hostility ... lay in the fact that the Jews persisted in speaking Yiddish ... even their men of education ... All of these things together contributed to the creation of a feeling of animosity, it was for that reason that I and my party encouraged the boycott, which has been a very severe one and terrible in its operation, and I am frank to say that it continues to this moment and has been growing worse instead of better."

Marshall responded,

"It came to me ... as a great shock when I first learned of the details of the boycott ... and if you will permit me Mr. Dmowski to use the expression, I regard the action of your party and of yourself as simply monstrous".

Dmowski interrupted,

"I think that your characterization is not out of place. In fact I like the word monstrous."

Marshall pointed out the errors in his reasons for establishing the boycott, and that Polish immigrants continued to speak Polish in America:

> "You have introduced poison into the system of the Polish people, who you say had been free from prejudice against the Jews.... It passes beyond the control of him who first administered it, and in the end is destructive not only of the immediate victim, but of those in whom the venom has been engendered ... it is you who lowered the moral fiber of the Polish people, and it is you alone who ... should persuade them of the error of their ways and induce them to terminate this horrible boycott and to fraternize with the Jews of Poland. The Pope, a few years ago, recognized the injustice of this boycott, and as I understand it, through the leading clergymen of Poland, sought to put it down, but they did not succeed because of the opposition of your party."

As Dmowski walked back and forth in the room, he said,

> "Yes I know what the Pope did, but you are perhaps unaware of the fact that I am no persona grata at the Vatican ... if I were now suddenly to change ... and deal with the boycott as you suggest, my party would immediately say that I was bought."

Marshall replied that (he) could not see how that would be possible if his party had confidence in him and if he was its leader,

> "They (know) as well as (you) the motive which had led them to unleash the bloodthirsty tiger and it was in their power not only to make amends but to help the cause of Poland by destroying that tiger with their own hands. Moreover, the moral soundness of a policy which united the Polish people and which did away with the wickedness of the boycott could be made clear by the Polish press, on the forum and in the churches, and the same agencies that had created it could be directed toward its elimination."

Dmowski responded,

> "... after all the real cause of the boycott rested in the poverty of the country and in the fact that there were not enough crumbs to go around, and that, therefore, the Poles were obliged to save themselves from starvation by engaging in competition, however destructive against the Jews who were engaged in commerce and industry. But, I am sure that if the New Poland is created, with all the resources that it would have, we should occupy almost

the same position as does the United States and there would be no such conflict of interest as that which now exists."

He showed Marshall a map of the New Poland. It would include "Russian Poland", and sections of Galicia and Posen, and the city of Danzig. These would give the new nation tremendous coal fields, salt mines, copper and iron mines, oil fields, and an outlet to the Baltic Sea. He therefore thought it important that the Jews ... should, in the interest of their own brethren, assist in the accomplishment of his plans, and ... that they should furnish capital with which to develop commerce and industries in Poland.
Marshall commented,

> "... before the Jews (can) be asked to take any position on this subject ... the Poles should put an immediate end to the boycott, ... they should show by their attitude toward the Jews that the era of hate and conflict ... (is) at an end."

Dmowski said,

> "it would all come in due time, but the only sure way of ending the struggle was to put an end to the real cause of it, which was the poverty of Poland."

They conversed for more than two hours. Dmowski said that he was very glad to have had this opportunity for an exchange of views, and that he was very anxious that there should be more conferences in the hope that a complete understanding could be reached; that it was his idea to take immediate action for the purpose of combating the boycott by indirect methods.
Marshall replied,

> "I (consider) it the part of wisdom to take immediate and direct action to accomplish that end, because so long as the boycott prevailed no Jew could look upon Poland as other than hostile."

Marshall pointed out to Dmowski the importance of purging Poland of an evil which would certainly lead to destruction, and to consider the effect that the exclusion of the Jews had upon Spain and Portugal, and other countries during the centuries when they were not permitted to dwell there. The Jews of Poland could become for Poland a source of strength as they have become for the United States.

Dmowski said,

> "... there are no Jews in Japan and Japan has prospered but perhaps I am wrong there, because I recognize the fact that but for Mr. Schiff, Japan would not be what it is today." [This was a reference to Jacob Schiff's financial support of Japan in the war between Japan and Russia in 1904].

Dmowski escorted Marshall to the elevator, saying that he wanted to remain in this country for some little time, and that he was very anxious to resume their discussion.[15]

There were no more meetings between them.

On November 11, 1918 the fighting ended, as an armistice was declared. By December the Jewish organizations had agreed to the creation of the American Jewish Congress, and that Marshall would be one of the delegates to the Paris Peace Conference. On December 15 be delivered a lengthy, illuminating address to the American Jewish Congress:

Mr. Chairman and Fellow Delegates:

> It is a source of great satisfaction to me to me to be permitted to call to your attention a number of facts on which all of us should soberly reflect before we are qualified to act at this Congress with respect to the most important ... of the subjects on which we have been summoned to deliberate. The future of Palestine is no longer a mooted question. The action of the British Government, as announced by its eminent spokesman, Mr. Balfour, endorsed as it has been ... by the Allied Nations,—approved ... by the President of the United States—will undoubtedly receive at the Peace Conference which is about to assemble at Versailles, the sanction of all the nations of the world.

> We here in America sympathize with every Jewish aspiration. Many of us who in the past have been disconnected with the Zionist organization have nevertheless felt that it would be a privilege to assist in the rehabilitation of the land of our fathers.

> This is not on my part an eleventh hour recantation ... of principles. There are some of us who have in the past been classed as anti-Zionist—which we never were—who have gladly inaugurated work in the Holy Land for the purpose of developing it agriculturally and educationally ...

> I pass from the subject of Palestine to that which should give us all the greatest concern,—the welfare, the protection, the emancipation of the Jews of Eastern Europe. This is the time, if the time shall ever come in our sad

history, when light can be made to break upon it. This is the accepted time and hour when the united will of the Jewish people must be heard at the peace table.

Russia is now in turmoil. She has been split into several, yes, into many states. I am confident that if the orderly elements of Russia shall once more come into power ... the (same) men whose first act when they came into office was to abolish all of the hateful and oppressive laws against the Jews and to wipe them from the statute book, if men like these shall return to power with a strong and liberal government, then it is certain that the rights of the Jews of Russia will be fully protected. Today, however, Russia is divided into many territories, each with its own problem.

Then there is Jugo-Slavia, Czecho-Slovakia, new states desiring recognition at the Peace Congress, States ... in which the Jews of those regions will be concerned to the same extent as all other people residing within the boundaries ... that shall eventually be assigned to these new states.

Then there is the question of Roumania ... There are now between 250,000 and 300,000 Jews in old Roumania. Should the new Roumania be organized with additional territory, the population ... would include 750,000 Jews. Hence the Roumanian problem as affecting our people, serious and tragic as it has been, becomes even more significant. The amelioration of the fate of the Jews of Roumania now assumes for us a task of huge dimensions.

But the greatest, the most important, the most difficult of our complications are those which revolve around the new state of Poland which is to be created. As projected, that will include Russian Poland ... Galicia, a part of Silesia, a part of Prussian Poland ... Danzig. A Poland thus constituted would have a Jewish population of practically four million. It is the future of these our brethren that we should take to heart tonight ... until the Peace Conference shall have pronounced the verdict of immediate, complete and unconditional emancipation ...

We all know of the patriotism of the Jews of Poland and their devotion to the land of their birth. We also know, alas, that ever since 1912 there has been in active progress in Poland that horrible economic boycott which has threatened the absolute annihilation and extermination of our brethren in Poland ... We know how it has poisoned the very roots of government, how it has incessantly worked into the consciousness of the entire population ... We know further what a tremendous burden of sorrow and destitution it has imposed upon the Jews of Poland. We have also heard during the past weeks ... that pogroms and massacres have been taking place in Poland, Galicia and Roumania, accompanied not only by loss of life, but by the looting and destruction of property.

It is denied by some Polish leaders that such Pogroms have actually occurred. It is admitted that lives have been lost and that there have been outbreaks, but it is alleged that they have been the concomitants of Civil War and that in the natural course of such warfare Jews have been injured and killed ... This information does not correspond with that which has come to us from other sources, reputable and trustworthy. At all events grave conditions unquestionably prevail.

Some of us have given careful study to the Polish situation, as we have that of ... other lands ... It has been our purpose to secure guarantees that if new Governments are created ... it must be upon compliance with conditions precedent which will in law or in fact secure to the Jews those equal rights for which they have so long striven and to which ... they are justly entitled. We shall not accept any false promises or any transparent shams. We shall not content ourselves with anything less than adequate guarantees, enforceable by the powers and shall insist upon the giving of such guarantees.

Since last April a number of us ... have been in conference with the leaders of the Polish Party ... including Mr. Paderewski, the representative in America of the National Polish Committee, of which Mr. Dmowski is the Chairman, and others. We received sweet words of promise from them eight months ago, but we were not given the assurance of an immediate termination of the boycott ... We were informed that a favorable recommendation would be made to the Polish National Committee of Paris, but we heard nothing from that body or its agents ... Then followed a series of conferences with Mr. Dmowski, with Mr. Paderewski ... Then came a new turn of the political kaleidoscope of Poland, and General Pilsudski appeared at the head of political and military affairs there, with an army at his command.

Of course nobody can say how many more twists there will be to that kaleidoscope ... That does not concern us. If there is to be a new and independent and enlarged Poland, it matters not (who) shall be at the head. Whoever it may be, justice must be done to the Jews. (The various Polish) organizations apparently have come together ... that they may secure for Poland the rights which they shall ask at the Peace Conference ... they realize that they cannot afford to disregard the Jews who are as much a part of Poland as the Poles, and that mere promises will not now prove sufficient. They no longer doubt that ... no people whoever they may be are entitled to national existence and to national rights until they are prepared to respect and give full recognition to the rights of minorities.

I do not care to what extent they may be permitted to save their faces provided we can accomplish what it is so essential to accomplish, the emancipation of our brethren in Poland. We have no feelings of animosity against any people in the world even though we have for ages been grievously wronged ... We know that for twenty centuries we have been ready to show by our example that, knowing what national hatreds are, we seek their extirpation. We are prepared to forgive the past. We only ask that our future may be secure. In Palestine the Jews have pledged themselves to recognize the rights of every people and of every creed.

We are, therefore, not opposed to any Poland that the Peace Conference may be prepared to organize, provided only that the Poland so created ... shall recognize the fundamental rights of all of its inhabitants, and shall confer them with proper guarantees upon every man, woman and child within her boundaries, however humble they may be.

Marshall read from a letter from John Smulski, the head of the National Polish Department. It said that from various sources there have been communications to the effect that pogroms have been conducted in Poland and Galicia. They would not admit to the truth of the reports since "such practices are contrary to the traditions and inconsistent with the character of the Polish people." They proposed that a commission be constituted composed of Jews, Poles and Americans ... to investigate the conditions in Poland affecting Jews. The commission was never organized.

From the Peace Conference Marshall wanted a Polish Government that would:

> hold in abhorrence ... pogroms and boycotts, recognize the principle that the Jews must have full and equal rights of citizenship in Poland ... and that those rights are to be protected ...

That is probably all that can be expected from any Peace Conference, provided that it shall write these conditions into the Treaty ... and which is to constitute the Charter of the new Government to be created in terms that will not brook violation ...

> ... we must look at this as a practical question. We cannot change humanity over night. A Peace Conference cannot make men different from what they are. We cannot as Jews afford to invite animosities ... to say that this or that shall not be done ... or that this or that state shall not be formed ... We are not seated at the peace table. Various new or expanded Nations are about to be organized. The Jews constitute but a fraction of each of them ... They can only insist ... that if these Nations ... are formed, then the Jews must be assured by these Nations of rights in every way equal to those of any other inhabitant of the State in which they may dwell.

Marshall spoke of the character of the members of the delegation and their willingness to know the significant details of the matters to be addressed, and gain the respect of "our fellow citizens."

In the conclusion of his lengthy and dynamic presentation, he said:

> Our efforts must be directed with humanity of spirit and in the confidence that justice and humanity will triumph at the Assizes of the Nations at which, I am confident, will be proclaimed liberty throughout the world and to all the inhabitants thereof.[16]

Marshall's misgivings about an American Jewish Congress and traveling to Europe faded away, with a lessening of his opposition to the Zionist aspirations for a Jewish nation. In a letter to his friend A. Leo Weil, dated December 21, 1918, he explained his position:

> I had not intended to go myself [to Paris]. But now that the [American Jewish] Congress has selected a delegation of nine members, of whom I am the only non-Zionist, I feel that it is my duty to go in order that the welfare of six million Jews of Eastern Europe shall not be lost sight of in the effort to emphasize the Palestinian question. I should like very much to have Dr. Adler and Oscar S. Straus accompany me as representatives of the American Jewish Committee. We would then be able to give due effect to the vital subjects as to which favorable action is demanded by the sad lot of our brethren in Russia, Poland, Roumania and other Middle Eastern and East European lands.[17]

The Jewish organizations of America, despite the difficult and at times angry discussions as to what to do when the war ended, had resolved their differences and were united in support of the suffering Jews in Europe. Their delegation would sail to Paris to participate with the nations in creating the final peace treaty between the victorious European Nations and the defeated Germany and her allies.

Louis Marshall and Cyrus Adler made preparations to sail for Europe together. Born in America to families of modest economic and social circumstances, they were now part of the team that would represent the Jews of America in a crucial international conference. Their mission was to improve the lives of the Jews who did not have the good fortune to live in the United States. In the contentious proceedings that would wring peace from the winners and the embittered losers, the Jewish delegates did not represent a political nation, and would have to struggle to be noticed.

The delegation consisted of prominent, successful American Jews, including some who were admittedly not religious and had little or limited relationships with their forebears in Europe, but they would spend money and time to help Jews who were strangers. While there were probably many different reasons; the "Jewish Soul" could have been a common thread.

The American delegation's essential goal was that clauses would be written into the peace treaty stating that all minorities living in the European countries should have rights equal to those of the majority in every country.

Considering the history of Europe, it was a formidable task.

Notes

1 House & Seymour Pgs 220-221
2 Reznikoff V2 Pgs 581-582
3 Ibid Pg 583
4 Ibid
5 Ibid
6 Ibid
7 Ibid
8 EJ V2 Pg 827
9 Janowsky
10 Janowsky
11 EJ V2 Pg 827
12 Reznikoff V2 Pg 519
13 AJA-MC
14 The Poles Pg 312
15 Reznikoff V2 Pgs 585-593
16 Reznikoff V2 Pgs 526-536
17 Ibid V2 Pgs 538-539

Versailles 1919: The Jewish Aspect

Jacob Schiff, the important leader and great philanthropist, wrote a letter to Louis Marshall on January 2, 1919:

> I learn with mixed feelings of your decision to go abroad as one of the delegates of the American Jewish Congress before the Peace Conference at Versailles. The sacrifice you are bringing is very, very great in many respects, but the cause you are going for is no doubt worth it, and I am very certain that no one else can so ably and effectively represent the interests not alone of American Jewry, but indeed of world Jewry, with your great ability and energy, and your big Jewish heart.[1]

Cyrus Adler and Louis Marshall sailed from New York City for Paris on March 10, 1919 on the S.S. Caronia, an old steamer that had been a converted cruiser in the war. It was a chilly voyage, made uncomfortable due to a longshoremen's strike that created a shortage of coal and at times they were subjected to below freezing temperatures.

Adler's cheerful letters to his wife Racie were not cold:

> Friday night there was another moving picture which was so poor as to be funny ... then someone began to play popular songs on the piano and the whole crowd joined in somehow, and it gave me a better feeling than being in the dining room. This morning I am warm. We had Shabbos dinner in my cabin yesterday; bread, tongue and fruit. I attended services—Episcopal of course. The people were very devout, but I thought the service rather uninspiring. There was no sermon. The 'lesson' was from Deuteronomy and most of the service consisted of Psalms. Here endeth the lesson.[2]

Upon their arrival in London they met with Claude Montefiore, Sir Stuart Samuel, and Anthony Rothschild who were prominent members of the Jewish community and supporters of the British Delegation to the Paris Conference.

They agreed that they wanted all the Jews of Eastern Europe to have equal rights as citizens. Montefiore touched upon the serious point of contention between Jewish delegations from Western and Eastern Europe when he stated that the Jews are a religious people. The delegates from the countries in Eastern Europe, where pogroms proliferated as part of the national culture, considered the Jews to be a nation, expressed as Zionism and bolstered by the Balfour Declaration proclaimed in 1917.[3]

The Orthodox and the Zionist members of the United States Delegation were in agreement with the Eastern European Delegations, that the Jewish People are a distinct nation and would eventually live in Palestine where the Jews would be responsible for their own destiny. The Zionist Organization of America sought to petition the Peace Conference to recognize the Jewish people as a national entity, but it was opposed by the Jewish representatives of England and France.

Most of the American delegates had come to Paris in January, well before Marshall and Adler, and those Americans agreed to a meeting with the Eastern European Delegations at Zionist headquarters in Paris to try to create a united Jewish presence in Versailles.

Within the American Jewish Congress delegation there were divisions as well. Designated Chairman Judge Julian Mack, who was a member of the American Jewish Committee, was a dedicated Zionist. Marshall and Adler were not. Many of those Americans who had come to Paris in January well before Marshall and Adler, saw that it would be difficult to unite the various die-hard factions.

Marshall firmly believed in a Jewish people that was a significant, strong, enduring religious body. He was neither a Zionist nor an Orthodox Jew and opposed to a Jewish "national entity." However, as a deeply religious man faithful to Reform Judaism, he believed that all branches of Judaism should be supported. As a leader of the delegates from his own United States, who were divided over the issue, he found himself in the difficult position of trying to bring their delegation together with the Jewish delegates from the European Countries who were similarly divided.

France's *Grand Rabbin* Israel Levi called for a conference, and asked Marshall as one of the vice-presidents of the American Delegation to be the chairman, and Marshall agreed.

Marshall, Adler and the other delegates would address the task of bringing about Jewish unity. Adler's comments were:

> Mr. Marshall was invited to act as chairman of the meeting, at which he was wonderfully efficient. His knowledge of French and German was excellent, and he also knew Yiddish pretty well. It was in many ways the most

important Conference that the Jewish representatives had, and while it did not result in agreement, I think it resulted in understanding. A most earnest discussion was held at which different points of view were presented.... representing the strongly nationalistic, and the Jewish religious.[4]

Even with the dark history of the terrible actions of Poland and Roumania before the Paris Peace Conference, it could have been possible for the negotiators to leave things as they were and not provide for any enforceable protections for minorities. However, in the proposed charter of the League of Nations the Allies would provide that all the minority clauses were expressly framed as "obligations of international concern ... and placed under the guarantee of the League of Nations."

The Eastern European Countries were either the defeated or newly created or reawakened from divisions of the past. Their Jews were persecuted because they were separate in language, education, and dress perhaps even disloyal to the government. Also of course, because it was traditional. With little internal support except from their own, Jews were convenient scapegoats especially in times of economic and political trouble. Even in periods when there were more tolerant regimes, and conditions would improve the Jews had limited rights.

The larger of the nations of Eastern Europe, Poland, Roumania, Hungary, and Czechoslovakia were to be independent or re-formed nations and hopefully this would be a fitting time to give equal rights to their minorities. It would not be easily done. In Poland, Jews were Germans or Russians, not Poles; to the Czechs, Jews were Germans; to the Slovaks, they were Magyars, and so on.[5] Inserting minority rights clauses into treaties with any of these Eastern European countries would be a struggle and an even greater struggle to have them applied.

In the United States on January 24, 1919 The Central Conference of American Rabbis submitted "a memorial" to the representatives of the United States at the Peace Conference, praying for the emancipation of the Jews of countries in which they suffered oppression, and for the rehabilitation of Palestine on the foundation of freedom and of liberty and equality for all inhabitants.

The American Delegates to the Peace Conference responded; "... the appeal has had the attentive reading of the American Commissioners, who will use their utmost endeavor to obtain for all peoples quality of treatment in accordance with their determined rights without regard to race or religious beliefs." [6]

The Jewish Delegations to the Peace Conference needed substantial support from the Allied Countries, most importantly from the United States. President would have to be the primary ally for the American Jewish delegations; he was the key to a solution for the European Jewish communities.

On May 20, 1919, *The New York Times* reported a speech made by a rabbi [not identified] at the Union of American Hebrew Congregations in Boston:

> ... the American Nation ... has constituted itself not on the basis of race, the blood in the veins of men and women ... but on the basis of the rights of men, and the duties of men. Our republic is the first humanitarian nation in history. The conception of humanity is its cornerstone. We must bravely demand, if it is not too late, complete rights for the Jew in every country. We must look to our own country ... to exert the influence of her moral leadership on behalf of persecuted Jewry ..."

As the peace treaties between the victorious nations and the defeated were being negotiated and hopefully soon to be completed, the pogroms against the Jewish communities in the liberated nations from the fallen empires or the ones newly created by the redistribution of territory, or both, did not completely abate. The Peace Conference was in full swing, as were the attacks upon the Jews of the Eastern European Countries. The American Jewish Yearbook [7] reported that in May 1919 the pogroms were the cause of many protests in America:

> May 6, 1919—Washington, D.C.—Conference of representatives of Jewish organizations sends cablegram to President Wilson ... protesting against Jewish massacres in Pinsk, Lemberg, and other places.
>
> May 11—Syracuse, N.Y.--Meeting of the representatives of the YMHA, YWHA, and the New York State Judean Organization adopts resolutions protesting against the 'many shocking massacres of Jewish people in various communities in Poland.' May 12—Sioux City, Iowa. Meetings of representatives of Jewish organizations send telegrams to President Wilson, to Secretary of State Lansing, and to Louis Marshall protesting against the pogroms in eastern Europe, especially in Poland. May 13—Atlantic City, New Jersey—Annual convention of order of B'rith Abraham sends cablegram to President Wilson asking him to appeal to the new Polish Government to use energetic efforts to prevent massacres of Jews in that land.
>
> May 14—Schenectady, New York—Mass meeting to denounce massacres of Jews in Poland.

There were demonstrations in Binghamton, Boston, Chattanooga, Chicago, Denver, Detroit, Fort Worth, Hoboken, Jersey City, Lewiston, Milwaukee, Philadelphia, Pittsburg, Rochester, Syracuse, Troy, Waterbury, and Youngstown. In San Francisco the American Union of Roumanian Jews sent a cable to President Wilson asking that efforts be made at the Peace Conference to stop the massacre of Jews of Roumania and occupied parts of Bessarabia. The Philadelphia Branch of the American Union of Roumanian Jews sent a similar cablegram to the President.

In the same week Adler received a two thousand word cable from New York City. It said that there were very large demonstrations in New York because of the constantly reported pogroms in Eastern Europe. It reported:

> On May 21 in New York City Jewish workingmen cease working at one o'clock as a protest against pogroms in Poland and Galicia and the Ukraine. Mass meeting in Madison Square Garden addressed by Charles Evans Hughes, Jacob Schiff and others, adopts resolution of protest.

May 24, 1919. In Paris Marshall delivered an address to the *Ligue Des Droits De L'Homme* (The League of the Rights of Man). It was convened to protest against the massacres perpetrated against the Jews in Eastern Europe:[8]

> Mr. Chairman, Ladies and Gentlemen,
>
> For a stranger to speak in a foreign language is a serious task, but when an American speaks in English to a French audience, he hopes that he will be welcomed. English, French and Americans have fought together on the consecrated soil of France for human liberty, and have gathered here tonight for which the Ligue des droits de L'homme is one of the finest exemplars. I wish it to be distinctly understood that the Jews of America and of the world sympathize with every people seeking independence. I care not where gathered under heaven. We have gathered tonight to say that no people, whoever they may be are entitled to liberty and independence unless prepared to grant the sweets of those blessings to all their citizens. We representatives of the Jews of America have come to Paris to ask for the emancipation of the Jews, and of all minorities, whoever they may be. I am sure we shall succeed in that end before we leave this city. But it is not sufficient to get a paper constitution, to get the assurance of equality and of civil and religious rights. We must insist upon guaranties and sanctions, such as will come from the League of Nations.
>
> I am not here tonight to speak about the Jewish people, to bestow on them encomiums of praise. If their history of many centuries, if their literature, their Bible, if all that they have done for liberty and justice and righteous-

ness do not make them deserving to live, then let them die. I have come here tonight to speak for all men, for humanity. We Jews have protested against Armenian massacres, we have protested against the boche [German] treatment of Belgium, and we ask tonight that the world unite with us to give us the rights of human beings. While Poland, Roumania, Czecho-Slovakia, Ukrainia and Lithuania have come to seek independence, murder and pogrom against the Jews have been taking place in Poland, Roumania, Czecho-Slovakia, Ukrainia and Lithuania.

Shall it be permitted to continue? Shall it be said that the ears of the world are deaf to the cries of the victims, the eyes of the world blind to what has been happening before them? Your presence here is proof that it is not so. Whatever atrocities occur, that land must be told from the seat of the Peace Conference that such things must not be tolerated. I make no distinctions between the countries in which the atrocities occurred. All are alike to me. I am trying to hit outrage, enormity, brutality, cruelty. Let us speak plainly. Let us consider a few of many facts.

Pogroms have occurred in over 150 places since last November. Since the suspension of hostilities [and] the armistice, murder, wholesale murder, has begun in these places. When the news of what happened was first communicated to America, I spoke with Paderewski and Dmowski [Polish leaders] in New York, and asked them to tell their people they held such crimes in horror. They said, "There are no pogroms in Poland." Dmowski, the father of the economic boycott [of Jewish businesses] that has operated ever since 1912, said, 'There never has been a pogrom in Poland.' No voice has been raised against the pogroms that have occurred since. Take an instance. I speak from the official, unprejudiced reports of qualified observers. The American Jewish Relief Committee, of which I am chairman, sent representatives to Europe to aid in distributing food to the starving and clothing to the naked. A man of high character, Mr. Zuckerman, went to Pinsk. With the authorization of the authorities he proceeded to organize committees to distribute food and clothing. On the afternoon of the day on which he left Pinsk the committee met there in broad daylight, engaged in the work of benevolence. They were there unarmed, unprotected, and unwarned, when a sound of soldiers, led by an officer who avowed himself an anti-Semite, arrested them without resistance, marched them to the public square, and thirty-seven young men of character were shot down by a machine gun operated by the soldiery who should have protected them. Old men and women were put in prison, and beaten upon their naked bodies. They were released the next day, when the Rabbi informed the soldiers they were people of good character. Then the military authorities imposed a fine of 100,000 marks upon the Jews of Pinsk. The American Jewish Relief Committee sent 100,000 marks to be distributed to the needy, and the military seized this small sum. There are many other towns in which such scenes were enacted.

Yesterday I heard from Wilna (Vilna), from an authoritative source, that after the legionaries reached Wilna they armed the mob, which killed two hundred Jews, mostly old people and children, destroyed a congregation praying to God, sacked every Jewish shop, pillaged every Jewish home, and drove five thousand Jews out of the city. They castigated the Rabbis and leading citizens because they would not say that those killed were Bolsheviks.

You in France, whence liberty and light came to the human race, think of this enormity. The same things occurred in the Ukraine, the same things are threatened in Roumania, the same things are possible in Russia. We have not only to protest against what is past, but also to raise our voices against a continuation of it. It is for that we are here, to say to the Great Powers, 'Listen to these facts, and notify these people, these governments, that this must not continue and that someone must be punished for these crimes against the human family.' We also ask that the Peace Conference put into the treaties to be made by the Great Powers with the new countries of Eastern Europe clauses requiring that the rights of ethnic, religious and linguistic minorities be fully and fairly protected, with a provision that will make pogroms in the future impossible.

I have a cheering bit of news to give you. I received tonight a long cable from America telling that on Wednesday of this week, there was held in Madison Square Garden, probably the largest auditorium in the world, a meeting of 15,000 people, which 200,000 found it impossible to enter. Every Jewish workman in Greater New York stopped work on that day. Every Jewish place of business was closed tight. There was a parade of the Jewish veterans of the Civil War, the Spanish-American War, and the world war to protest against the pogroms. There spoke at the meeting the Governor of New York, the Mayor of New York, Secretary of the Treasury McAdoo, and Judge Hughes, a former candidate for the Presidency ..., to raise a violent protest against the iniquity. Every newspaper in New York published editorials indorsing the action of the committee and demanding that the wrong be righted. The voice of America was heard at the time of the massacre at Kishinef, it was heard when raised to save the world for democracy, it will be heard now when it demands the ending of this wrong against humanity.

The difficult issues, notably concerning Poland, were brought to President Wilson's attention before the Peace Conference, in letters from Marshall. On November 7, 1918:

> It is generally recognized that one of the most important subjects to come before the Conference of nations to be held at the close of the war, is the restoration of Poland. It necessarily affects the future of all of the inhabitants within the area of the recreated Polish State ... Approximately four million Jews who now dwell within that territory will be directly concerned. Hence, whatever the geographical extent of the new State or its form of government, the civil, political and religious rights of these Jews must be safeguarded.... [9]

Marshall wrote again on November 14:

> On the 7th instant I submitted to you on behalf of the American Jewish Committee a communication relative to the status of the Jews of Poland, which followed on the 11th instant by a telegram which set forth the terms of a cablegram ... which threatened attacks upon the Jews of Poland and Roumania.... [10]

It was important to bring the pogroms and protests to the attention of President Wilson who was in Paris, and was very busy. Marshall and Adler were told by those who tried to meet with him that it was difficult just to get an appointment. Adler said, "Why do we not just do as we would if we were in Washington?" "What?" Marshall asked. Adler responded, "Call up his house and ask for an appointment." They did call one evening and were given an appointment with Wilson the next afternoon.

Adler wrote about it:

> We had an interview with the President at his home ... The President received us very cordially, meeting us half way up the steps, and took us into his working room. Marshall told him of the very long cablegram that reported a large demonstration in New York City protesting the pogroms in Eastern Europe. He read some of the salient features of the cable to Mr. Wilson, dwelling on the magnitude of the demonstration, and gave him a copy.[11] They conferred for half an hour. Wilson expressed his sympathy and said that he would give the matter his fullest support.

When it became known that they had spent the time with the President, they were asked if there was any news, and replied that if there was any it would have to come from the President. Marshall, who had been an opponent of the proposed League of Nations did say, "Well, if it is news, you may say that I have become a convert to the League of Nations."[12]

As the Peace Conference progressed, the Jewish Delegations, American, British and French and the Eastern European Jewish Delegations pleaded for the granting of equal rights to all minorities. Marshall, not the sole fighter for the cause, was their leader, meeting with the delegates of all nations who were party to the negotiations for the treaty agreements.

Marshall's letter to his family three days later began in a somber tone. On May 27, 1919, he wrote:[13]

My dear Children,

This is the saddest day of all the year—the anniversary of Mother's death. Her memory grows more precious with each passing day. Every joy and every sorrow brings her to my side and I feel her ennobling presence. It is now nearly twenty four years when we came to Paris together and all the past becomes again the present. I have just received Robert's lovely letter of May 6th in which he speaks of his and George's visit to Mother's grave on that day of days. I am sure that these anniversaries will ever be observed with reverence and love by those upon whom she showered all the wealth of her sweetness and loveliness and undying devotion.

Yesterday was an important turning point in my work. I had a most satisfactory interview with President Wilson which lasted half an hour. Dr. Adler accompanied me. The President was exceedingly gracious and at his best ... His physical condition is excellent and when I commented upon it, he remarked that it was due to the fact that he had preserved his sense of humor. His attitude was most favorable and I am satisfied that with a few exceptions my entire programme is likely to be adopted unless unexpected obstacles develop. We discussed the pogroms, bolshevism ... the attitude of the Poles and of the Roumanians; the necessity of protecting minority groups, the League of Nations and its functions in affording sanctions for the guarantees that are to be given in the Constitutions of the new East European governments.

Marshall also told of the various scenic trips in France, that he and Adler took to admire the flora and stroll through "the forest under the fine Lindens". He concluded with:

> There are many Americans here who are pining for their native soil. The streets crowded with members of the A.E.F. They have but one thought and that is to get across the Atlantic with the utmost expedition ...
>
> With proudest love, I am
Your devoted
Father

Cyrus Adler recalled a time in France when they were not addressing the problems of the Conference:

> Mr. Marshall and I took a trip to the Argonne, with (Chaplain Rabbi Elkan) Voorsanger. Marshall asked Voorsanger if he knew of a Rabbi for Temple of Concord in Syracuse. He replied that he knew 'the finest young Rabbi' who was in his company in France. As a result Marshall recommended Benjamin Friedman, who traveled to Syracuse in his army uniform, and was engaged immediately. Friedman became friendly with Marshall on his many visits to Syracuse. Friedman was Rabbi of the congregation for almost 50 years.[14]

The foremost aspiration of the Jewish Delegations was to have clauses included in the treaties that would declare that all citizens or residents of all European countries would be protected from discrimination and persecution attributable to their ethnic, religious or legal political persuasions, a status for the individual that many of the governments and their popular majorities had seldom, if ever, granted.

Poland, with its large Jewish population, had been infected with discrimination for decades, whether Poland was or was not under Russian rule. Even in 1918, their thirst for national independence did not include tolerance for minorities, especially for the Jews.

They resisted the insertion of the minorities clauses in the peace treaty until the last days of the negotiations, but in the end Poland agreed to a statement of minority rights in Article 93 of the Treaty with Germany:

> Poland accepts and agrees to embody in a treaty with the principal Allied and Associated Powers such provisions as may be deemed necessary by the said powers to protect the interests of inhabitants of that state who differ

from the majority of the population in race, language or religion ... (detail provisions) so far as they affect persons belonging to racial, religious, or linguistic minorities constitute obligations of international concern and shall be placed under the guarantee of the League of Nations.

The Treaties signed later in 1919 with the other newly formed or revised nations contained the same provisions.

Thus a state's legitimacy was made to rest on its obligation to respect the rights of minorities ... [and] subject to enforcement by the newly formed League of Nations. The Jewish delegation to the peace conference had contributed a notable achievement to the development of international law.[15]

The existing conditions from late 1918 and into 1919 when the treaties were nearing completion were recounted in the American Jewish Yearbook:[16]

> [it was] ... a period of transition ... uncertainty, confusion, and rapid transformation ... upon the life of the Jewish people throughout the world. Confusion and turmoil are most apparent in eastern Europe where old frontiers are being rapidly effaced and new boundaries created, and where hitherto suppressed peoples are experiencing a rebirth of intense national feeling, as result of which many new wars on a smaller scale have taken the place of the titanic struggle which ended but yesterday ...
>
> Due to a combination of political, economic, social and religious factors, the Jewries of Eastern Europe appear to be among the greatest sufferers from there chaotic conditions.
>
> ... we find the Jews being ground between the upper and nether millstones. It will be many years before the peoples of eastern Europe will forget ... the thousand and one commercial, industrial, and domiciliary restrictions which hedged the Jews about for so many generations. *The true emancipation of the Jews of Eastern Europe will come only with the emancipation of the non-Jews from the role of oppressor, from the psychology of the persecutor.* [author's italics]
>
> In Poland, the artificial breach consciously created between Jews and Poles by [Czarist Russia] has resulted in a deep-seated mutual suspicion and distrust, which has been accentuated by the Polish chauvinists.... Poland is warring against all her neighbors-against Lithuania ... Russia ... and Ukrainia (sic) ... As a consequence we have frequent outbreaks of anti-Jewish riots, wholesale looting of Jewish commercial and domestic property, summary executions without trial ... taking of hostages, arson, rapine (sic) and murder ...

The economic conditions of our brethren throughout Eastern Europe are so degraded as to beggar description. The task of reconstruction which lies before us is huge enough to overtax all the philanthropic resources of the more fortunate countries of Western Europe and America for at least a generation.

After conclusion of hostilities the Jewish communities of western Europe and America strained every effort to secure from the Peace Conference a charter of liberty for the Jews, as well as for all other racial and religious minorities. The success of the Jewish delegations to the Peace Conference … is demonstrated in the opening clauses of the Treaty with Poland; similar clauses will form part of the treaties with Austria, Czecho-Slovakia, Hungary, Jugo-Slavia, and Roumania. In these charters of liberty, by which the minorities may appeal from injustice and discrimination at the hands of their governments to the League of Nations, lies the hope of the future regeneration of our down-trodden and persecuted brethren.

The final Treaty with Poland, as stipulated in the Treaty with Germany, contained twelve articles that speak to the rights if minorities. Foremost were:

Article 2.—Poland undertakes to assure full and complete protection of life and liberty to all inhabitants of Poland without distinction of birth, nationality, language, race or religion.

Article 7.—All Polish nationals shall be equal before the law and shall enjoy the same civil and political rights without distinction as to race, language or religion.

Article 11 —Jews shall not be compelled to perform any act which constitutes a violation of their Sabbath, nor shall they be placed under any disability by reason of their refusal to attend courts of law or to perform any legal business on their Sabbath.

The Treaty also provided for protection of the rights of citizens, nationals, and any residents born in another country but were not citizens of that country.

It was finally signed on September 28, 1919, as agreed in the Peace Treaty with Germany. The treaties with the other nations containing similar clauses protecting the rights of minorities were also signed in 1919: Austria, September 10; Jugo-Slavia, September 19; Czecho-Slovakia, September 19; Bulgaria, November 27; Roumania, December 9.[17]

When it is realized that in 1914 the Jews suffered almost immediately from the effects of the war, the agreements must be considered an historic achievement. At last, the Jewish people of Europe had documents executed by the Eastern and Central European nations that said flatly that they were to be accorded the same rights, privileges, and obligations of citizenship enjoyed by the majority of their citizens and that these rights were for all of European humanity.

Historian Ismar Elbogen wrote:

> The treaty between the Allies and Poland firmly anchored the principle of equality of all minorities ... as individuals and as a group ... Nevertheless the Poles continued their obstructionist tactics ... (having) only at the last moment decided to put their signatures to the treaty that was set before them ... Courtesies were exchanged between Paderewski and the Jewish delegates, and it appeared 'that a better era was now dawning'. But it was only the laws and not the people that were changed, and so this hope was not fulfilled.[18]

Mr. Elbogen's somber words were written in 1944.

It is to the credit of the American Jews that in 1914 they joined forces, set aside their doctrinal differences, and united with the Western European Jews to support their suffering brethren; that after five years they led the fight to convince the victorious nations to acknowledge the rights of minorities, not only Jews, as integral to the Peace Treaty and that all minorities must be accorded their rights as citizens of the world.

The Jewish people of the United States were now firmly established as the leader of world Jewry. From the month that the war began American Jews gave extensive support without hesitation. Those having achieved position and financial success joined with the workers, the recent immigrants, in working to alleviate the suffering in Europe. Financial contributions reached unexpected and unprecedented levels. The Joint Distribution Committee which had a goal of $15,000,000 raised more than $47,000,000 by the time the war ended.

Marshall wrote to his children:[19]

> My Dear Children,
>
> This is a great day in the history of the world and ... in the history of the Jewish people. The treaty of peace with Germany has been agreed (to) and concurrently with it the treaty between the Principal Powers and Poland which confers complete emancipation upon the minorities of that country, and is to be followed by treaties which are to be in the same terms with Roumania, Greece, Czecho-Slovakia, Jugo-Slavia, Austria, etc. It carries out

my programme in a very important feature; it goes further than I had the right to expect. What has been denied is undoubtedly in the long run for the best. It is a special grain of satisfaction that Paderewski and Dmowski have to sign it. Last fall I tried to build a golden bridge for them which if availed of would have made things easier for them and would have added to the prestige of Poland. It would also have prevented many a bloody pogrom. I am now about to tender to them once more the olive-branch and to present to them a practical method for bringing about a better understanding between the Poles and the Jews and the eventual prosperity of the country. It is for them to decide.

I have been overwhelmed with congratulations. The East Europeans are most grateful, and although they realize that they still have many obstacles to overcome, they know that they have at least secured a charter of liberty which will eventually become operative. They rightly behold in the clauses which make the obligations of the treaty matters of international concern having the sanction of the League of Nations, to be enforced by the Permanent Court of International Justice.... I feel grateful to the Almighty that he has enabled me to lead on this sacred course for right, justice and equality.

I wish to add that without the firm and unfailing support of President Wilson success would have been practically impossible; we would have had a colorless and ineffectual result, which would have been worse than failure.

All Paris is now rejoicing ... The city is a mass of color, all arranged with exquisite taste; the pavements have been converted into improvised dancing pavilions. The students are marching and skipping along singing the Marseillaise and other stirring airs....

You, James [his oldest son], are, I fear, greatly mistaken in your estimate of Clemenceau. I look upon him as a great figure, as the embodiment of ... justice and not of that type of politicians among whom you class him. He is seeking to prevent a recurrence of war and he insists that the only way to do it is to understand that he who lives by the sword must perish of it. Germany ... must now pay the piper. If lax and flabby methods were to be employed she would laugh in derision. Her crime has been monumental, her punishment must, therefore, be terrible lest she forgets and lest we forget, for the world must know that retribution for [crimes] committed is inevitable.... The next remaining problem is that of Russia. I have been giving it much thought and am having daily conferences with the Russian leaders who are now here. Bolshevism must be destroyed.

July 12th is the date I shall soon embrace my dear children.

The Jewish people, numerically tiny, with enormous pride, without any homeland, had been degraded and driven without mercy from place to place for almost two millennia. This attention paid by the countries of Europe was something that would not have been thought possible even two years earlier.

The Treaty with Germany was signed at Versailles on Shabbat, June 28, 1919. Marshall and Adler did not attend; they heard the announcement in Paris by the boom of the guns. They would now turn from the needs of the Jews in Europe to those of the Jewish community in America. They would devote themselves to Jewish education.[20]

The execution of the treaties was an important accomplishment, but the willingness by the signatories to comply was not. The future would be changed only when the participating countries would regard the clauses to be more than ink on paper. The new decade brought little change in the attitudes of many of the Easter European countries.

The United States did not sign the Paris Peace Treaty in 1920, was not then a party to the minority rights treaties, and did not belong to the League of Nations.

Notes

1 Adler-Schiff Pg 306
2 Adler-Letters V1 Pgs 363-364
3 Adler Pg 308
4 Adler Pg 310
5 Elbogen Pg 503
6 AJYB V21 Pg 191
7 AJYB V 21 Pg 192
8 AJA-MC
9 Reznikoff VII Pg 593
10 Ibid Pg 595
11 Adler Pgs 313 fwd

12 Ibid Pg 316
13 Ibid
14 From a conversation in 1988 between Rabbi Benjamin Friedman, age 94 and the writer. Friedman said that he did not know Marshall then, and found out sometime later that Marshall had recommended him to the Temple Society of Concord.
15 Dawidowicz Pgs 84-85
16 Dawidowicz Pgs 84-85
17 AJYB V22 Pgs 102 fwd
18 Elbogen Pg 509
19 AJA-MC
20 Davis Pg 406

Return to Blessed America

The creation of the peace treaty with Germany required almost the first six months of 1919. The final document began with the Covenant of the League of Nations, committing the world's leading countries to resolve problems between them peacefully and to protect one from the other. Then peace treaties were negotiated with several of the Eastern European Countries that had been expanded, reformed, or newly created and signed by the end of 1919.

After months of participation in the Peace Conference, Adler and Marshall were the only American Jewish Delegates remaining in Paris. They enjoyed a sense of great accomplishment that was unimaginable before the Peace Conference began in January 1919. Near the end of June; it was time to make arrangements to go home. Adler wrote:

> There were not many vessels available ... Finally I succeeded in getting passage on the *Lafayette* ... to Havre and (there we) boarded the boat ... (but) owing to a strike the boat could not sail ... and the French Line would not be responsible ... we had no place to go ... and Havre was crowded to the eyes. Finally an official arranged that we should stay on board, but go on land for food. Later we were transferred to (a ship), with equally bad accommodations, and sailed at last.... We had not been afloat more than a day, before a strike broke out on the boat. The stewards refused to work ... Red Cross and YWCA girls on board pitched in, and gave us coffee and eggs and sardines. After forty-eight hours the stewards returned to their jobs and made up for their dereliction by being especially attentive, no doubt with a view to their tips....
>
> Everybody was in high spirits. The war was over, the world was at peace. America had come out creditably, and this crowded boat of Army officers and War workers were on top of the wave literally and figuratively ... I was the first person off the ship at New York. A few days later a great public reception was held in New York for Mr. Marshall and the other members of the delegation.[1]

That reception was succinctly described by Marshall in a letter to his cousins and close friends Rabbi Joseph Stolz and his wife Blanche on July 28, 1919:

> I have just received your words of welcome and of praise, for which I thank you most heartily. All that I can say is that I have tried to realize the dreams which my mother instilled in me as a child. I believe that the work of emancipation has been accomplished. In order to guarantee the covenants on the Polish and other treaties which are intended to safeguard the rights of racial, linguistic and religious minorities in Eastern Europe it is of the utmost importance that the League of Nations comes into existence with the powers sought to be conferred upon it by the treaties which have been entered into. I shall at an early day elaborate my views on this subject. It is necessary that public opinion shall be properly educated so that the treaties shall not be deprived of the sanction essential to them.
>
> While in Paris I was so occupied day and night that I had no time to write letters except to my children. I did not have proper secretarial assistance … otherwise I should have written to you from Paris.…
>
> I wish that I could get out of the banquet and mass meeting which are to be held in my honor this evening. I hate these functions more than I can tell. I had the great satisfaction of arriving at the dock before the committee of arrangements knew about it, with the result, as I understand it, that a boat with a huge committee and a brass band floated around the harbor in a frantic attempt to reach me long after I had reached my house.
>
> I thank you for your congratulations on James' engagement. I am very happy that he has made so excellent a choice. Lenore is in every way charming and has a brilliant mind.[2]

On Monday evening July 28, 1919, at Carnegie Hall, there was a "Mass Welcome to Louis Marshall on his return from the Peace Conference." It was preceded by a dinner at the Waldorf-Astoria Hotel, where there were brief speeches of welcome. The program for the event included the names of almost eight hundred members of the reception committee from all sections of the United States, including several friends from Syracuse. The welcome at Carnegie Hall began with a cantorial "Boruch Haba" [Welcome Back]. The printed program said:

> The Jews of America hail the return of the American Jewish Delegation from the Peace Conference at Paris in a spirit of deep thankfulness and appreciation. The work accomplished on behalf of the Jewish people by its

spokesmen in Paris marks the crowning effort in the movement for Jewish emancipation which was inaugurated in the capital of France over a hundred years ago. Among the names of the brave men who have appeared as the champions of the Jewish cause before the assembly of nations in Paris the name of LOUIS MARSHALL will stand out in golden letters. The work of securing liberty and equality for the Jews of Eastern Europe ... is a fitting climax to a life spent in the service of Jewry ... He has dedicated his great gifts of mind and heart to the interests of his fellow-Jews.... Mr. Marshall has proved himself to be what some of his friends have called him—a martial Jew.

On July 29, 1919, *The New York Times* reported the event.

Jews Pay Tribute

To Their Delegates

—

Marshall and His Associates

Praised Warmly For Work

In Paris

—

Want League Adopted

Louis Marshall, Chairman of the American Jewish Congress, which sent him to the Peace Conference on behalf of the Jews, received last night, together with those of his associates of the Jewish Delegation now in New York, an enthusiastic welcome from the Jews of New York ... at the Waldorf-Astoria and then Mr. Marshall and his co-delegates were greeted at Carnegie Hall, where in spite of the sweltering weather, more than 4,000 men, women and children had gathered to hear Mr. Marshall's report of his work at Paris.

The speakers voiced the demand that the treaty of peace, including the covenant of the League of Nations, must be ratified without amendment. Mr. Marshall, Rabbi Stephen S. Wise, Cyrus Adler, (and others) praised the wisdom and sympathy of President Wilson and his quick perception of the plight of the Jews in Europe.

In replying to his welcome at the dinner Mr. Marshall said he was sure that the treaty would be ratified because it was right, but he thought that the time for rejoicing would not come until the work was completed.[3]

In Carnegie Hall Marshall delivered a momentous message in his usual eloquent voice. The following are excerpts:

It may seem ungracious for me to express regret that I have been made the recipient of this remarkable demonstration of your affection and good will, which has come to me as a great surprise, but I can assure you that if any avenue of escape had been open to me I, who have never wavered before an enemy, would have fled precipitately from my friends. I do not regard this extraordinary outburst of your enthusiasm as in any way personal to myself. My associates and I are merely the symbols who represent in your minds the emancipation of the racial, religious and linguistic minorities of the world, which has been brought about by an enlightened public opinion and which is the expression of that genuine democracy which now controls the actions of mankind....

You, my friends, are celebrating an event which the Almighty has in His wisdom willed. The Peace Conference, the nations gathered in council at Paris and Versailles, have been but the instruments of Divine Providence, to whom belongs the honor and the praise and the glory ... we in the House of Israel should unite in joyous thanksgiving. For the first time the nations of the world have recognized that, in common with all other peoples, we are entitled to equality in law and in fact.... we have been assured not only religious but civil and political rights ... life and liberty are secured to all. The right to employ one's own language is effectually established. The desecration of the Sabbath is prohibited. Education along cultural lines is guaranteed ... the observance of these obligations is made a matter of international concern, and the League of Nations has conferred upon it jurisdiction to protect and enforce the rights secured ... a new principle in international law has been established.[4]

Marshall then reminded the assemblage that as recipients of these rights the Jewish citizens of the "new States" must accept responsibilities:

> I am confident that I speak for every true Jew when I say that henceforth the Jews of Poland, Roumania, Czecho-Slovakia, Jugo-Slavia and other new States, will vie with their fellow-citizens in the effort to establish but one standard of citizenship and to cultivate friendship and brotherhood. Let us forget the nightmare of the past.
>
> And now a word as to the duties of American Jewry to their suffering brethren ... Their sufferings are without parallel. Liberty ... will not in itself alleviate the pangs of starvation. One further effort, but it must be a vigorous one, must be made for the extension of adequate relief to the suffering. This means their industrial rehabilitation. It now becomes incumbent upon us to make careful studies to bring about the economic reconstruction of the Jewish communities of Eastern Europe ... it cannot be done on the basis of charity. It must be on a purely business basis. Influential men in these States are prepared to cooperate but a large part of the capital required for this work must be supplied by American Jewry ... to the end that self-respecting, self supporting, self determining and patriotic communities may be built upon the ruins of the past.

In his comments, Marshall did not neglect the sharing of praise with the other members of the Jewish delegation, especially Judge Julian Mack was named as chairman when the delegation was elected in 1918. The singing of "Hatikvah" and the "Star Spangled Banner" concluded the evening.

President Wilson may have been exhilarated about the results, but he was undoubtedly exhausted when he returned to America after the Peace Conference ended. He was aware of the negative comments about the peace treaty in the United States and in France, but he was not inclined to compromise with the critics in the Senate. Wilson returned from Europe, and despite the advice and suggestions from others to be conciliatory in negotiations with the Senate, he intended to fight for the approval of the treaties.

For instance, Colonel Edward M. House who was Wilson's political advisor and friend from his reign as the Governor of New Jersey, was with him in Paris. In the course of the Peace Conference their relationship cooled as Wilson lost confidence in him. Before leaving France, House "pointed out that if Wilson were as conciliatory in dealing with the Senate as he had been with his foreign colleagues in Paris, all would be well. Ominously, Wilson rejected this counsel of compromise and concession, and said 'House, I have found one can never get anything in his life that is worth while without fighting for it.' House replied that 'Anglo-Saxon civilization was built up on compromise ...' Into these few words were compressed the divergent viewpoints of the two men."[5]

"At that suggestion the President stuck out his jaw and said that he was going to fight for the treaty. That he did, to his death."[6]

The League of Nations was presented by Wilson in 1918 in his Fourteen Points, but was not a new idea. In 1915 there were American leaders such as former President Taft, who spoke and wrote about a "League to Enforce Peace". Senator Henry Cabot Lodge also addressed it in 1916 when he said that George Washington's warning to avoid entangling alliances was not meant to suggest that America should not join with other nations in "a method ... to diminish war and encourage peace."[7]

There were prominent citizens, including political figures, who met in 1918 to pursue the idea to "win the war for permanent peace." [8] It was discussed favorably in many circles and in the press, but the enthusiasm dwindled by the time the Versailles Peace Conference was concluded. The marriage of the peace treaty to the Covenant of the League of Nations was not unfavorable to many Americans, but there were also arguments against American approval. However there a was a growing chorus of disapproval from liberals, from some German-Americans who criticized the severity of the punishment of Germany, from Italian-Americans who where angry because Italy was not given a disputed city, from Irish-Americans who were unhappy over the treatment of a unit of the Irish Revolutionary Army, and, of course, Republicans and other politicians.

Wilson's political enemies were an effective group that included key Senators Lodge, Borah, Johnson. La Follette fought against ratification, possibly because the treaty with Germany was part of the document that created the League of Nations. While Lodge had spoken positively about some form of alliance of nations in 1916, the covenant of the League contained a provision, Article X, which created an obligation for a "military alliance" with France. When the treaty with Germany was not yet finalized, there was an agreement of alliance in case of attack on Britain, France and the United States. It was actually a Security Treaty with and for France, negotiated after serious discussion and trade-offs between the parties. It was intended as a temporary provision until the League was solidly in place, but those who opposed the Treaty viewed it as taking away the right of the Senate to declare war.

Thus, President Wilson's presentation of that treaty to the Senate was looked upon as a sign of his low regard for the authority of the Senate, and a snub of the

Nation's venerated Monroe Doctrine policy [9], which warned European nations that acquiring nations of the Western Hemisphere that were then independent or attacking any of these nations of the Western Hemisphere would not be tolerated by the United States. That Security Treaty was submitted to the Senate's Foreign Affairs Committee, rejected, and never seen again.

President Wilson was determined that the Senate would eventually approve the Paris Peace Treaty; a document to maintain peace and bound nations together in a league that was to keep peace.

In the fall of 1919 Wilson decided to go to the people with a speaking tour through the American Midwest and West. It went well when he was greeted, cheered and listened to from place to place, but he was also dogged by opponents who followed him, speaking against the treaty and against him as well. He insisted that if the League of Nations was not endowed with the presence of the United States there would be a war within the foreseeable future with terrible consequences. With eloquence and great conviction, he told his audiences:

> "I can predict with absolute certainty that within another generation there will be another world war if the nations of the world do not concert the method by which to prevent it. What the Germans used were toys compared to what would be used in the next war."[10]

One day in late September he spoke in Pueblo, Colorado, and that night he collapsed. There was a public announcement that the President had suffered a stroke, and Mrs. Wilson and entourage took him to Washington, but after more than two months he could function only in a limited capacity. Vice-President Thomas R. Marshall was kept in the dark, as was most of the nation. Mrs. Wilson functioned for the President.

While he was ill, the Senate considered the Paris Peace Treaty, and when he was somewhat improved his friend Senator Gilbert Hitchcock suggested to him that he could compromise with the Senate on some of the disputed items. His wife asked him to accept the reservations of those who were against the treaty and compromise. Wilson's answer was, "Let Lodge compromise! Better a thousand times to go down fighting than to dip your colors to dishonorable compromise."[11] There were two unsuccessful attempts to get the Senate to confirm the treaty, but the Senate would not consent. The League of Nations, the most far-reaching agreement ever created among the world's nations was without the United States, and, therefore, was crippled.

With the loss of America's membership in the League of Nations, keeping the peace and protecting minorities, the outlook for minorities and certainly the

Jews of Eastern Europe, was not as bright as was hoped in the euphoric time of mid-1919.

The rejection of the Treaty of Versailles—League of Nations agreement by the U. S. Senate, the fate of many of the inhabitants of western Europe for the next thirty years, and beyond, was sealed.

For Marshall and his brethren the work of maintaining equality and peace for the Jewish people of Europe would have to go on. Nicholas Titulesco, the Roumanian Ambassador to Great Britain, spoke at a luncheon of the American Committee on the Rights of Religious Minorities in December 1925. He insisted that there was no cause for complaint on the part of the minorities of Roumania.

Louis Marshall responded:

> Mr. Chairman: It is with much interest that I have listened to the remarks of M. Titulesco and of the other various gentlemen who have discussed the attitude of Roumania toward her religious minorities. For many years I have followed the march of events in Roumania and had hoped that upon the signing of the Treaty of Peace, by which the boundaries of Roumania were greatly extended and the execution by Roumania of the guaranties intended to protect her racial, linguistic and religious minorities ... a new era of good will and prosperity would dawn on the inhabitants of the greater Roumania.
>
> There was every reason to expect that under the Minority Treaties ... those for whose benefit these treaties were executed would at once become ... entitled to equal rights with those who constituted the ... majority of the country ... So far as the Jews are concerned, they are still subjected to hateful discriminations ... They are constantly attacked by mobs and rioters ... Their lives are threatened, their houses are broken into, and it is a matter of daily occurrence that those engaged in peacefully following their business are ... subjected to every manner of violence. No action to relieve this condition has been taken by the Government.[12]

Marshall sent a supplemental letter to Titulesco on January 5, 1926:

> Give to the Jews of Roumania the full benefit intended by the framers of the Treaty of 1919, and Roumania will find in them a tremendous asset ... Give them freedom of action, remove from them the incubus of fear and terror and uncertainty, and you will find that they will be a blessing to the land in which they and their ancestors have lived for centuries and which they continue to love even though untoward circumstances have compelled them to seek their happiness under other skies.[13]

In 1927 Marshall wrote to a friend, Solomon Unger:

> I am extremely anxious that no further mistakes shall be made with respect to the relations between the Roumanian Government and the Jews of that country. The subject is one that has occupied my thoughts for many years. You probably know that it was I who drafted the treaties for the protection of the various minorities of Roumania, Poland, Czechoslovakia and other Eastern European countries, and that I spent four and a half months in Paris in 1919 in order to secure the adoption of these treaties. I had previously presented the whole subject to President Wilson in a memorandum prepared by me.[14]

There was little respite of the anti-Jewish discrimination through the twenties and the thirties, with little help from The League of Nations. The League made contributions in fields of refugee rehabilitation, public health, and international labor problems, but settled only a few minor disputes between nations. It had no enforcing power against aggressive nations' policies. It failed to stop the invasion of Ethiopia [1935] by Italy, Manchuria [1931] by Japan, and could not stop the Spanish Civil War [1936-39]. In the late nineteen thirties several nations resigned including Germany, Italy, and Japan. The League was formally dissolved on April 18, 1946.

The Minorities Treaties were primarily documents that displayed the unfortunate events that would occur if the treaties' provisions could not be applicable. And so it was.

Only Estonia granted its minorities, including Jews, complete autonomy. Latvia, in 1921 narrowed the granting of rights, but to those who could prove residence over a period of 20 years were provided allowances for minority schools. Latvia never enacted laws regarding religious or cultural or organizations. In Lithuania there was great hope in 1922 when Jewish Communities were allowed to administer their own cultural social, educational and welfare affairs. All came to a halt in 1924 when the Jewish national Council and the ministry of Jewish Affairs were abolished. In Poland anti-Semitism was rampant, especially in the economic sphere. Almost all Polish Parties opposed the granting of equal minority treatment to Jews.[15]

With the rejection of the Treaty of Versailles—League of Nations agreement by the U. S. Senate in 1920, the fate of many of the inhabitants of Western Europe for the next thirty years, and beyond, was sealed.

Upon his return home Louis Marshall settled into the routine of rendering legal service for clients and government, community work for many minorities, leadership of the American Jewish Committee, president of Temple Emanu-El in New York City, chairman of the board of the New York State College of Forestry at Syracuse University and a growing interest in the Zionist movement.

Notes

1 Adler Pgs 326-327
2 AJA-MC
3 *The New York Times* July 29, 1919
4 Reznikoff VII Pgs 307-308
5 Bailey Pgs 307-308
6 Oxford Pg 880
7 Ibid Pg 881
8 Ibid
9 Proclaimed by President James Monroe and Secretary of State John Quincy Adams in 1823
10 Ibid Pg 882
11 Ibid Pg 883
12 Reznikoff VII Pgs 647-648
13 Ibid Pg 655
14 Reznikoff VII Pg 656
15 EJ

The Rosenbluth Case

America entered World War I in April 1917 and Americans suffered personal tragedies, as did the Europeans, from the military casualties and the international influenza epidemic. At a United States Army camp far from the battlefields of Europe, toward the end of the War, an American army major died. It would eventually involve the United States War Department, the United States Attorney General, a foremost industrial tycoon, several prominent affluent citizens and lawyers, two accused soldiers, the deceased's parents and Louis Marshall. Ripples from the incident soon spread into the upper levels of the Government and Congress and was paraded prominently in the national press from 1920 through 1924.

On October 25, 1918 Major Alexander P. Cronkhite, a twenty-five-year-old West Point graduate the commander of the 213th Engineers at Camp Lewis in Washington State, died while on duty, necessitating a military investigation. Had he died in the war in Europe, the effects of the tragedy would have been confined to his family. His father, Major General Adelbert Cronkhite was at greater risk to be a casualty of the war, since he was in France commanding the U.S. 80th division that was part of the assault on the German army in a final, furious campaign by General Pershing's First Army. The fighting officially stopped seventeen days after Major Cronkhite's death.

General Cronkhite was a career soldier. In 1891 he was a young officer serving in the last campaigns against the Sioux Nation and went on to serve in a variety of positions in the Army. He rose to the rank of Brigadier General and, in 1918 held the wartime rank of Major General. He returned to the United States early in 1919.

The General's wife, who was descended from a line of prominent Americans in government and the military, told him that she could not agree with the official report of the reasons for their son's death. As a career soldier, General Cronkhite had the experience and knowledge of the military to enable him to pursue an investigation. He decided to investigate.

The fallout from the general's investigation would descend upon many people. Two prominent Americans, Louis Marshall and Henry Ford, would become involved. Marshall was acknowledged as the outstanding constitutional lawyer and defender of human rights in America. Ford was the American industrialist extraordinaire, a true representative of American capitalism. They knew each other in 1919 only by reputation, and would not physically meet until 1927.

Henry Ford, who was 52 years old when the war started and considered to be one of the leading citizens in America, professed to be a pacifist, but when the United States entered the War in 1917, he supported his government's decision, even converting his factory to the manufacture of vehicles for the military. However, he would not give up his advocacy for peace. He created the well-known *Peace Ship* and sailed to Europe in attempting to convince the warring nations to end the war. The effort did not succeed, ending in Norway without success, and it was an embarrassing and bitter defeat for Ford. He became a candidate for the U.S. senate in 1918, but suffered another bitter defeat. He did not give up his political aspirations, and by 1922 he was a willing candidate for the Republican nomination for president in the 1924 election, even in opposition to the nomination of his fellow Republican, the incumbent President Warren G. Harding.

In 1918 Henry Ford purchased a weekly newspaper in Michigan, *The Dearborn Independent*. The first issue under his ownership in January 1919 was criticized as unfocused and unprofessional and was not well received. Ford decided that for the paper to grow, it needed content that would attract national attention. In 1920 he hired more experienced employees. Above the name of the paper at the top of the front page was the motto, *The Ford International Weekly* and at the bottom was the motto *Chronicler of the Neglected Truth*. Ford and key members of his staff decided that the Jews were to be a target. The few members of the staff who did not agree left the paper either immediately or after the program got underway.

In a private interview with a reporter from *The New York World*, Ford said that he would speak out on the neglected truth, "international financiers are behind all war. They are what is called the international Jew: German Jews, French Jews, English Jews, American Jews. I believe that in all those countries except our own the Jewish financier is supreme ... here the Jew is a threat." Several reasons have been advanced for Ford's anti-Semitism: his rustic boyhood, his failure with the peace ship, his disappointment with Jews with whom he had dealt, and the anti-Semitism of key employees on the *Independent*. Several of his friends who were prominent industrialists did not express their disagreement with him, but were not as blatant and outspoken as he was.

The newspaper began a series of attacks on May 22, 1920 with an article that said, "The Jew is the world's enigma. Poor in his masses, he yet controls the world's finances. Scattered about without country or government, he yet presents a unity of race continuity which no other people has achieved. There are ancient prophecies to the effect that the Jew will return to his own land and from that center rule the world." A succeeding article said, "... most of the big business, the trusts and the banks ... are in the control of Jewish financiers or their agents." The articles went on in this fashion for ninety-one weeks, then ceased abruptly in January 1922. They would resume when the Cronkhite case was in the public eye.

After the publication of the second anti-Semitic piece Louis Marshall immediately responded with a telegram to Ford:

> In the issues of May twenty-second and twenty-ninth of the Dearborn Independent which is understood to be your property or under your control there have appeared two articles which are disseminating anti-Semitism in its most insidious and pernicious form. They constitute a libel upon an entire people who had hoped that at least in America they might be spared the insult the humiliation and the obloquy which these articles are scattering throughout the land and which are echoes from the dark middle ages. On behalf of my brethren I ask you from whom we had believed that justice might be expected whether these articles have your sanction.... Three million of deeply wounded Americans are awaiting your answer.[1]

Ford replied to Marshall in a telegram to the American Jewish Committee. It said:

> We regret the words in which you have seen fit to characterize the Dearborn Independent articles. Your terms insidious, fabrications, etc. we resent and deny. Your rhetoric is that of a Bolshevik orator ... These articles shall continue and we hope you will continue to read them and when you have attained a more tolerable state of mind we shall be glad to discuss them with you.[2]

Ford continued these pieces until late in 1921, then ceased. He may have stopped either at the urging of friends, or at the request of President Harding. When the pieces were resumed, it was in connection with the Cronkhite tragedy.

In 1922 Robert Rosenbluth, a captain in Major Cronkhite's regiment, and Roland Pothier, a sergeant in the regiment, were charged with the Major's murder. Rosenbluth was Jewish, Pothier was Catholic. The national press reported what was happening in the investigation of Major Cronkhite's death. Two were charged, but in the press it was *The Rosenbluth Case*. Ford seized upon the opportunity to resume the anti-Semitic articles. Starting in December 1922, *The Independent* attacked Rosenbluth, his Jewish attorneys, and supporters.

Rosenbluth engaged a young attorney, Jonah Goldstein. His wife was Harriet Lowenstein who had been a secretary and worker for the Joint Distribution Committee, and one of the Jewish delegation's workers at Versailles. Marshall and the others praised her outstanding work at that time. It was probably through her contacts with the leaders of the JDC and the delegates to Versailles that Goldstein was asked to represent Rosenbluth.

Marshall, in the midst of his busy life in 1922, was asked by Goldstein, to participate as adviser in the Cronkhite matter.

On October 17, 1924, *The New York Times* printed a long letter from Louis Marshall. In it he reviewed the entire Cronkhite matter from the beginning in 1918 to its conclusion just a few days prior to writing his letter. He began by criticizing the national press for prominently publicizing the case from 1922 through 1924 and then underreporting the final outcome:[3] "In October 1918, [Captain Robert] Rosenbluth, age 31, was stationed at Camp Lewis, Washington, with the U.S. army's 213th Engineers. His superior was Major Alexander Cronkhite, a promising (25 year old) officer, who was universally beloved and to whom Captain Rosenbluth was greatly attached. On October 25, 1918, the Major having had a recent attack of influenza, asked Captain Rosenbluth to lead the regiment on a march of considerable distance from the barracks. An hour after the column started, the Major decided to take a walk. He asked Sergeant [Roland] Pothier, who had not followed the regiment [to accompany him] and after some time reached the place not far from where it was at rest and the Major and Pothier proceeded to fire with revolvers at an empty tobacco can."

The column was approximately fifty yards away from where Cronkhite and Pothier were shooting. Rosenbluth ran to ask them about the shooting, and as he neared them, he saw the Major fire at a tobacco can. Cronkhite fired again, hitting the can and said, "I got it this time Rosie," and then there was a revolver shot. Major Cronkhite fell to the ground, calling out, "My God, I'm shot."[4] The surprised Rosenbluth did not know the source of the shot, and seeing no sign of a wound, he thought that the Major had a heart attack. He called back to the road for a doctor, who double—timed up with two medical orderlies. Pothier stood nearby. Rosenbluth, on the ground holding Major Cronkhite, suggested that the doctor give him a stimulant, and two men were told to attempt artificial respiration. An injection was given, and when the men unbuttoned the major's shirt, they discovered a bullet hole in the upper right chest. One of the men said, "Why this man has been shot." Later, the inquirers found it difficult to believe that the doctor did not look carefully for the wound, but since it was about three inches above the right nipple, there was almost no external bleeding, and the undershirt was only slightly stained. After it was agreed that the major was dead, his body was straightened, covered with a raincoat. At the board of inquiry, one of the sergeants said that he closed the major's eyes. An ambulance arrived to transport the major's body, his belongings, and some of the pertinent evidence to the hospital.

The autopsy was completed four hours later. The official inquiry concluded, "Major Cronkhite met his death by reason of an accidental self-inflicted wound."[5]

With the inquiry ended, all of the pertinent material, including the tobacco can, the revolver, exploded shells, the major's hat and jacket, were stored in several desk drawers in various offices of the regiment. The jacket with the bullet hole hung in an office for some time, and was never given to the major's parents. It disappeared.

When the major's mother was told of his death, she is reported to have said, "I don't believe it, he was too much of a man to kill himself, and too expert with arms to accidentally shoot himself in that way." She left her young daughter, who was ill with pneumonia at home, and traveled alone to West Point to meet the train that carried her son and to prepare for his burial. There had been an error in the notification to her of the arrival day of the train, and when she got to the railroad station, she was told that the train had arrived the preceding day, that the accompanying officer had left the body of Major Cronkhite at West Point and gone on a five day leave. Mrs. Cronkhite was not allowed to speak with any member of her son's regiment, nor did she hear any words of explanation or consolation. She was not given her son's personal effects. She was told that his uniform had been burned as ordered by an officer in command. No reason was ever given.[6] She did not believe the "accident" report, was suspicious about the stated cause of his death, and she believed that her son had been murdered.

When General Cronkhite returned from France in the summer of 1919, he agreed with her. He examined the War Department file and found it to be incomplete. There was no information as to Major Cronkhite's revolver, hat, and uniform. General Cronkhite wrote to members of the regiment asking for details and from their replies he pieced together certain sentences from some, and phrases from others.[7] Former members of the regiment were interviewed, and from these sources there were recollections: that Rosenbluth was very near to the major when he was shot, that Rosenbluth's efficiency rating in the unit was not very high, and that weapons similar to the one carried by Pothier on that fateful day were commonly carried by former Army officers like Rosenbluth.[8] The General became convinced that his son did not die from an accident and that therefore, this was a case of murder.

He hired his own private investigators and then descended on the War Department, demanding an investigation. The War Department referred him to the Department of Justice, where he spoke to Attorney General A. Mitchell Palmer.[9] In deference to General Cronkhite's long and distinguished career the Justice Department under Palmer agreed to an investigation. However, in this era of the "Red Scare," the Justice Department under Palmer was primarily interested in anarchist and Bolshevik activities. A cursory investigation into the Cronkhite case revealed no evidence of murder, no apparent motive and no involvement of Rosenbluth in any radical activities. The matter was quietly dropped.[10]

In July 1920 General Cronkhite was able to get a court order to have his son's body exhumed. He engaged a physician, who had been a medical assistant to the district attorney of New York County, to give an opinion of the accuracy of the army's report as to the cause of the major's death. After exhumation and examination of the remains, the doctor concluded that the Major could not have pulled the trigger of the revolver and accidentally inflicted a wound where the bullet entered his body while it was in the position cited in the report.[11] General Cronkhite was now certain that his murder theory was correct, but could not get satisfaction from the governmental departments. For the present his investigation was blocked.

Things changed in 1920 when Warren G. Harding won the nomination as the Republican Party's candidate for President in the November election. It was a surprise. Before the Republican convention he was hardly favored to be the nominee and he would not have been, or become President, if it wasn't for Harry M. Daugherty.

Harry Daugherty was born in 1860 in Washington Court House, Ohio. He had to work through school, and became a lawyer without attending an undergraduate school. He was elected to the Ohio Legislature twice, but not elected to any office again. While practicing law, hardly his real love, he became part of the political machine, and achieved a reputation as a man who could get "things done". He met Warren Harding at a small political rally in Ohio, and they became friends. Allegedly, Daugherty was enticed by his presidential mien. Harding moved up the political ladder with Daugherty as his guide and campaign brains. In 1914 Harding ran for the United States Senate, and with Daugherty as campaign manager he won. Daugherty looked ahead to the 1920 presidential convention, although Harding preferred to stay in the Senate: "A position more to my liking than the Presidency possibly could be."[12] There were eleven prominent men who were the front runners in the Republican hierarchy, but Harding, undoubtedly encouraged by Daugherty, became interested and announced his availability. Daugherty spoke with Harding's friends in Congress, suggesting that even if Harding was not a first choice for the nomination, they should keep him in mind.

Daugherty raised campaign money from wherever he could, including $50,000 of his own, "every cent I had in the world."[13] In February 1920, Daugherty made a prophetic statement, "I don't expect Senator Harding to be nominated on the first, second or third ballots, but … about eleven minutes after two, Friday morning of the convention, when ten or more weary men are sitting around a table, someone will say 'Who will we nominate?' At that decisive time, the friends of Harding will suggest him." [14]

The convention opened in Chicago in June. It went through a number of ballots throughout the week, and neither the favorite, General Leonard Wood, nor his opponents were able to accumulate enough votes. On Friday the chairman of the convention called for an adjournment until the next morning. The weary group of insiders met that night in a smoke filled room in the local hotel. Harding waited gloomily throughout, but Daugherty continued his machinations, cajoling, trading votes wherever he could, not giving up. And on that Friday night, actually Saturday morning, at 2:11 A.M., the prophecy was fulfilled, within the hour of the time he had predicted. Harding was approved and nominated the next day, on the tenth ballot. After a spirited contest, Massachusetts Governor Calvin Coolidge, one of the failed aspirants for the presidential office, was nominated as Harding's running mate.[15] In November 1920 Harding was elected handily. He defeated James M. Cox, who could not overcome the negative aspects of 's legacy.

Harding had problems selecting his cabinet. He had obligations to his political pals in Ohio, known in political circles as "The Ohio Gang." He did appoint qualified people who were not from that gang. Charles Evans Hughes (Secretary of State), Andrew W. Mellon (Treasury), Herbert Hoover (Commerce) were considered to be admirable choices, but there were others that he would come to regret. Harry M. Daugherty certainly considered himself worthy to be the Attorney General, and as expected he was chosen. Senator Myron T. Herrick, who once ran against Daugherty for the Ohio senatorial nomination, told Harding that as a cabinet member, "Harry Daugherty will wreck your administration."[16]

As things turned out, Daugherty was not the Harding administration's wrecking instrument.

Daugherty's legal experience was limited, his reputation from his early political days was tainted, and he was considered to be a ruthless political enemy. He was a questionable choice to be the chief lawyer of the United States. Soon enough, he became a target of critics in Congress for neglecting to pursue war fraud cases. He answered by arguing that some of these cases rested on shaky legal grounds, and he believed that with the war over everything connected to it should be forgotten as quickly as possible. The criticism was not totally ignored; it caused him to exert some legal effort, and ultimately the Justice Department recovered a few million dollars.[17] There were further criticisms of him. Samuel Gompers attacked him through the American Federation of Labor publications, wherein their executive committee called for his removal. Unhappy Republicans asked the President to excise Daugherty before the forthcoming congressional elections. Daugherty met all of the criticism with scorn, telling reporters, "'I wouldn't have given thirty cents for the office of Attorney General, but I wouldn't surrender it for a million dollars.'"[18]

In 1921 Daugherty was still being criticized for his lack of progress on the war fraud cases and wanted to silence the critics. To garner some positive publicity for himself, he decided to use his authority to help General Cronkhite investigate his son's death. Daugherty met with the general and assigned Justice Department agents to look into the War Department's files and to investigate in the Tacoma-Seattle area of Washington State.

In a report in the press in February 1923, General Cronkhite referred to a letter written to the President in November 1921, in which he complained that the War Department failed to follow up on his request for an investigation. Secretary of War John W. Weeks then directed that "the investigation would be most thorough and would extend to files prepared before he became Secretary of War."[19] Even Congressional action was called for by a few of Cronkhite's friends, but it was delayed until the War Department could complete its investigation. By April, Weeks reported that the War Department's records were "intact so far as the War Department could ascertain." By then Congress was in recess.[20] The issue was closed as far as the War Department was concerned. In that same War Department, General Cronkhite's superiors were displeased with him because he was not available for active army duty, and they were sensitive to his criticism of the Army's Board of Inquiry into Major Cronkhite's death. In an interview published in *The Dearborn Independent* in 1923, Chief of Staff General John J. Pershing, said: "he has the deepest sympathy of everyone. But this matter has dragged on for two whole years, and the Department cannot afford to consider the personal affairs of its officers."[21] The War Department informed the Justice Department that "the Government has had no value received from General Cronkhite since April [1921] he has been given very explicit orders that if [he] desires to remain on the active list of the Army he must go to Panama."[22]

General Cronkhite would not bow to the pressure. He did not obey the order to go to Panama, continuing rather to look for evidence against the alleged killers. The objects of his suspicions were Captain Robert Rosenbluth, the man who had held Major Cronkhite in his arms as he died, and Sergeant Roland Pothier, who had accompanied the major on his final hike. They were not aware that they were under investigation.

Robert Owen Rosenbluth was born in New York City in 1887 to Russian immigrant parents. After high school he entered Pennsylvania State Agriculture College, majoring in forestry. For his junior year he transferred to the Yale Forest College, and in 1907 he graduated with a degree of master of forestry. He entered the U.S. Forestry Service and volunteered for duty in the Philippines. He returned to the United States in 1910 and was put in charge of surveys in Utah, Nevada and Arizona. Subsequently, he joined the New York State Forest Service as director of forest investigation. He developed a plan to use land around state prisons as a means of prisoner rehabilitation, and after a riot at Dannemora State Prison, he was allowed to test his theory. Using twenty prisoners, he successfully trained them in forestry techniques. He continued to work in prison reform as a forester, and he discovered original survey marks around Dannemora prison land area and he found that recorded surveys were seriously in error. Without official support, on his own, he created a legal case for New York State against a railroad company whose mining firm subsidiary had been cutting timber on state land. As a result the courts awarded the state thousands of acres of timberland and substantial cash awards. There were other successes in his career as forester and social reformer. By the eve of the World War, he was physically and mentally strong, and stubborn enough to resist any suggestion of compromise in any matter involving his view of right and wrong.

When the Unites States entered the war, he enlisted in the army, only to be told that with his background and expertise with loading and terminal problems he could be assigned to the Port of New York with the rank of major. He asked to go to France, but he was refused. He asked Assistant Secretary of the Navy Franklin D. Roosevelt, who spoke to the assistant secretary of the Army. He was reassigned and allowed to leave for France at once as a first lieutenant. In the early days of 1918, Rosenbluth was with the First Division, First Engineers. He received excellent reviews from his superiors and a promotion to captain. As a result of a gas attack and artillery bombardment, he was injured and hospitalized. Because of his combat experience he was sent back to the United States to be an engineer instructor. Thus he became a member of the 213th Engineers under Major Cronkhite at Camp Forrest, Georgia. Rosenbluth and Cronkhite became friends and when the unit was transferred to Camp Lewis, Washington, Cronkhite asked that Rosenbluth be included. Also in the unit was Sergeant Pothier, with whom Rosenbluth had almost no contact.[23]

Roland Roch Pothier was born and grew up near Providence, Rhode Island, as part of a lower middle-class family. He enlisted in the U. S. Army in 1913, serving for three years, with the special rating of musician. He was court-martialed several times for minor offenses and for one charge of sleeping while on guard duty. After leaving the army, he enlisted in the United States Navy. In 1918 he was given a bad conduct discharge after a court martial found him guilty of "having the property of another in his possession." Ironically in the summer of 1918, he was drafted into the army and assigned to the 213th engineers at Camp Forrest. He was made bugler and promoted to sergeant by his commanding officer, Major Alexander Cronkhite.[24]

When the World War ended, Rosenbluth returned to civilian life as did Pothier. Rosenbluth's career took him into various positions in government service. At one time he worked for Lewis L. Strauss, who was part of the American Relief Administration under Herbert Hoover in his effort to reduce the suffering from starvation of millions in Europe. Many years later Strauss wrote in his autobiography that he was involved in organizing and raising funds for an "American United Effort for the Repatriation of War Prisoners from Siberia." When the money was found, Strauss needed capable people to do the work:

> We were able to enlist the services of two quite extraordinary men (who) made the enterprise successful. One of them was Daniel O'Connell Lively. The other man was Robert Rosenbluth, a tough, resourceful Army officer. These two men chartered ships for us at a fraction of the cost ... they fitted out the ships with racks of bunks ... found supplies and provisions in unlikely places and at bargain prices ... supervised the loading and clearing, and worked for nothing but bare expenses. The dollars would have been quickly exhausted but for Lively and Rosenbluth. Former Captain Rosenbluth had been an army instructor during World War I at a military camp in the West. One of the officers was killed. Rosenbluth was accused of murder by an enlisted man who was with the group and who later changed his testimony. [I] do not know whether he is living, but if he is, I hope that

he derives the satisfaction to which he is entitled for the important role he played in an enterprise which saved many lives.[25]

In 1920 Rosenbluth worked for the American Relief Association in Siberia, where he derived satisfaction, and was praised for his work. When he returned to the United States in March 1921, he heard that the Cronkhite case had been reopened, but he was unaware of his role. Soon enough he would find that he was a target in the investigation of the case.

On March 17, 1921, agents of the Unites States Justice Department went to Providence, Rhode Island, to interrogate former Sergeant Pothier. He was married and worked for a railroad. In short order he admitted to the agents that he shot the Major by accident, and he signed a statement to that effect. That was his first confession. Several days later he agreed to sign a statement that Captain Rosenbluth had ordered him to shoot Major Cronkhite during the hike. There were several subsequent confessions that varied with the others. Finally he said that Captain Rosenbluth had planned the murder in advance, ordered him to borrow a pistol, and planned that he kill the major in a particular secluded clearing.[26]

Marshall's 1924 letter to *The New York Times* continues, "As the uncontradicted testimony showed, Pothier was subjected to the third degree by a number of Secret Service men and five so called confessions were extracted from him giving five different and conflicting versions. These confessions were retracted by Pothier as soon as he was relieved from the duress under which they were made."

Pothier was taken to New York to testify against Rosenbluth, who was arrested and jailed.[27] Rosenbluth did not know that Pothier told the authorities that he would not stand by the confessions that implicated Rosenbluth.[28]

On March 20, 1921 *The New York Times* reported, "Ex-Sergeant Roland H. Pothier ... pleaded guilty this afternoon to involuntary manslaughter in connection with the death of Major Alexander P. Cronkhite ... he signed a statement concerning the death ... [he] maintains that the shot was fired accidentally while he was cleaning his pistol ... From information gathered here [in Providence] and in Washington it is understood that Federal investigators are proceeding on the theory that Major Cronkhite's death was due to a conspiracy ... Bail fixed at $10,000 and failing to find surety he was committed to Providence County jail." There was no mention of a co-conspirator.

On March 24, 1921 *The Times* reported, "Robert Rosenbluth[42] ... was locked up in Police Headquarters last night by agents of the Department of Justice on a warrant charging him with the murder of Major Alexander P. Cronkhite." Near the end of the report, in referring to the arrest of Pothier, it said that "the authorities here are believed to have sought only to hold Pothier until the man 'higher up' was apprehended." On March 25th, *The Times* reported, "Jonah Goldstein appeared as counsel for Rosenbluth. He said 'my client has talked freely to the agents of the Department of Justice ... he has nothing to conceal.'"

The next day, the paper reported, "While Mr. Rosenbluth was being questioned by the federal prosecutor, Colonel Herbert Lehman of Lehman Brothers bankers, a friend of the accused man, announced that he was confident a mistake had been made and offered to furnish bail for his release. Mr. Goldstein, the accused man's attorney, explained that if the Government consented to the release of Mr. Rosenbluth under bail that the latter would start for the State [Washington] at his own expense, with the intention of removing any suspicion that attached to his presence in Camp Lewis on the day of the shooting."

The next day, a court hearing for bail for Rosenbluth was adjourned by the Federal prosecutor, saying that he was awaiting advice from Attorney General Harry M. Daugherty. Three days later, Rosenbluth was released on $25,000 bail that was provided by Felix M. Warburg, Colonel Herbert H. Lehman and Walter E. Frank.[29]

The Federal Government's attorney in Seattle was instructed to advise the State of Washington prosecutor, Mr. James Selden, that the Justice Department's entire file covering the case would be forwarded to him, with advice from Daugherty as to how to proceed. The months passed, but the Justice Department did not send anything, possibly because it had little of substance to send.[30] The accused were in limbo.

The arrests were made in March 1921, but there was little activity until the fall. On September 24, *The Times* reported that "Jonah J. Goldstein, counsel for Captain Robert Rosenbluth, said that he had made several attempts to get the Government to call his client in the Federal Grand Jury inquiry ... but that all communications had been ignored, although Rosenbluth offered to waive immunity that fact has been stated repeatedly to Attorney General Daugherty ... at least a score of telegrams had been sent to ... Daugherty, the foreman of the Grand Jury, and other authorities ... but that all efforts had failed."

The Department of Justice had to consider whether the State of Washington or the Federal Government had jurisdiction to prosecute the Cronkhite case. The alleged crime was committed on a U. S. Army base, but it was uncertain that the property had been deeded to the Federal Government prior to Major Cronkhite's death. If the Camp property had not been conveyed to the Federal Government prior to Major Cronkhite's death, the Justice Department would have to turn the Cronkhite case over to the Washington State authorities in Tacoma. This question of jurisdiction would be raised, resolved, and survive to be re-raised several more times. Finally, Attorney General Daugherty sent a wire to the Federal Government's attorney in Seattle informing him that the Federal Government did not have jurisdiction in the case.[31] Washington State would have to prosecute.

Rosenbluth had engaged Jonah J. Goldstein of New York City as his attorney.

After several months, the Federal Government notified Goldstein that its charges against both men were dropped.[33] However, the Justice Department did not officially close the case.

In Tacoma, State Attorney Selden was outraged by the Justice Department's failure to send him materials as promised. and in fact he never did receive the files. He did an analysis of the case with whatever information that he had. Three months later, in late December, he issued a lengthy report entitled, "An Exoneration of Captain Rosenbluth in the Matter of the Death of Major Cronkhite"[34] and it was published in the Tacoma and Seattle newspapers. The report concluded, "All of the statements made by Pothier must be repudiated. They do not ring true. They would not be sufficient … to even justify the filing of any charge against him. As to Captain Rosenbluth, he should be, and is, so far as we are able to do it, entirely exonerated from any connection whatever with the death of Major Cronkhite … A great injustice has been done to him which should be righted."[35]

Rosenbluth wanted, as Selden said, that "it should be righted". On December 13, 1921, *The New York Times* reported, "James W. Selden, Prosecuting Attorney of Pierce County [Washington], announced today he would not initiate prosecution as a result of the killing at Camp Lewis in October, 1918, of Major Alexander P. Cronkhite. Mr. Selden's announcement was accepted by officials of Pierce County as an exoneration of Captain Rosenbluth. Following receipt of the news from Tacoma … Captain Rosenbluth announced last night that he would demand an investigation 'I shall ask … as to how the machinery of the Department of Justice can be so terribly perverted, first to wrong a citizen of our country, and then to prevent … the righting of that wrong. Prosecutor Selden's expression of the broad duties of prosecutors to help undo the wrong is a direct challenge to Attorney General Daugherty to invite a sweeping and impartial investigation, preferably by Congress.'"

Goldstein advised Rosenbluth to forget the whole business, but Rosenbluth was, as Goldstein termed him, "an idealist."[36] He wanted the Justice Department to attest to his innocence. Rosenbluth was determined to clear his name. His career was at a standstill, he could not find permanent work, and he was said to be exhausted physically and financially.[37] He was convinced that by continued pressure on the Department of Justice his good name and reputation would be restored.

An assistant attorney general initiated a private meeting with Rosenbluth. He told Rosenbluth not to repeat their conversation. If he did that, the Justice Department would deny that it ever took place, and "who would believe an accused murderer?" He said that the Justice Department would issue a statement exonerating Rosenbluth if he in turn would issue a statement exonerating it from any and all charges of improper conduct. Should he refuse, the department would reverse the position taken earlier as to whether the Federal Government had jurisdiction to prosecute the Cronkhite case. They would have him indicted by a Federal grand jury, jail him in Tacoma, and delay trial, leaving him to "rot in jail."[28]

Rosenbluth did refuse. As it turned out it made no difference, because Attorney General Daugherty had no intention of simply closing the case. He was still facing criticism from Congress for failing to prosecute the fraud cases. Even within the Justice Department, employees who had worked on these cases were discouraged by Daugherty's refusal to prosecute. One employee resigned and then had a letter entered in the Congressional Record. The letter ended with the statement: "So far as the Department of Justice is concerned, it no longer functions except in the capacity of first aid to crooks."[39]

At a high level meeting in April 1922 in Washington, the Federal attorney from Seattle, Thomas Revelle, met with General Cronkhite and three army officers. They decided to bring the case to a Federal grand jury in Tacoma seeking Federal indictments against Pothier and Rosenbluth. By August their plans were underway.[40]

In September a Federal Grand Jury was convened in Tacoma and met for two weeks. Witnesses were brought from all sections of the country. However, almost four years had passed, and the testimony by these witnesses about the events surrounding the shooting was inconsistent. Revelle could not find a motive for the crime alleged to have been committed by Rosenbluth and Pothier, and he could not even establish that there was any relationship, any connection between the two within the regiment.

General Cronkhite was considered to be a key witness for the Federal Government, but when he was called to testify, he brought no evidence to support his contentions of foul play, even though he said earlier that he had accumulated evidence. He said that other Justice Department lawyers had told him that his evidence would not be needed, and in any case he had not had time to collect it. He took the opportunity to strongly criticize the army board that conducted the inquiry at the time of his son's death, and he complained about its failure to return all of his son's possessions. He spoke about his son, "He always devoted a great deal of time to things athletic; just a great big boy; still a boy when killed. That was his nature—just to be a boy."[41]

Meanwhile, Rosenbluth and Goldstein remained in New York. Goldstein felt that the issue of jurisdiction was still a question. The Department of Justice's one time admission that it did not have jurisdiction, and it's own reversal of that early in 1922, had not been challenged or affirmed in any court. In mid-1922, when Goldstein was informed that the Justice Department would pursue the case, he asked Louis Marshall to assist him in pleading the jurisdiction issue. Marshall accepted, suggesting that it could be resolved in the defendants' favor without even going to Tacoma. However, they would have to wait for the grand jury to make a determination.

Marshall wrote to James W. Selden, the state attorney, in Tacoma on September 8, 1922 about Rosenbluth, and complimenting him for his investigation and report exonerating Rosenbluth:

> Within the past few days I have been consulted on behalf of Captain Robert Rosenbluth, not on retainer, but simply for the purpose of giving my unprejudiced opinion on the question of the jurisdiction of the Federal court to proceed against him. I learn that Attorney General Daugherty has instructed the United States Attorney in your district to present the case to the Federal Grand Jury. You performed an act the moral grandeur of which should never be forgotten by those who still believe that law and justice must be supreme if our civilization is to be preserved. I congratulate you.[43]

In Tacoma the grand jury proceedings continued, but the Federal government attorneys were doubtful about their case. No solid motive was established, and there may not be enough evidence to convince the grand jury to indict, and even if there were an indictment, the aforementioned weaknesses would not be enough for a trial jury to convict. But, on October 12, 1922 the Federal Grand Jury returned indictments against Pothier and Rosenbluth.[44]

Almost two years would pass before they would be put on trial.

In January 1923, Federal Judge Brown of the U.S. District Court in Rhode Island ruled that the Federal Government had jurisdiction. Pothier was arrested in Rhode Island. Since he could not provide a bond for release, he remained in jail. Rosenbluth surrendered to the Federal authorities in New York, was put in jail and then released on bond of $40,000. The bond money was furnished by Felix Warburg, who put up his home on Fifth Avenue in New York City as security.

In January 1923 Goldstein and Marshall filed a petition in New York for a hearing on Rosenbluth's behalf before Commissioner Samuel Hitchcock of the U.S. Court of Appeals, claiming that the Federal Government could not prosecute Rosenbluth because it did not have jurisdiction in the case. After hearing the arguments from both sides, Commissioner Hitchcock said, "I have not the slightest doubt that the Federal courts have no jurisdiction ... the only testimony ... tended to show the innocence rather than the guilt of the defendant. Nevertheless ... I should not undertake to pass on this most important question of jurisdiction. I now direct that the matter be placed before a district court judge."[45] He also said, "I want this man held in such a way that action will be taken at an early instant by the Circuit Court of Appeals." [46]

More than a month went by, but the Justice Department did not transfer the matter to the circuit court. In apparent frustration Hitchcock issued a ruling denying the jurisdiction of the Federal Courts and ordered that Rosenbluth be discharged.

General Cronkhite's response to the order to release Rosenbluth was explosive, and he was aggravated for another reason. On February 3, 1923, *The New York Times* reported: "... Major General Adelbert Cronkhite went on the retired list today ... by order of the President." Despite pleas from senators and congressmen, he was forced to retire from the service.[47] Two weeks later, on February 14, *The Times* reported that friends of General Cronkhite "allege that he has been railroaded into retirement as a result of his efforts to obtain justice for his dead son." There were even calls for a Congressional investigation, which did not happen.

Louis Marshall commented in a letter to his son, Robert, who was visiting Syracuse at the time: "Captain Rosenbluth was discharged yesterday and his bail bond cancelled. Justice has triumphed, although there is no telling what the insanity of General Cronkhite will next conjure up. Just now he is attacking the Secretary of War (Weeks), Mr. (Herbert) Hoover, the Attorney-General and the President for retiring him."[48]

Up to this point, Goldstein, Marshall and Rosenbluth did not feel that Rosenbluth's Jewishness was a significant factor either in the prosecution or the public's perception of the case. It became an issue on December 22, 1922.

Henry Ford's *The Dearborn Independent* renewed its dormant series attacking Jews. It proclaimed in a headline, "THE MYSTERIOUS KILLING OF MAJOR

CRONKHITE AND AMAZING ACTIONS OF CAPTAIN ROSENBLUTH." The article said that "thousands of aliens ... are being taught in their vernacular press that the United States is persecuting deliberately a member of their race."[49] It asserted that the motive for the "killing" was friction between West Point graduate Cronkhite and enlisted soldier Rosenbluth.

The next issue, December 30, headlined, "WHAT THEY CALL A DREYFUS CASE! Here for the First Time ... Are Presented the Facts in the Amazing Death Mystery Known as The Rosenbluth Case ... a powerful racial organization, with fanatical leaders and unlimited resources ... promises that the evidence shall never see the light, that the witnesses shall never be heard."[50]

The State of Washington had issued a report that cleared both men of the murder charges, but the *Independent* called that report a "fake." Sympathetic newsmen were labeled as "strange exotic types, reporters for the vernacular press." Louis Marshall was characterized as "sneering, imperious."[51] One article contemptuously referred to Marshall's efforts in the Leo Frank case in 1915. It said that when Frank was dragged from prison and then lynched it was done by "sensitive Southern people who were outraged by the efforts of Jewish lawyers."[52]

After Commissioner Hitchcock's order to release Rosenbluth from jail, *The Independent's* headline said, "TWO MEN INDICTED, THE JEW WALKS FREE, THE NON-JEW HELD IN JAIL FOR TRIAL."[53]

After April 1923 the attacks by Ford's paper abated, but national media attention continued. On February 16 *The New York Times* ran a report of calls for two Congressional investigations. Friends of General Cronkhite asked Senator William Calder of New York State to halt an appointment for a replacement for the General pending an investigation alleging that he was "railroaded into retirement" as a result of his efforts to continue his investigation into the cause of his son's death. The same report printed a wire from Louis Marshall to the same Senator, in which he welcomed the request, adding "Speaking as counsel for Captain Rosenbluth, I am authorized to say that he heartily welcomes a full and unlimited Congressional investigation of the cruel charges and insinuations that have been made against him."

Senator Carter Glass of Virginia said that he would insist upon an investigation of the facts behind the retirement of General Cronkhite: "He feels that General Pershing has put a blot on his record in the reasons given for the action of the President in ordering his retirement at the age of 62 years. General Cronkhite has criticized the War Department and has criticized Attorney General Daugherty for alleged negligence in the prosecution of the men who were arrested in connection with the death of his son." Neither of the requested investigations came to pass.

Throughout 1923, the furor and the national press coverage continued, although the *Dearborn Independent's* attacks did not recur. President Harding died suddenly on August 3, 1923. His successor was Calvin Coolidge, and of the bequests left by Harding to Coolidge, one of the most troublesome was Daugherty. The new President did nothing. He would make no direct move although Chief Justice William Howard Taft and other advisors suggested that a change should be made. Coolidge said, "He was Harding's friend. He stands high with the Republican organization. I don't see how I can do it."[54] A Senate Committee intent on exposing and deposing Daugherty, accumulated information about his incompetence, his affluence since attaining office, and his questionable associates. It wanted explanations. When he was requested to appear before the Committee, Daugherty avoided it. After an agent of the committee raised many questions when he examined the records of his brother's bank, the agent was barred from the bank. Questions were not answered, and Daugherty again refused to appear before the committee. In March 1924 Coolidge asked for his resignation, assuring him that his personal integrity was not in question.[55]

Harlan Fiske Stone was appointed attorney general, and he wanted the Rosenbluth case expedited.

Although the jurisdiction hearing in New York had resulted in favor of Rosenbluth, Pothier in Rhode Island had not fared as well. In the U.S. District Court for Rhode Island Judge Brown ruled that the Cronkhite death took place on a Government reservation over which the Federal Courts had jurisdiction. The Court refused to release Pothier on bail. An appeal for a writ of habeas corpus for Pothier was made to the U.S. Supreme Court. That appeal was denied and sent back to the Court of Appeals in Boston. That court reversed Judge Brown's decision. Months passed while the Justice Department decided whether to appeal the Boston Court's decision. It did, and on April 7, 1924, the Supreme Court ruled that the question of jurisdiction would have to be determined in the court appointed to try those indicted in the Cronkhite case. That meant a Federal Court in Washington State. Pothier and Rosenbluth were ordered to stand trial in Tacoma.[56]

In the spring of 1924 Marshall wrote to attorney L. L. Thompson, in Tacoma. He reminded Thompson that they had once met on a train from Washington, D.C. to New York City, and at that time Marshall had told him of the Rosenbluth case. He recited the history of the case, the issue of jurisdiction, and the role of General Cronkhite: "... General Cronkhite moved heaven and earth to procure the indictment and by dint of his unrelenting activity an indictment was finally found. I seriously doubt as to whether the case will ever come to trial, but it is ... necessary to provide against any emergency. I have asked Rosenbluth to ask you to appear for him ... he is without means. All the work that I have done for him has been gratuitously done. It is not, however, to be expected that you would put your time in without compensation. This matter has been a horrible illustration of what can happen when a man in high position, suffering from a terrible affliction—the loss of an only son—is acting under an insane obsession that a murder has been committed, and then looks around to find a victim."[57]

Thompson accepted and contacted Jonah Goldstein. Goldstein responded, "I have been ... Rosenbluth's friend and personal counsel. Mr. Louis Marshall, big minded and big hearted man that he is, consented to bear the burden with me, all without compensation, when the sole issue was the lack of Federal jurisdiction."[58]

As Rosenbluth and Goldstein made preparations for the trip to Tacoma, Rosenbluth told Goldstein and Marshall that he did not want to raise the issue of the Federal Government's lack of jurisdiction in his defense in Tacoma. Marshall's response to Rosenbluth was, "Your letter indicates that it is your idea that you are to do the thinking and that your counsel are to carry out your decisions. I am unwilling to become a part of such a program."[59]

Rosenbluth answered, affirming his gratitude for all that Marshall had done for him, ... "as a friend, providing real inspiration to light the darkest corner of my life, but to sanction a motion for dismissal purely on the grounds of jurisdiction as Mr. Thompson has proposed ... is more than I can stand ... and all the thinking since has not altered my opinion. I regret it if this runs counter to yours. Whatever else you think of me, please do believe ... that I will be man enough to take the consequences of my acts ... and that I will always ... be deeply indebted to you beyond all possibility of recompense."[60] The attorneys found this acceptable.

Two weeks later Marshall wrote to Thompson, "Captain Rosenbluth has just been here to say good-bye. He is leaving for Tacoma. I have called his attention to the fact that in his ordinary conversation, due to nervous reaction, he is constantly laughing, when as a matter of fact he does not consider this prosecution a laughing matter, and that this apparent levity would be apt to make a bad impression on the court and the jury."[61]

Pre-trial activities began. Rosenbluth and Jonah Goldstein traveled together to Tacoma; the Federal Government transported Pothier.

General Cronkhite, was the key witness for the Government. He had initiated the investigation, his agents had secured the original confessions from Pothier.

He had arranged to have his son's body exhumed, resulting in the independent physician's expert opinion that Major Cronkhite could not have shot himself. He was subpoenaed as a witness by the prosecution, but did not respond, saying that he "misunderstood the nature of the summons."[62] He asked the attorney general's office for a list of the Government's trial witnesses, was given the list, and insisted that the list was incomplete. On the day that the trial began he was asked to submit names of other witnesses, but he did not comply. He wired the assistant attorney general that he wanted assurance that the case would be properly handled, insisting that prosecuting attorney Osborne was mishandling the case and should be removed.

The Government prosecutors did not press the issue of his non-response to the order to appear, because they feared publicity about his idiosyncrasies and attitude toward the prosecution. They could not leave for Tacoma until October 4th because Mrs. Cronkhite was ill, and having come to Tacoma, General and Mrs. Cronkhite did not attend the trial. The prosecution was without their most important witness.

There was another person in Tacoma for the trial. The local newspaper reported that Mr. S. Rosenbluth, father of Robert Rosenbluth, was there. His picture was in the newspaper: an older man, formally dressed, dark mustache, bald. He was quoted as saying, "Over forty years ago, when I settled in a homestead in Oregon, and then returned east to engage in other work, little did I dream that my next trip west would be on an occasion such as this. I have come to be with my son when he needs me most." [63]

Robert Rosenbluth and Jonah Goldstein arrived in Tacoma on September 23, 1924, one week before the trial was to begin. Goldstein later wrote in an autobiographical article that it was "on the eve of [the] Jewish New Year 'Rosh Hashonnah [sic]' when we arrived in the little town where the trial was to take place. We went to the Temple; that in itself evoked the respect of the Christian population." [64]

That "little town" of Tacoma was the center of national attention, the atmosphere was charged. *The New York Times* reported that the case was "one of the most remarkable criminal cases in American jurisprudence."[65]

Federal Prosecutor James Osborne himself felt that the government did not have a strong case. Almost five years had passed since the alleged crime, there was little direct evidence, and there was not a credible, provable motive. Osborne knew that the War Department did not have a deed of ownership of the camp property at the time of Cronkhite's death, therefore it was quite possible that the trial judge could dismiss the case because the Federal Government did not have jurisdiction. Osborne advised the United States Attorney General's office that he would try the accused separately because there was really no case against Rosenbluth, and if the two were tried together, there might be a directed verdict by the court in favor of Rosenbluth. That would eliminate any chance of success against Pothier.[66]

Pothier would be tried first. Jury selection began. Prosecuting Attorney Osborne focused mainly on one point. He objected to the selection of any who were World War veterans. Defense Attorneys Maurice Langhorne and L.L. Thompson consistently asked prospective jurors if they had any racial and religious prejudices. Selection of the jury was completed in one day.[67]

In the prosecution's opening statement, Osborne emphasized that it was impossible for Major Cronkhite to have accidentally fired the revolver if it was in his hand in the position as stated in the official report. It follows that someone else had shot him, and he offered as the motive that there was friction [not defined] between Rosenbluth and Cronkhite. Therefore, Rosenbluth had ordered Pothier to shoot him.

In his opening statement defense attorney Langhorne said that there was no reason for Rosenbluth to order Pothier to kill Cronkhite, because there was no evidence of friction between the two officers.

The prosecution called a number of soldiers and veterans of Major Cronkhite's regiment to testify about the relationship between the major and the captain, and they all offered nothing conclusive as to any quarrel between the two. Furthermore, the prosecution could not prove that there was ever any relationship between Pothier and Rosenbluth. Rosenbluth did not even know Pothier's name although Pothier invoked Rosenbluth's name in one of the confessions extracted by an agent.[68]

The defense called several character witnesses. Their key witness was Captain Eugene Caffey, who was in the regiment at the time of the incident and now a regular army officer who was brought in from his station in the Panama Canal Zone. Untrue statements made to him by a U.S. Justice Department agent who tried to blacken Rosenbluth's character had angered him. Caffey was called by the defense hoping to prove that it was possible to fire a revolver when held in the position that Major Cronkhite had held his weapon when he was shot. Caffey said that even those who were experts with guns could become careless after firing at a target and then bringing the weapon back too far. "I once shot away a lock of my own hair," he said. In cross examination, the prosecutor placed the weapon in Caffey's hand and told him to hold it in his hand as the Major was alleged to have done. "Now," he ordered, "pull the trigger!" With little effort, Caffey pulled the trigger, provoking laughter in the courtroom.[69]

With that testimony the defense unexpectedly rested its case, catching the prosecution by surprise, since they had expected Rosenbluth to testify. In his closing statement Osborne attacked Rosenbluth. He said to the jury "You know and I know and everyone in this courtroom knows that he didn't testify because he didn't dare." He said that the defense testimony was perjured and he attacked the original army board of inquiry: "... this was the most slipshod investigation ever made by a military board of inquiry into the death ... of a brilliant young officer. Not a single exhibit has been preserved."[70]

Defense Attorney Thompson responded with, "From the number of agents who have been working on the case ... it is fair to assume they have combed the field to find any cause of enmity between the principals in this case ... there is no evidence ... [that] anything occurred to mar the amicable relations ... between Major Cronkhite and Captain Rosenbluth."[71]

Marshall's October 17, 1924, letter to *The New York Times* goes on. "The trial proved an utter fiasco. Practically every witness called gave proof favorable to the prisoners ... [a star witness] for the prosecution to whom it was alleged that Pothier had also made confessions, testified that he did not believe them, and that he did not consider either Pothier or Rosenbluth had anything to do with the death of Major Cronkhite."

With closing statements done, the Judge instructed the jury that if they believed that Pothier had accidentally shot Major Cronkhite the charge of manslaughter would normally apply, but it was not applicable here because it was beyond the statute of limitations.[72] Pothier would be judged as either guilty of murder, or acquitted.

At 2:45 on a Saturday afternoon, after less than two weeks of trial, the jury retired to deliberate. The next day the *Tacoma Sunday Ledger* reported as follows:

> After the jury retired, a group of officers and noncoms of the 213th Engineers, witnesses for the Government and defense, gathered around the door of the district attorney's office close to the jury room and sang old army ballads while the jurors were deliberating with Pothier's life.
>
> The catchy tunes ... floated down the corridors and filtered through the transom of the room where Pothier stood in his barred cage awaiting the word that would send him back to his little family in New England or to the death cell ... Pothier smiled as the familiar words (of the ballad) caught

his ear ... [they] were singing the regimental marching song which ends (with):

'The infantry, the cavalry in a 100,000 years, they couldn't build a mess shack without the engineers.'

Pothier's ears ... caught ... the patter of a bailiff's feet along ... the ... corridor.

The jury had decided his fate.[73]

At 4:15, one and a half hours after retiring, and after one ballot, the jury returned to the courtroom. That evening, in New York, Louis Marshall received a telegram:[74]

> "8:57 PM, Tacoma Wash, October 11, 1924
> POTHIER ACQUITTED.
>   (signed) JONAH GOLDSTEIN
>   LL THOMPSON"

The *Tacoma Sunday Ledger's* report continues:

There was no demonstration as the words 'not guilty' fell from [the foreman's] lips. Pothier smiled, Captain Rosenbluth sighed. As the jurors filed past Pothier, he thanked them and shook their hands. Captain Rosenbluth hurried about greatly excited. Many people shook (his) hand.[75]

Two days later Attorney L.L. Thompson wrote a letter to Marshall:

As I wired you, the jury brought in a verdict of acquittal in the Pothier case ... unanimous upon the first ballot. The Government has not yet formally dismissed the charge against Captain Rosenbluth, however I have little doubt that this will happen tomorrow. I became convinced some days before the trial opened that it was as much a trial of Captain Rosenbluth as of Pothier, and that if Pothier be acquitted, Rosenbluth would not be tried. I accordingly determined to actively assist Pothier's attorney. I did this because the Government's case was against Rosenbluth as well as Pothier.

I am frank to say that I was greatly disappointed in Captain Rosenbluth. I am certain that he is entirely innocent. I appreciate the fact that he has been a victim of injustice, but ... he had better forget this matter, if he is able, and particularly refrain from any further interviews or letters demanding vindication. The verdict, to my judgment, constitutes a complete vindication. I am certain that neither Henry Ford nor General Cronkhite are in a position to say that ... any technicalities interfered with the final hearing of this case ... I trust that the course which I have followed meets with your approval.[76]

He concluded with high praise for Jonah Goldstein.

Within a few days the Federal Government dropped all charges against Robert Rosenbluth. Marshall's 1924 letter to *The New York Times* concludes:

"For three long years Rosenbluth was relentlessly subjected to the torments of hell, but when the day of reckoning came, the infamous charge vanished like the mists of the morning. This prosecution has cost the government nearly $200,000. It has practically wrecked the career of Rosenbluth, who now stands before the public an innocent man, exonerated by his Federal prosecutors of criminality, as he had been by the State authorities.

But there is an even more sordid aspect of this case which should not be overlooked. There lives in Michigan one Henry Ford, who for several years past has been amusing himself by publishing a personal organ known as The Dearborn Independent, which likewise bears the caption The Ford International Weekly. Learning that Rosenbluth is a Jew, that damning fact was enough. For weeks and months Ford's columns were filled with cunningly contrived appeals to passion and prejudice, with attacks upon those who ventured to stand at the side of the man who had been unjustly accused of a heinous crime.

Rosenbluth's counsel, who likewise happened to be Jews and who came to his rescue as a matter of simple justice in recognition of their oaths of office were showered with insults. Other good citizens who came forward were denounced as tools of a Jewish conspiracy. Will Ford now make a retraction? Will he do anything to rehabilitate the victim of his savage and baseless attacks?"

The Dearborn Independent ran a brief report saying that the two defendants were acquitted, but "the hysterical efforts to make of Captain Rosenbluth an American Dreyfus was amply illustrative of the length to which an alien type of mind will go. There can be no pretense of believing that the trial cleared up the mystery of Major Cronkhite's death."[77]

The Jewish Tribune responded with an article by Marshall that said in part, "*The Dearborn Independent* editorial ... is an illustration of the disgraceful methods of that publication under cover of which Henry Ford manifests his fanaticism. Ford, the intellectual brother of the Ku Klux Klan, the inspirer of Hitler, and Ludendorf [the German General known for his anti-Semitism], persists in his crusade against him upon whom he has inflicted so terrible a wrong. There is not a decent man who would not rather stand in the shoes of Captain Rosenbluth than those of Ford, even though he be the richest man in all the world."[78]

On October 18, 1924, Marshall wrote a letter to Felix Warburg:

> I know how delighted you must be in the vindication of Rosenbluth. I thought that it was necessary to put on record the accurate history of the prosecution. It appeared on the editorial page of yesterday's *New York Times*. While Mr. Ochs was very kind in giving it the space which he did, he felt that my denunciation of Ford was too savage, and it was necessary, in order to have the article appear promptly, that I tone it down somewhat ... I enclose an exact copy of that part of the original article ... I wish to express to you my personal appreciation of the fine manner, characteristic of all your acts, in which you stood by Rosenbluth in the days when he needed friends, and you evinced confidence in his innocence.

> [Ford] learning that Rosenbluth is a Jew, that damning fact was enough to serve the malign purposes of this ignorant fanatic to embark on one of his characteristic crusades to compass the destruction, nay, the judicial murder if possible, of a fellow-being. A ... question ... arises ... to what extent a man richer than Croesus may shelter himself behind a corporation ... instead of being brought to the bar of justice for the most infamous of all crimes, that of conspiring to murder innocent men by egging on an utterly baseless prosecution and by resorting to means more pernicious than the use of dynamite?[79]

On October 21 Marshall wrote again to Warburg: "You will be interested in reading the enclosed editorial which appeared in the *Tacoma Times* on the day succeeding the dismissal of Captain Rosenbluth. In view of the fact that the alleged crime took place in the immediate vicinity of Tacoma, it is important to note the impression made upon that community."

The editorial, titled "The Truth about the Pothier Case," said, "The plain truth about the Pothier case ... is that there never was any doubt that the accused veteran was innocent. The grief stricken General Cronkhite, a man with a long and honorable record in the army had a human and natural desire to know just what had happened. But he did not get courteous treatment from the politicians back in Washington. The more opposition he met; the more suspicious he became. Then the high officials had General Cronkhite kicked out of the army without a hearing in spite of his honorable record. Then the irresponsible propaganda paper published by Henry Ford jumped into the case and attempted to create another Drefus [sic] affair, raising the race question. There would have been no Pothier case, the name of Rosenbluth would not have been besmirched, and General Cronkhite would still be serving his country ... had the department of justice been efficient in the handling of the entire affair. But it wasn't. It had Daugherty at its head and a typical Daugherty mess resulted." [80]

On December 15, 1924 Robert Rosenbluth wrote to Felix Warburg from Pittsburgh, where he was interviewing for a job with the local YM/WHA, as recommended by Warburg: "You may be interested to know that I was summoned before the various committees ... and have been committee-d for the past three days. From reports I have, the prospects seem very favorable. Please let me thank you again for your great kindness to me, on that, and every other occasion." [81]

In September 1925 Marshall wrote to Rosenbluth in Albany, New York where he was the executive director of the Jewish Community Center: "I think I informed you ... that some of your friends and well-wishers contributed to a fund ... for your defense. All of the expenses ... have been defrayed, and there remains, the sum of $5435.46. I have spoken to the contributors and it is their desire that the money shall be either invested for you or turned over to you ... with the hope that it may prove a convenient nest-egg ... to begin your married life. With best regards to both of you, I am ... Louis Marshall." [82]

Robert Rosenbluth became the director of the Jewish Community Center in Albany, New York. After several subsequent jobs, he settled in Chicago. Rosemary Reeves Davies interviewed him in 1968. She said that he was a genial man and that he had written an unpublished autobiography.[83] He retired in the 1960s as deputy director of the Cook County Welfare Department. He died in Sun City, Arizona in June 1975 at the age of 88. His survivors included two sons, Marshall and Lehman Rosenbluth.

General Adelbert Cronkhite, even after the cases against Rosenbluth and Pothier were over, continued his efforts to find his son's "slayer." These efforts were not successful. His wife died in 1930, and he remarried a year later. He died in 1937 at age 76 and was buried at West Point,[84] a soldier from 1882 with an unblemished record.

Notes

1 AJA-MC
2 AJA-MC
3 *New York Times* October 17, 1924, Pg 20
4 Davies Pg 16
5 Report by James W. Selden, Attorney, Pierce County, WA "In the matter of the death of Major Cronkhite" AJA-MC
6 Davies Pg 30
7 Davies Pg 36
8 Davies Pg 41
9 Ibid
10 Davies Pg 43
11 Davies Pg 41
12 Adams Pg 37
13 Adams Pg 120
14 Adams Pg 123
15 Adams Pg 130
16 Adams Pgs 163-167
17 Adams Pg 197
18 Murray Pg 293
19 Ibid
20 Ibid
21 Davies Pg 178
22 Davies Pg 97
23 Davies Pgs 8-11
24 Davies Pg 3
25 Strauss Pgs 74-76
26 Davies Pg 49
27 Davies Pg 73
28 Davies Pg 76
29 Ibid
30 Davies Pg 96
31 Davies Pg 78
32 Jonah Goldstein, Autobiography in *The Day*, January 13 & 20, 1951 AJA-MC
33 Davies Pg 94
34 Davies Pg 110

35 Selden Report
36 Jonah Goldstein in *The Day*, January 13 & 20, 1951 AJA-MC
37 Davies Pg 115
38 Davies Pg 116
39 Davies Pg 117
40 Davies Pg 126
41 Davies Pg 146
42 Marshall letter to Selden, September 8, 1922 AJA-MC
43 Davies Pg 138
44 Davies Pgs 162-164
45 *The New York Times,* January 4, 1923
46 Davies Pg 176
47 Marshall letter to Robert Marshall, February 14, 1923 AJA-MC
48 *The Dearborn Independent,* December 22, 1922
49 *The Dearborn Independent* January 6, 1923
50 Davies Pgs 170-171
51 Davies Pg 172
52 Ibid
53 Adams Pgs 412-413
54 Adams Pgs 414-415
55 Davies Pg 187
56 Marshall letter to L.L. Thompson, April 21, 1924 AJA-MC
57 Goldstein letter to Thompson May 5, 1924, Goldstein File-AJA
58 Marshall letter to Rosenbluth, August 19, 1924 AJA-MC
59 Rosenbluth letter to Marshall, August 24, 1924 AJA-MC
60 Marshall letter to Thompson, September 8, 1924 AJA-MC
61 *Tacoma Sunday Ledger,* October 12, 1924, AJA-MC
62 *Tacoma News Tribune,* October 1, 1924, AJA-MC
63 Goldstein letter to *The Morning World,* (New York), June 14, 1940, JJG File-AJA
64 Davies Pg 194
65 Davies Pg 193
66 Davies Pg 196
67 Davies Pg 209
68 Davies Pg 206
69 Davies Pg 210
70 Davies Pg 209
71 Davies Pg 211

72 *Tacoma Sunday Ledger,* October 12, 1924, AJA-MC
73 Postal Telegraph to Marshall at his residence, October 11, 1924, AJA-MC
74 Davies PG 211
75 Thompson letter to Marshall, October 13, 1924, AJA-MC
76 *The Dearborn Independent,* November 8, 1924, AJA-MC
77 *The Jewish Tribune, New York City,* November 21, 1924
78 FWP-AJA
79 bid
80 Ibid
81 AJA-MC
82 Davies Pg x
83 *The Chicago Tribune,* June 19, 1975
84 *The New York Times,* June 16, 1937

Henry Ford's Belated Apology—Fini?

The saga of Henry Ford and his newspaper continued well into the last half of the 1920s.

In 1923 Adolph Hitler, a rising star of Germany, praised Ford as his greatest supporter. Hitler told a Chicago reporter, "I wish that I could send some of my shock troops to Chicago and other big American cities to help in the elections. We look on Heinrich Ford as the leader of the growing Fascist Party in America."[1]

Louis Marshall, citizen, president of several Jewish organizations, expert trial lawyer and renowned constitutional lawyer continued his attacks on Ford even in the highest circles. He wrote a letter to newly inaugurated President Coolidge on Marsh 18, 1925. He began by expressing his admiration:

> The noble words contained in your inaugural address are still ringing in my ears.
>
> 'The fundamental precept of liberty is toleration. We cannot permit any inquisition either within or without the law or apply any religious test to the holding of office. The mind of America must be forever free.'
>
> This redeclaration of the spirit which permeates our system of government leads me to bring to your attention to a condition the continuance of which it is earnestly hoped by hundreds of thousand of American citizens may be obviated by such action as you may be able to take.
>
> It is well known that for several years past _The Dearborn Independent_, which is the personal organ of Mr. Henry Ford, he being the president of the corporation which issues this publication and his name appearing upon its editorial page, has been engaged, week to week, in a systematic attack upon the Jews. The articles published abound in monumental falsehoods and malicious inventions, couched in violent terms and designed to arouse suspicion, hatred and prejudice against those of the Jewish faith. There is no libel,

no product of superstition, or base concoction, that has ever been made at the Jews, that has **not** been rehashed in the columns of this sheet. Men who have striven to perform their duties as citizens or in the discharge of their public obligations have been shamefully maligned. These articles have been reprinted by Mr. Ford in a series of booklets entitled "*The International Jew*" and have been spread broadcast throughout the world ... translated into various European language by professional anti-Semites for the purpose of provoking enmity against the Jews, to such an extent as to frequently to result in concerted attacks upon them, in many cases involving the loss of life. The Ford Motor Company thus seeks to coerce its agents ... into becoming distributors of propaganda calculated to poison the public mind against the Jews designed not only to arouse the spirit of intolerance, but to inflict lasting injury upon the entire country by sowing the evil seeds of racial and religious animosity. I am confident that it is within your power to abate this iniquity.[2]

It is not known if Coolidge made any serious gesture to abate Ford's vicious assaults. Having succeeded to the Presidency when Warren Harding died, Coolidge had been the logical 1924 Republican nominee, but Ford, his fellow Republican, had also wanted the nomination and had had enthusiastic support. Ford also wanted to take over the Muscle Shoals dam from the jurisdiction of the Tennessee Valley Authority, and Coolidge said that he would not oppose Ford's bid. On December 20, 1923, Ford took his hat out of the ring.[3]

It was the fourth year of the anti-Semitic campaign by Ford's *Dearborn Independent,* shocking the Jewish community, as well as many who were not Jewish. Marshall sent a telegram in response to the first article, offering Ford the opportunity to retract the abusive articles. Ford answered with a nasty telegram that attacked Marshall and others as Bolsheviks, who were therefore the mortal enemies of America. Soon, prominent Jews, including Marshall, became targets of the *Independent's* pieces. There were complaints and criticism from prominent non-Jewish persons and a move toward a public boycott. Privately, Marshall said that it was one's right to avoid buying a Ford car, but the American Jewish Committee kept a low public profile, believing that publicity was what Ford wanted.

Public protests against the selling of the *Independent* on the streets of certain larger cities. On March 20, 1921, *The New York Times* reported from Detroit:

> Men selling Henry Ford's Dearborn Independent on downtown streets have been warned by the police to refrain from quoting that publication's reference to Jews.

[The] Superintendent of Police stated that many of the men have been shouting quotations from the Dearborn Independent in such loud voices that Jewish citizens complained. He has threatened to arrest the criers for disturbing the peace if such practice is not immediately stopped.

Also via Detroit, *The New York Times* reported on January 6, 1922:

'I believe that it is an error to say that the present financial system was founded by the Jews,' said Rabbi Leo Franklin, Detroit's leading rabbi today … commenting on an interview which Henry Ford is said to have asserted that the Jews created the present financial system and that they should be willing to aid in constructing a new one. Mr. Ford was also quoted as saying that the *Dearborn Independent* would cease it attacks on the Jews after the Jan. 14 issue. His publications have besmirched the names of Jews in the minds of the great majority. He has fed the flames of anti-Semitism throughout the world. All men, Jew or Gentile, would be glad to know that Ford has had the courage to admit he has been wrong in his attacks.

Rabbi Franklin, a friend and neighbor of Ford, had once said that Ford might not have continued with his diatribes but for Louis Marshall's inflammatory criticism of Ford. Rabbi Franklin later retracted that opinion, one may suppose, after hearing from Marshall.

It was known that Ford required his employees and sales agents to sell subscriptions to the newspaper. The agents' failure to do so resulted in admonishment from Ford "that [you] had not sent in a single Dearborn subscription. You are fully expected to live up to [an] agreement to sell monthly subscriptions … and live up to monthly estimates … until you have reached your quota."

In 1923, the personal attacks in *The Dearborn Independent* provoked the first of two libel actions against it and Ford. Herman Bernstein, the editor of *The Jewish Tribune*, instituted a libel suit in July 1923 against Ford engaging Sam Untermyer, Marshall's former law partner, as his lawyer. *The New York Times* reported that Bernstein wrote a letter to Ford, that said:

In an issue of The Dearborn Independent of Aug. 1921 you published a scurrilous and libelous article concerning me, in which I was represented, among other things, as a sort of spy in the service of your mythical combination of Jewish bankers against whom you have been directing grotesque assaults based upon a tissue of fabrications that indicate an extent of … race hatred and bigotry that are beyond human understanding. I am determined to seek redress for the injury you have done me … and to expose the wanton falsehoods you have been spreading over the country concerning the Jews of the land. It is high time for the American people to get a true picture of the manner of man you are, and I feel that I am performing an important public service.

The suit would not be settled for four years.

The second libel suit was brought in 1925 by Aaron Sapiro, a lawyer and a leader and activist in the farmers' cooperative movement. He had received national recognition for his leadership in organizing farmers who were growers of fruit, potatoes, wheat, tobacco and cotton in California, Maine, Canada, and places in the south. Many of the farmers had improved their lot under Sapiro's leadership, and he was endorsed by numerous farmers' organizations.

In April 1924 Sapiro was attacked in *The Dearborn Independent:*, "Jewish Exploitation of Farmers' Organization. A band of Jews—bankers, lawyers, moneylenders, advertising agencies, fruit packers, produce buyers—is on the back of the American farmer." In 1925 Sapiro sued Henry Ford for libel; not only on his own behalf, but also as a member of the Jewish people.

Marshall was against Sapiro's suit from its beginning. In a 1926 letter Marshall said,

> I have long known Mr. Ford has been very anxious to have the Jews of this country take issue with him in the public press, in the hope that thereby his propaganda may be extended and the free advertising from it can be capitalized. He has now been engaged in this anti-Semitic campaign for five years and has easy by saying that he has been merely attacking Jewish bankers. He has defined Jewish bankers to include J.P. Morgan and all of Wall Street. He has written many an article against me, his principal grievance being that I am credited with having urged the Jews not to pay any attention to him. I shall continue to pursue that course. The best way to deal with that sort of gentry is to treat them with silent contempt.[4]

In March, 1927 when Sapiro's action came to trial Ford was represented by a prestigious team of eight lawyers led by United States Senator James M. Reed. Sapiro was represented by William H. Gallagher, a well—regarded lawyer from Detroit.

Gallagher argued that Sapiro, known as a distinguished humanitarian, had been libeled by the attacks on him, as well as scandalous attacks on the Jewish people, in the *Dearborn Independent.*

Senator Reed answered, "if Henry Ford authorized an attack on the Jewish race, that is something for which no individual can recover damages." Judge Fred

Raymond agreed. He would not allow Sapiro's arguments against Ford for what the newspaper had published about the Jews. Gallagher repeatedly raised the issue despite the judge's rulings.

As the trial continued, it seemed to be going well for Sapiro, but in April, there was an upheaval. It was alleged that one of the jurors "had lied during the jury selection process, and had then been offered a bribe by a Jew." Ford's lawyers presented affidavits to the judge,[5] who prohibited any publication of the matter. It was to no avail because the story was leaked to the press. The juror was dismissed, and despite Sapiro's willingness to continue with eleven jurors, Ford's lawyers instantly moved for a mistrial. The judge granted their motion. The new trial was scheduled for September.[6]

This was a climactic time for Ford. His concern was for the new product, and a bump in the road caused by his reputation as a bigot might alienate a segment of the public, potential customers for his new and improved product. Ford cars were not selling as well as in the past, and he had serious competition, especially from Chevrolet. His decision to cease publication of his newspaper may well have been attributable to the introduction and marketing of the new automobile, but his simple statement to Black had wide-ranging affects on Sapiro's suit, and Herman Bernstein's libel suit. The stage was now set for the final act in the seven plus years drama of America's most notorious anti-Semitic campaign.

Although Ford's decision in 1927 marked the beginning of the end of this major anti-Semitic campaign in America, it would not, however, be over in Europe. Early in Ford's newspaper's life, several of the anti-Jewish pieces were put together in a book called *The International Jew, the World's Foremost Problem*. Ford was also involved in the importation, printing and promotion of a book, *The Protocols of the Elders of Zion*, one of the most notorious and flagrantly false propagations of anti-Semitism ever created.

The door would be closed on Ford's anti-Semitic actions in America, but in Europe his programs lived on, and grew. Distribution of the appalling books did not stop, and the German nation's slide into Nazism rolled on. Ford's anti-Jewish employees left the newspaper, but did not leave the anti-Jewish programs or Ford's employ, despite his promises. Copies of both books were exported to and distributed in Europe, to be circulated and believed for decades, to the present day, wherever the hatred exists.

Louis Marshall would be greatly involved, almost by accident. He and Ford had been enemies from the time that the *Dearborn Independent* began the anti-Jewish pieces. Marshall had at least twice written publicly of his abhorrence of Ford. Yet when the opportunity arose for him to repudiate him and deny Ford any forgiveness, he would accept Ford's change of heart. Ford could simply ignore the past, wiping it away with the stroke of his pen. He signed an apology, was not vilified, his company flourished, and his hatred for Jews never diminished. In fact he would be honored by the future German fuehrer. It may have been a period when Marshall was absorbed in other, more significant events. He was partner with Chaim Weizmann in the development of the Jewish Agency for Palestine, he had several important pleadings before the United States Supreme Court, his leadership in the AJC, the JTS, the NY State Forestry and his legal career. He seemed to be mellowing, to be more tolerant of those who disagreed with him, even villains.

In June 1927, former U.S. Congressman Nathan Perlman was approached by two men representing Ford, who wanted to arrange for Ford to make peace with the Jewish people. They were Earl J. Davis, once an assistant U.S. attorney general, and Joseph Palma of the New York office of the Secret Service.

On July 27, 1927, almost a month after negotiations with Ford were concluded Perlman summarized the affair in a letter to Marshall, after expressing his feelings:[7]

> I am amazed at the contents of your communication relative to my participation in the negotiations which resulted in the Ford retraction and apology … You have done me a great injustice.

At the end of the letter Perlman makes reference to Marshall as a leader whose:

> accomplishments have made you an outstanding figure and shining light in American Jewry … I sincerely regret that you do not now entertain the high opinion which you say you had of me, for I value your friendship very much indeed.

The letter recites the Ford apology incident as follows:

> About 8:30 a.m. on May 20, 1927, Mr. George C. Nordlinger, one of my friends, called at my home and told me that Messrs Palma and Davis were in New York City and desired to discuss with prominent Jews the controversy between the Jewish people and Mr. Ford. I have known Mr. Palma for a long time and had come in contact with Mr. Davis when he was Assistant United States Attorney General. Accordingly, at about 10 a.m. that morning Messrs. Davis, Palma and I discussed the articles that had been published in *The Dearborn Independent* and their effect on the Jews. They told me that Mr. Ford was not antagonistic to the Jews; that he had the kindliest

feelings for them and that he did not know the contents of the articles that had been published. They told me that Mr. Ford had been deceived by Mr. Cameron [the editor] and asked me what I thought Mr. Ford could do to make amends. I advised them that Mr. Ford should make a strong public retraction and apology; that Mr. Ford should discontinue the publication of *The Dearborn Independent*. Davis and Palma informed me that they believed that he was prepared to make a public retraction and apology such as I suggested when my conversation. with Messrs Davis and Palma was about to be concluded, your name was mentioned for the first time to them. This suggestion came from me, please understand that. I told them that I would telephone to you. Later that day I telephoned to you and told you of the conference at my office with Messrs Davis and Palma. You stated that you would be pleased to see [them], and I then communicated with Mr. Davis and arranged an appointment for the following day. At that conference I repeated what I had said to them previously at my office. You talked at length and read the telegrams which you had sent to Mr. Ford when the first articles were published. You suggested that Mr. Ford make a public retraction and apology. Mr. Davis and Mr. Palma reported that they would go to Detroit and confer with Mr. Ford and would get in touch with us in a few days.

Several days after this conference Mr. Palma phoned me and asked that I arrange for another conference at your office. It was then that [they] told us that Mr. Ford would make a public retraction and apology and that after it was signed by Mr. Ford, Arthur Brisbane would give us publicity. It was agreeable to you. No publicity until after Mr. Brisbane had published Mr. Ford's statement."[8]

Perlman's letter was prompted by Marshall's criticism of him because he gave an interview to a reporter without clearing it first with Marshall. Perlman denied giving an interview to the reporter, saying that he only responded to questions in a telephone conversation.

It appears that in all of the publicity in reaction to Marshall's role, Perlman's role was hardly mentioned, but Marshall did make a statement reciting all of the apology negotiations, published in the *American Jewish Yearbook 1927-28*:

About a month ago [Davis and Palma] came to my office, introduced by former Congressman Nathan D. Perlman, who had informed me that they desired to meet me in order to present various facts to my attention. They told me that they came as representatives of Henry Ford.

Arthur Brisbane, a well-known newspaper columnist, and an old friend of Ford, had disagreed with Ford from the beginning in 1920, for his anti-Semitic tirades. He said that Ford was wrong to publish the articles and the *International Jew, The Protocols of the Elders of Zion,* and the other rants against the Jewish people. At last, in May 1927 Ford himself had told Brisbane that "he had made up his mind to discontinue all articles such as those that had given offense to Jews. No one can charge that I am an enemy of the Jewish people. I employ thousands of them. Among them can be found many of my most talented associates." [9]

Through his emissaries, Ford requested that Marshall compose the apology. Henry Ford must make a "complete retraction, ask for forgiveness, see to it that such attacks are not made in the future."[10]

In the latter part of June, Marshall wrote the apology, and on June 30, he sent it to Harry Bennett, Ford's close associate, at Ford's office in New York City. A copy was transmitted to Brisbane, who then called Ford and started to read the apology to him. He tried to tell Ford "that it was pretty bad" but Ford stopped him, saying, "I don't care how bad it is, you just settle it up."[11] The apology was publicized by Brisbane on June 30, 1927.

On July 1 Marshall wrote to Sam Untermyer, his friend and former partner, and Herman Bernstein's representative in his suit against Ford, telling him all about the Ford matter:

> I have been trying to see you for some days, but you have been so occupied that I never got a chance. I wished to inform you of what I have been doing in connection with procuring from Henry Ford a statement of which I do not believe he can feel very proud and which will have a most wholesome effect upon the anti-Semites of the world and especially Eastern Europe. There Ford has been made into a demi-god. His reprint of the *Dearborn Independent* articles in *The International Jew* has been translated into half a dozen languages and has been circulated, as I have reason to believe, with his money.
>
> On several occasions I have been approached by men claimed to be in the counsel of Ford, with the suggestion that they thought the time was opportune to make peace with him. I was visited by Earl J. Davis. He was accompanied by Joseph Palmer [Palma] who has apparently done a great deal of work for Ford and is in his confidence. They told me that they thought that Ford would be willing to do whatever was right [to] put an end to existing conditions, that he had found that Cameron, the editor of the *Dearborn Independent* had been deceiving him and that he had no idea of the real

character of the publications which appeared. I told them that I was interested in procuring a document which would be acceptable to the Jews and which would so far as possible make amends for the harm that he had tried to do them.

I also said that, although not interested in the case, I thought that he would have to make a settlement with Sapiro and Bernstein on terms satisfactory to them which would include a full retraction of the charges made against them I insisted that before anything should be done with regard to the settlement of the cases, such a document as I would prepare should be signed.

Marshall wanted that order of settlement because he did not want the "document intended to set the Jews right in the public mind made a subsidiary to any settlement of a law suit."

Accordingly I prepared the paper, of which I enclose a copy, and submitted it to Mr. Palmer [Palma]. He immediately proceeded to Detroit presented it to Ford. [Palma] called me, stating that Mr. Ford had agreed to make the statement just as it had been prepared, without any changes. I asked whether the statement had been signed by Ford and he told me that he had merely signed a letter in which he authorized the statement to be regarded as made by him. I told him that that would not be satisfactory, but that the document would have to be signed by Ford and dated by him. Immediately thereafter [Palma] telegraphed me that the document had been signed and would be sent to me by air mail special delivery. I just received it and am having photo static copies made.

Marshall's letter went on to discuss his contacts with the lawsuits against Ford:

In the meantime I had put myself in communication with Fred Butzel ... a friend of Sapiro, who is delighted ... He has taken the matter up with Gallagher (attorney for Sapiro) who is very much pleased, and at my suggestion Gallagher is now conferring with Davis with a view to bringing about a settlement. Sapiro has said that he does not desire anything for himself, that he wishes to be reimbursed for his expenses, and to receive a fund which he can devote to some public purpose.

Herman Bernstein was in the office the other day and I intimated to him what was in the wind, and he is extremely anxious to get the benefit of any settlement that can now be made ... Under the circumstances I think it would be a very simple thing for you to secure a very satisfactory adjustment of the Bernstein case.

If I had his money I would not have made such a humiliating statement for one hundred million dollars. I have prepared a letter which I am sending him … so far as my influence can further acceptance of his request for a pardon, it will be exerted, simply because there flows in my veins the blood of ancestors who were inured to suffering and nevertheless remained steadfast in their trust in God.[12]

Marshall, then at his summer home at Lower Saranac Lake, soon received a telegram from Untermyer. Though he approved of Marshall's plan, he declared:

My dear Louis,

I approve general plan and believe it will be productive of great and permanent results for Jews the world over. The reason given for the apology is ludicrous beyond words. The only impelling reason is to escape being exposed from the witness stand for what he is, a mean, petty, bigoted ignoramus … I am not so sure that we could not have accomplished still more by exposing him to the world's contempt instead of setting him up as a big broadminded hero. I was right in bringing the Bernstein case against your protest wasn't I. Our first duty here is to Bernstein and nothing more must be done until he is satisfied nor until Shapiro (sic) is satisfied for to him belongs the sole credit of bringing this thing to a head and I object to anything being done that does not accord them that credit. Am sending for Bernstein to come here.[13]

Untermyer had second thoughts, and on July 2 he wired Marshall:

I do not think that you should make any definite commitment until I have talked with you. Further reflection inclines me to the view that you are unnecessarily building up Ford on a hypothesis that we all know to be false. He was not deceived by his subordinates, nor was he ignorant of what he was doing.… Whilst this apology will aid the Jews it will needlessly aid Ford still more.

You should not have gone so far as you have gone without consulting me.

I do not care what you do although you will have done more to build him up by his apparent 'generosity' than he could have ever done for himself …

Untermyer called upon Marshall to consult with him, as Bernstein's counsel:

> By insisting as usual on 'going it alone' I think you have made a mistake. However if you arrange so that our statement commenting on this will be understood and not be regarded as a breach of faith by you or me I do not see that I have any right to object. Otherwise I do object, decidedly.[14]

On July 3, Marshall received another telegram from Untermyer. He had seen Bernstein, who insisted that Ford retract his libels and settle up or he would publicly attack the sincerity of Ford's apology. Untermyer also charged that Marshall should have consulted with him:

> B claims great losses from libels. He represented about fifty newspapers when F charged he was not representing newspapers as war correspondent or at peace conference. B said that when you spoke to him you said you were going to consult me which you should have done.

Untermyer finished with diatribe against Marshall, saying that Bernstein's suit is:

> More important than anybody's lawsuit I have. If you knew my reaction your offence in proceeding without my knowledge is greatly magnified. But for your confession I would not have believed it possible not-withstanding frequent recent evidences of your ruthless disregard of my views and wishes which I have attributed to an ego, but never dreamed it originated in ill will.[15]

Presumably, the final outburst in this conflict was in a telegram from Marshall to his old friend on July 4:

> For once I insist that you do not interfere. This is a matter affecting the destinies and honor of hundreds of thousands infinitely more important than anybody's lawsuit and there should be no cross-purposes. Stop. Of course the statement as was intended makes F. appear ridiculous. That very fact, his confession of wrong ... avowed repentance ... retraction ... humble apology must accomplish untold good ... his desire for settlement both suits coupled with full retractions you will have no difficulty fixing terms ... Stop. I tried to inform you of proceedings but apparently you had no time for me, besides it was certain what your natural reaction would be and I did not regard your recent treatment conducive to confidences. Stop. I informed B what was brewing and that I intended telling you. S. Friends appreciate this.[16]

While this conflict between old friends was most likely patched up, the differences that arose between Marshall and Sapiro would never end.

The "Statement by Henry Ford to Louis Marshall"[17] was publicized on July 8, 1927 throughout the United States, and much of Europe. Even in spite of Ford's self-serving excuses of his ignorance the apology still bears the mark of Marshall's outrage over his anti-Semitic publications. What follows is Ford's confession of sins from 1920 on:

> For some time past I have given consideration to the series of articles concerning Jews which since 1920 have appeared in *The Dearborn Independent.* Some have been reprinted in tablet form under the title *The International Jew.* Although both publications are my property, it goes without saying that in the multitude of my activities it has been impossible for me to devote personal attention to their management or to keep informed as to their contents. It has therefore inevitably followed that the conduct and policies of these publications had to be delegated to men whom I placed in charge of them and upon whom I relied implicitly.
>
> To my great regret I have learned that Jews generally, and particularly those of this country, not only resent these publications as promoting anti-Semitism, but regard me as their enemy. Trusted friends with whom I have conferred recently have assured me in all sincerity that in their opinion the character of the charges and insinuations made against the Jews, both individually and collectively, contained in many of the articles which have been circulated periodically in *The Dearborn Independent* and have been reprinted in the pamphlets mentioned, justifies the righteous indignation entertained by Jews everywhere toward me because of the mental anguish occasioned by the unprovoked reflections made upon them.
>
> This has led me to direct my personal attention to this subject, in order to ascertain the exact nature of these articles. As a result of this survey I confess I am deeply mortified that this journal, which is intended to be constructive and not destructive, has been made the medium for resurrecting exploded fictions, for giving currency to the so-called '*Protocols of the Wise Men of Zion*' which have been demonstrated, as I learn, to be gross forgeries, and for contending that the Jews have been engaged in a conspiracy to control the capital and the industries of the world, besides laying at their door many offenses against decency, public order and good morals.

Had I appreciated even the general nature, to say nothing of the details, of these utterances, I would have forbidden their circulation without a moment's hesitation, because I am fully aware of the virtues of the Jewish people as a whole, of what they and their ancestors have done for civilization, and for mankind and toward the development of commerce and industry, of their sobriety and diligence, their benevolence and their unselfish interest in the public welfare.

Of course there are black sheep in every flock, as there are among men of all races, creeds and nationalities who are at times evildoers. It is wrong, however, to judge a people by a few individuals, and I therefore join in condemning unreservedly all wholesale denunciations and attacks.

Those who know me can bear witness that it is not in my nature to inflict insult upon and to occasion pain to anybody, and that it has been my effort to free myself from prejudice. Because of that I frankly confess that I have been greatly shocked as a result of my study and examination of the files of *The Dearborn Independent* and of the pamphlets entitled *The International Jew*. I deem it to be my duty as an honorable man to make amends for the wrong done to the Jews as fellow-men and brothers, by asking for their forgiveness for the harm that I have unintentionally committed, by retracting so far as lies within my power the offensive charges laid at their door by these publications, and by giving them the unqualified assurance that henceforth they may look to me for friendship and good will.

It is needless to add that the pamphlets which have been distributed throughout the country and in foreign lands will be withdrawn from circulation, that in every way possible I will make it known that they have my unqualified disapproval, and that henceforth *The Dearborn Independent* will be conducted under such auspices that articles reflecting upon will never again appear in its columns.

Finally let me add that this statement is made on my own initiative and wholly in the interest of right and justice and in accordance with what I regard as my solemn duty as a man and as a citizen.

Signed, "Henry Ford, June 30, 1927, Dearborn, Michigan." [18]

The *Jewish Daily Bulletin* of New York City in an article on July 10 announced Louis Marshall's acceptance of Henry Ford's apology for his anti-Jewish attacks and quoted his answer to Ford:

> I am in receipt of your letter to Mr. Earl J. Davis accompanied by your statement, etc … It is my sincere hope that never again shall such a recrudescence of ancient superstition manifest itself upon our horizon.[19]

Ford's announcement to the country and even to the world had an impact in the Jewish community ranging from approval to outright disbelief. Some major newspapers either praised it enthusiastically and without reservations, others with reservations or expressions of caution.

Many people wrote letters to Ford and most approved, with reservations, of his apology. Marshall received hundreds of letters from both America and Europe, expressing gratitude or praise.

On July 22, Marshall, from his summer home in Lower Saranac Lake replied to one such letter of praise from the illustrious philanthropist Julius Rosenwald:

> I thank you for your congratulations upon the retraction and apology of Ford, which in my judgment will prove far-reaching in its effect. You say that Ford has written himself down as an ass and a liar. That is precisely what I intended he should do … I deemed it important to show the world the kind of man he was, willing to indulge in a series of disgraceful and criminal attacks upon a whole people and capable at the same time to resort to the most infantile of excuses. My great and outstanding objective has been accomplished with universal approval. Today the Jews stand vindicated and absolved. The lies uttered against them have been extirpated and by freely forgiving the monumental crime they stand forth morally as citizens greater than ever.[20]

In an editorial *The New York Times may* have had the most judicious response to Ford's apology:

> When a man alters a course which he has pursued for years in a public matter, withdraws statements and apologizes for having made them, it is inevitable that his motives will be questioned. There will be no end of wondering what lies behind his present action. But an apology is an apology, and Mr. Ford has made his so complete and handsome that those whom he has long been attacking through his publication will be fain to accept it. While it is better late than never … it is impossible to overlook the fact that in Mr.

Ford's case it is decidedly late. It is the more agreeable for the 'Times' to welcome Mr. Ford's repentance and vows to amend, since it urged such a reconciliation upon him at the time of the Sapiro suit against him for libel.

Indeed, Ford's apology led to settlement in Sapiro's lawsuit. Though Sapiro claimed to be out of pocket for more than $85,000, Ford did pay out $91,550 for damages. Still Sapiro was embittered. He was broke. His law practice was in ruins, and the cooperatives that he had enhanced had proven treacherous. Apart from these problems, he felt particular animosity against Marshall.

The Sapiro suit was ended, and Ford's agreement to settle was adhered to, but there was anger and animosity between Sapiro and Marshall. There was talk of an incident at that time in which Sapiro remarked about the "king of the Jews", referring to Marshall and possibly to others, that was then told to Marshall. In a letter dated February 21, 1928 to Herman Bernstein, Marshall wrote:

> I have read with interest your correspondence with Sapiro, and have heard and seen reports of what he has said. I deem it beneath my dignity to have anything to do with him. I have never spoken to him or seen him or had any correspondence with him. I know just exactly what his state of mind was with regard to his suit at the time when I was negotiating with Henry Ford. He was ready to settle for any amount. I had this from his personal friends and representatives, whom I informed of what was going on and who urged me to carry out the plan that I had of procuring Ford's retraction. Sapiro never had the grace to say a word to me in recognition of what I had done and of the way in which I had treated him and helped him out of what I was informed by his friends was a lamentable position. He has not hesitated to say all manner of things that no gentleman would permit himself to say. He tried to convey the idea that I personally profited by your settlement, when, as I informed you, I never accepted a cent. One of his friends asked me whether I would see Sapiro if he called on me and apologized. My answer was that I would not consciously meet him and would have nothing whatever to do with him.[21]

On July 19, 1927 Marshall wrote a letter of appreciation to Arthur Brisbane for his role in publicizing Ford's apology:

> The righting of a monumental wrong was my sole passion. To accomplish this end much more still remains to be done. [William J.] Cameron and Ernest G. Liebold are still associated with Mr. Ford. Until their relations are severed the public will question the sincerity of his recantation. *The Inter-*

national Jew translated into half a dozen languages has become the Bible of the anti-Semites of Eastern Europe and is still in circulation there. Theodor Fritsch, the infamous arch-enemy of the Jews expressed his unwillingness to believe that Mr. Ford had retracted.[22]

On December 21, 1927, Marshall took up his pen to complain directly to Ford: "Today's mail has brought me a copy of the issue of December 7, 1927 of the *Volkischer Beobachter,* published in Munich by the notorious Adolf Hitler. He is one of the most virulent anti-Semites that the world has ever known. He and his followers have resorted to libel, slander and violence of the most pernicious character, and throughout the civilized world he is regarded as a menace to society." Marshall then referred to a letter from Ford to Theodor Fritsch, who published and circulated *The International Jew* in Europe, in which Ford demanded that he stop publication and circulation. He also referred to a letter from Fritsch to Ford: "He is seeking to make it appear that you were forced by Jewish bankers to make reparation for the anti-Jewish articles published in *The Dearborn Independent*. His motive is obvious and I believe that an answer by you would be most desirable and illuminating".[23]

The Dearborn Independent stopped publishing as of December 1927. Cameron and Liebold were gone from their positions on the newspaper, but their association with Ford was not ended since his promise to discharge them was not kept. Cameron went on representing Ford and Ford's anti-Semitism in a surreptitious way, with a still hateful attitude, through the 1930s and into the 1940s, as did Liebold. It had little effect for Fritsch continued to be successful in circulating *The International Jew* and *The Protocols of the Elders of Zion* throughout the century.

In a letter to his son Robert in January 1928, Marshall, in a relaxed mood, tells of his final meeting with Henry Ford:

> On Tuesday morning at 9:30, Mr. Henry Ford, by pre-arrangement, called on me at the office, and we spent a most interesting hour together. He said that he felt better now that he had relieved his mind of the burden of the 'great mistake and blunder that he had made' in his anti-Jewish publications. He expressed his readiness to do anything that I might at any time suggest to enable him to minimize the evil that he had done. Ford is ready to sign anything that I prepare for him and has made 'a holy show' of Fritsch—the most bitter of German anti-Semites who has now shown himself to be a low blackmailer. The effect has been to bring consternation into the ranks of the European anti-Semites.

Ford invited me to see his new car and asked me to select any of his products that I might desire. I respectfully declined, informing him of my devotion to pedestrian locomotion. [24]

In a February 1928 letter to his friend Herman Bernstein Marshall referred to the same conversation:

> I was very much amused at what Henry Ford told me. He said that Cameron is out of a job and has indicated his willingness to write on the Jewish side of the subject. I replied that we did not need his help. You have probably noticed that Ford is carrying out his promises in every way. While in Washington yesterday I met Earl Davis, with whom I negotiated, who states that Ford has developed a great confidence in me. This is most amusing in view of what *The Dearborn Independent* said about me for a period of five years.[25]

In July, 1938 at a party to honor Henry Ford's seventy-fifth birthday, attended by more than 1,500 prominent Detroiters, Adolph Hitler awarded Ford the Grand Service Cross of the Supreme Order of the German Eagle. That award was created by Hitler in 1937 as the "highest honor given by Germany to distinguished foreigners." [26]

It is unfortunate that Ford's apparent reform and benevolence would not continue after Marshall's death. In fact Ford's post-apology statements about Cameron, Fritsch, and others were not true.

Henry Ford's attacks on the Jewish People were part of Louis Marshall's life for eight years, the longest period of all the sagas that he had undertaken for his people. It was one more instance in which he was supported by the American majority in reducing or eliminating attacks against the Jews.

More than four years before Ford's apology, Louis Marshall joined with Chaim Weizmann in a movement to end internal Jewish strife and unite the Jewish people.

Notes

1 Black Pg 27
2 Reznikoff V1 Pgs 368-370
3 Baldwin Pg 185
4 Reznikoff V1 Pg 371
5 Baldwin Pg 223
6 Ibid Pg 224
7 AJA-MC
8 AJA-MC
9 Baldwin Pg 235
10 Ibid Pg 236
11 Ibid Pgs 238-239
12 Reznikoff V1 Pgs 374-76
13 AJA-MC
14 Ibid
15 Ibid
16 Reznikoff V1 Pg 376
17 Ibid Pgs 376-79
18 Baldwin Pg 240
19 Reznikoff V1 Pgs 379-80
20 Ibid
21 Ibid
22 Ibid
23 Ibid
24 Reznikoff V1 Pg 388
25 AJA-MC
26 Reznikoff V1 Pgs 376-379

1922 and 1926

1922. In the years following the Versailles Conference, Marshall, now in his sixties, vigorously maintained his twin passions for justice and Judaism. His law practice was as busy as ever as he pursued his penchant for representing those who had been treated unjustly, either politically, financially, socially or racially. For his fellow Jews he would continue to attempt to apply himself to any needs that they would have.

His busy life did not exclude his closeness to his family. The children were doing well. His oldest son James and Lenore had two children, Jonathan and Ellen. His daughter Ruth was married to Jacob Billikopf, a social worker, a Jewish leader, and a valuable assistant to Marshall in many of his Jewish activities. They too had two children, Florence and David. Son Robert, not married, was becoming a leading environmentalist, having graduated from the New York State College of Forestry at Syracuse. George, the youngest child, also not yet married, was active in social affairs and would eventually become an economist.

The United States was about to enter a period that would be nostalgically remembered as unrestrained party time.

Much of the forthcoming gaiety could have been attributed to the famous and infamous Prohibition amendment, the Volstead Act, to the Constitution. The prohibition of marketing, manufacturing, and drinking encouraged violations of the law by ordinary citizens, and the successful growth of organized crime. Money became available for the criminals and smugglers, some even filtering down to ordinary workers. However, the era of the roaring twenties, the happy time, was ended abruptly by the depression in 1929.

In 1922, Marshall, as a founding member in 1914 of the American Jewish Relief Committee for War Sufferers, sent a special Rosh Hashanah greeting to several publications:

> More than 300,000 orphans in the Ukraine, threatened by death and moral decadence, look to the Jews of America for help. The special committee sent abroad early this summer to verify the condition of the war stricken communities has reported that our previous estimate of 300,000 Jewish orphans

in the Ukraine has been short of actual fact. These innocent victims are hungry, naked, and exposed to the dire peril of moral degeneracy unless they are at once properly assisted until we have saved them all by nourishing their bodies and feeding their souls. The Jews of America, who last fall pledged over $14,000,000 for war relief, will not permit this terrible tragedy of the children to persist. [It] has been assured by the leading Jews of Eastern Europe that but for the help rendered by American Jewry the greatest part of the Jews dwelling in that region would have gone down to death. They are not only the blameless victims of the war but also of that monstrous wave of religion and race prejudice which is the cruelest aftermath of the war.

When we shall assemble in our synagogues during these Holy Days to give thanks to the Ruler of the Universe for the blessings that have come to us let our hearts go out to our stricken brethren not only in Ukraine but in Poland, Lithuania, Austria, Roumania and Palestine. May our prayers be answered as we shall answer the prayers that come to us from across the seas.

1926. As the relief campaign begun in 1922 continued year after year, Marshall and his friends worked to raise money. In fact even *Time Magazine* took notice. It ran an article on May 24, 1926 with the catchy headline, "Jew and Jew":

a procurator wrote to his Emperor Trajan. 'Greek wars with Greek; ... Jew helps Jew'. He was not the first to observe the racial loyalty of the Jewish people, a loyalty that has kept them together, like a colossal freemasonry, while other nations light the world for a while, then crumble down. For some weeks past the Jews in various U.S. cities, animated by this tradition, have been working to raise money for the relief of the Jews in Eastern Europe.

Felix Warburg, Louis Marshall, William Fox and other rich Jews are on the committee which has sent its representatives up and down the country, *'There is one hope for the Jews of Eastern Europe,'* great posters state; *'that hope is in the drive for fifteen million dollars; women and children are dropping dead of hunger on the streets of Bessarabia. Others are found in Poland, typhus is sweeping over the Jews in both lands, hundreds are killing themselves, the Jews of America must respond.'*

The article concludes with the report that the $15,000,000 goal was reached and oversubscribed in the allotted two weeks; the leaders extended the campaign for another week, raising the goal to $ 25,000,000.

As the year 1926 progressed, members of the Marshall family prepared to celebrate an auspicious occasion. On December 14, Louis Marshall would reach his seventieth birthday, and many who knew him or of him joined in to honor him.

On December 13, the *New York Times* ran a picture of Marshall receiving a book from his friend Cyrus Adler. The accompanying article read in part: "An address signed by 8,112 persons in many parts of the world was presented to Louis Marshall yesterday in celebration of his seventieth birthday, which will be tomorrow. The address testified to his services to the cause of Judaism and commemorated his efforts to safeguard the religious and political rights of Jews. It extolled his brilliant record as a lawyer and his civic activities."[1]

The *Times* ran several columns citing tributes from many famous persons throughout the world. Every Anglo-Jewish newspaper and magazine featured lengthy pieces about his life, his work and his dedication to the United States Constitution.

Nathaniel Zalowitz, a reporter for an Anglo-Jewish newspaper, declared in a long multi-columnar article, "What Louis Marshall Has Meant to Jewry", a history of his accomplishments as a leader, and as an American Jew. "He has been a useful citizen of his state and country. But above everything else, Mr. Marshall has been interested in Jewish questions. It has been a consuming passion." Mr. Zalowitz concludes with, "The Jews of America, irrespective of party, have every reason to be proud of Louis Marshall's leadership. It is not every age which is fortunate enough to have such a leader."

Florence Marshall's closest sister was Beatrice Magnes. After Florence's death she and her husband Rabbi Judah Magnes maintained a close relationship with Marshall and his children. In honor of Marshall's birthday she composed a poem that included The following:

> Louis was a Syracusan,
> Playing ball and loving Jews an'
> Life was simple, life was sweet
> When he lived on Cedar Street,
> But G&U held out a hand.[2]
> His eyes beheld the promised land.
> Have you heard how Louis reached the City of New York?
> How he found the Kosher butchers selling sausages of pork?
> He got his little Scrap Book and wrote a Kosher Bill.

That was hotter than the hottest dogs upon a Kosher grill
He lifts his voice in clarion tones
To help the Jews in warring zones …
He brings the Jews from East and West
At Knollwood he should really be at ease.[3]
Surely there's the place to do, just as you please …
(friends and Rabbis)
Were begging Marshall for a statement
To strengthen Chewish Educatement[sic]
May his scrap book grow more weighty
By the time that he is eighty.[4]

Notes

1 AJA-MC
2 Attorneys Guggenheimer & Untermyer in New York City
3 AJA-MC Knollwood is the Marshall home on Lower Saranac Lake in New York State
4 AJA-MC

The Twenties—Toward The Jewish Agency

There were unprecedented achievements for minorities written into the Versailles Treaty, but the failure of the United States to accept the treaty and the League of Nations was a devastating obstacle in the path of the Jewish people in Europe. The minority rights that had been so fiercely fought for on paper could not readily provide security for the Jews in Poland and Roumania. In Poland, in fact, anti-Semitism was accepted as almost official policy.

In the United States, in the decade that began in the latter part of 1919, there would be progress and setbacks for American Jews. Marshall was the at the peak of his power and influence, and his friends were foremost among the leaders.

In his book, *A Time For Searching, 1920-1925* historian Henry L. Feingold would say it nicely:

> ... during the twenties the golden age of American Jewish stewardship was drawing to a close; Jacob Schiff died in 1920, Oscar Straus in 1926, and Louis Marshall, who took the most active leadership role, in 1929. Their roots were in the German Jewish community.... Its members were propertied, Jewish educated, and committed, and they possessed a sense of service.
> 1

In 1919 Marshall at 62, was admired as a fighter for individual rights, an outstanding constitutional lawyer, and his outlook seemed to be broadening. Indeed, he was mellowing. Still a staunch Republican, he could admire and praise prominent Democrats and Al Smith. As in the past, he was not a Zionist. He and Zionist leader Justice Louis D. Brandeis were not friends, but they did meet in 1918 in regard to the conflicts between the non-Zionists and the Zionists, and worked together to decide how to help the Jews of Europe when the war ended. Their differences were resolved when Marshall got non-Zionists to agree to compromises as to the make-up and the goals of a Jewish delegation to Versailles.

Marshall moderated his view toward Zionism. He was increasingly concerned about the need for a place for his brethren who wanted or needed to leave their native lands in Europe. For more than three decades the United States was the new home to go to, but for almost ten years there had been attempts in Washington to restrict immigration. In 1921 immigration from the eastern and low European countries would begin to be limited.

England's Balfour Declaration of 1917 opened a door of welcome to Palestine for the Jews. Herzl's Zionists had grown in number and popularity, and even after he died in 1904 at 44 the organization's membership grew, with branches in Europe and America. Jews were either Zionists, anti-Zionists, or non-Zionists. Some would shift from anti- to non-, or to full Zionists, but most would be steadfast. Many Jews who had come to the United States to make new lives as Americans were not involved, depending on their religiosity, income levels, or whim. More recent immigrants were supporters or members of Zionist Organizations, and they responded to the Zionist leaders.

The non-Zionists did not believe in a Jewish political nation. For them the United States was their national, permanent home. Judaism remained the religion of their people, but most would not consider moving to Palestine.

Marshall and many of the members of the American Jewish Committee were non-Zionists, but they did understand the desire for those who wanted to re-start in Palestine. They were the leaders, the most outspoken of non-Zionists, yet they would support the projects of those who immigrated to Palestine depending on the project or the development that was proposed.

The clauses written into the Versailles Treaty for equality for the minorities of certain European countries were to a significant degree from the efforts of the American Jewish delegation led by Marshall. It was arguably his finest contribution to Jewish life, and he was acclaimed for it. He returned home after four months to his family and law career

Meanwhile, in both America and Europe, the storm between leaders who were non-Zionists and Zionists was ongoing, and reconciliation would take almost nine years.

Zionism, as a modern movement, began with Theodore Herzl. In 1895 Herzl at 30, was a newspaper reporter, in the crowd of Parisians that witnessed the public degrading of French Army Captain Alfred Dreyfus who had been accused of being a German spy, convicted as a traitor, and sentenced to life imprisonment. Herzl was disturbed as the crowd reacted vehemently and joyously to the disgraced man's punishment. It appeared to him that the great public fury was aroused because Dreyfus was Jewish.

Herzl came from an Austrian assimilated Jewish family. Though educated as a lawyer, he preferred writing and journalism and became a correspondent for a Viennese newspaper and assigned to Paris. Herzl, of course had been aware of the discrimination and persecution of his fellow Jews in Europe. He had long been concerned about the anti-Semitism prevalent in European countries, including France, where the Jews had been allowed to live free in freedom as a result of the French revolution. The Dreyfus Affair was the catalyst that created in him what he perceived to be, the need for a Zionist movement.

The name Zionism did not originate with him. In fact, a yearning to solve the "Jewish Question" by finding a safe place to live had been the subject of other groups at least twenty years before Herzl. Then, in 1896, he wrote and had published a slim book, "Der Judenstaat" ("The Jewish State"). Surprisingly, the pamphlet, as he termed it, was enthusiastically received.

Herzl wrote that the Jewish people must cease their emigration from place to place because their very presence stirred up old prejudices and bigoted religious teachings. They must have a homeland, and the most appropriate place was their biblical land in Palestine. He soon developed a following, and by 1897 he convened a Zionist council in Basle, Switzerland. The council was divided over differences and conflicts as to how to proceed, who would be the leaders and who would provide the money needed to build a homeland?

For Jews living in the United States, Great Britain and France when conditions permitted, they considered their country of residence and citizenship to be home. Still they could share loyalties and obligations to the United States, England or France with a loyalty and obligation to their fellow Jews, "their brethren" in the lands where the monarchies treated their Jewish minority subjects as they wished. The Jews, as non-Christians were vulnerable everywhere, but as free citizens of western democracies they could be responsive when persecutions and pogroms arose in other countries. They sent money, they protested to their governments, and they formed organizations to help and support those afflicted. But for them Judaism was their religion; their homeland was the country where they lived.

In December, 1901 Marshall received an invitation to a Zionist gathering and on December 30, he responded:

> I am in receipt of yours of the 26th inst. inviting me to address a meeting of the Zionists on the 26th prox.to say that I cannot conscientiously avail myself of the invitation. While I sympathize with every movement which tends to ameliorate the condition of our co-religionists, I have been unable to convince myself that the nationalistic movement represented by the

Zionists possesses any element of practicability. The racial aspect of Judaism does not appeal to me as strongly as the religious side, and, much as I have been impressed by the enthusiasm of Herzl, Nordau, and Zangwill in respect to the Palestinian restoration, I can view it merely in the light of a poet's dream.[2]

Over the years, Marshall apparently received much information and solicitations from Zionists. When it concerned development of industry or education in Palestine he paid them some attention. For instance, in 1908 he wrote to his close friend Jacob Schiff recommending a book about the Zionist cause. Schiff's and Marshall's interest in Palestine was the same; as a home for Jews fleeing from persecution and discrimination. Marshall said:

[This book] is apparently a fair, dispassionate, clear, and logical statement of existing conditions.... It has given me new ideas, and has led me to regard the cause which it advocates, with better understanding, and much more sympathy than I have heretofore given to it....

In 1909 Marshall wrote to his friend, Sears Roebuck chief Julius Rosenwald, who was an anti-Zionist, introducing "my friend Shemaryahu Levin, with whose fame you are doubtless acquainted." Levin, a leading Zionist, had once been a member of the Russian Duma (a Russified version of a parliament) and very active in protest actions. Marshall wrote that Levin "was interested in the establishment of a technical school at Haifa, Palestine, which is intended to afford necessary instruction to the Jewish youth of the Holy Land, so as to enable them to help in the development of Palestine ... to the ultimate benefit of the Jewish people." Marshall goes on to say that Jacob Schiff contributed $100,000 toward the project and was enlisting a number of his affluent friends. Rosenwald had a great interest in supporting education in America, so it can be assumed that he became a supporter of the institution that was created and became the respected, renowned Technion [3]

Marshall would always remain a non-member of the Zionist Organization, but when he and his associates were spoken of, or even attacked, as anti-Zionist, he reacted with some vehemence. He was simply a non-Zionist, as were many of his friends.

While Marshall was engaged in his very active life and careers in the 1920s

There were to be a number of vital and even volatile incidents in his life starting in 1914 with declarations of war by the civilized, sophisticated, educated countries of Europe. Marshall would be into it, in support of the Jewish victims, within a few months, and would be involved until the signing of a peace treaty in 1919.

Ironically, Marshall would become increasingly associated with Zionism and the leader of The World Zionist Organization, Chaim Weizmann.

In his 1901 letter he said that he was not a Zionist, and never would be, and over the next 20 years he said that repeatedly. He supported various enterprises in Palestine, and he was not opposed to those who wanted to live in Palestine, but would not alter his opposition to the idea of a Jewish political entity. To him Judaism was a religion, and Jews were a nation with a small "n."

However, he had learned first hand and in depth of the suffering of Jews in eastern Europe, and as an avid, energetic advocate for the Jews, he could not, he would not, fail to support the movement that offered the prospect of life independent of the whims of kings, czars and dictators. As always for him, his involvement with the Zionists would not be a passing, casual relationship. Despite past reservations, he gave of his time, his money, and the time and money of several of his family members and his close associates.

Before the World War began, he stated feelings that can be seen as a re-positioning of his outlook. Nathan Straus was a leading merchant [R.H. Macy], a leading philanthropist, a supporter of milk pasteurization laboratories in the United States and Palestine, and reputed to have given two-thirds of his fortune to Palestine. On January 20, 1914, Marshall wrote to him. Marshall expressed his regret that Straus had temporarily given up going on a trip to Palestine because of his wife's illness. "It is my sincere hope that Mrs. Straus will be speedily restored to health, so that you may ere long be able to carry out your plans, which would be fraught with great blessings to our brethren in the Holy Land." Marshall then introduced another topic:

> I cannot refrain from (giving) expression to some of the thoughts which have occurred to me since our recent interview, which indicate to me that, to thousands of our people, the star of hope, points to the land of our fathers. As you know I am not a Zionist, certainly not a nationalist. I am a Jew with conviction and sentiment, one who takes pride in the literature, the history, the traditions, and the spiritual and intellectual contributions which Judaism has made to the world, and as I grow older, the feelings of love and reverence for the cradle of our race increase in intensity.

Marshall then wrote about the needs of the Jews in the ghettos of Russia and Roumania, and what they would face if restrictive immigration laws and similar restrictive laws were passed in America, England, South America, South Africa, and other lands:

> Hence it becomes the bounden duty of those of our people who have been blessed by Providence with worldly possessions, and who are at the same time imbued with the sentiments of love and loyalty for Judaism and its institutions, to concentrate their efforts toward the development of that land, which, after all, should rouse the most tender feelings in the heart of every Jew.
>
> To my mind this is a critical period in our history. I sincerely trust that God may strengthen you in your undertaking, and that the noble men who have hitherto acted as the vanguard of a great movement may continue their efforts in behalf of a great cause.[4]

In 1917 a convention was proposed for the following year in Pittsburgh to protest against Zionism. Marshall had no doubt that the Balfour Declaration was a milestone accomplishment, and any discord or disagreement by the Jews could be detrimental to the carrying out of its goal. He opposed the proposed convention because "the Balfour Declaration, and its acceptance by the other Powers, mainly the Allied Countries including the United States, is an act of the highest diplomacy. Zionism is but an incident of a far—reaching plan. It is merely a convenient peg upon which to hang a powerful weapon. All the protests that non-Zionists may make would be futile to affect any policy." These statements are another indication that Marshall was re-thinking his position on Zionism.

Marshall stated these objections and more in a letter dated September 25, 1918 to Max Senior who was a highly regarded merchant and a well-known Jewish supporter:

> I am not an alarmist, and even my enemies will give me credit for not being a coward, but my love for our people is such that even if I were disposed to combat Zionism I would shrink from the possibilities which might be entailed were I to do so. I have never been identified and am not now in any way connected with the Zionist organization. I have never favored the creation of a sovereign Jewish State. My interest in Jewish affairs is largely from the religious point of view. Yet I am so impressed with the reasons which I have sought to present to you, that I would regard public antagonism to Zionism at the present time as an act of treachery to the welfare of Judaism. Knowing as I do the sacrifices that you have made … the splendid service that you rendered in the interest of the Joint Distribution Committee, I

regard it as my duty to ask you to do all that lies in your power to defer the holding of any convention of the kind proposed until the war is over.

At Versailles the victors had responsibilities not just to their own lands, but to the territories that had been revived, created and reformed in the treaties. Palestine was taken from the once formidable Turkish Empire. It was neither a former nor a united nation within the resident Arabs. The Arabs' primary bond was their religion, since almost all worshipped Allah and followed the teachings of Mohammed, but not all practiced their religion within the same strictures.

At a conference of the war allies in San Remo, Italy, on April, 1920, the European Powers—Great Britain, France and Italy—confirmed the pledge contained in the Balfour Declaration, and decided to put Palestine under British mandatory rule. Thus Britain was made responsible for putting into effect the declaration made in November 1917. Final boundaries were determined in December, and the mandate was approved by the League of Nations in July 1922.

Chaim Weizmann, born in a *shtetl* in White Russia, was a student in Germany, an educator in Switzerland, and then a well-known scientist in England. In the post-war decade he became the most well-known and admired Jew in the world. In 1919 he was the leader of the World Zionist Organization. In his 1947 autobiography, he wrote:

> My acquaintance with Louis Marshall began in 1919, when he came to Paris as the head of the American Jewish Delegation to the Peace Conference. I saw little of him, for I did not take part in their work; the whole fight for minority rights seemed to me to be unreal. But I was greatly impressed by Marshall's forceful personality, his devotion to Jewish matters and the great wisdom he brought to bear in the discussions. Although counted among the 'assimilationists', he had a very clear understanding of and a deep sense of sympathy for the national endeavors of the Jewish communities in Europe who were struggling for cultural minority rights. He had learned Yiddish and followed the Yiddish press very closely, showing himself very sensitive to its criticism. Of a naturally autocratic habit of mind, firm if not obstinate on occasion, impatient of argument, he was, I felt, a man who once convinced of a rightness of a course, would follow it unswervingly. The main difficulty in working with him lay in his tendency to procrastinate-mainly due to his preoccupation with his profession and his various public activities This naturally added to the delays in our negotiations.[5]

Weizmann hoped to convince Marshall to aid him in his striving to acquire support from the leading American Jews who had wealth and influence. A few were Zionists, most were not, but they might support those Jews who were in Palestine or who would go there to live in freedom and to achieve economic progress. His autobiography continues:

> It was a profound mistake to think, as some Zionists did at the time, that Marshall was not 'representative' because he had not been elected, like members of the Zionist Executive. As one traveled up and down the States one could not but be impressed by the extent and power of his influence. The most important Jewish groups in every city in America looked to him for the lead in communal matters, and his attitude went a long way, in fact was often decisive, in determining theirs. [6]
>
> And yet in one sense he was not representative of his following. *He was much nearer to Jews and Judaism; nearer in fact than [Louis] Brandeis, an ardent Zionist, ever was.* [Author's italics] For Brandeis Zionism was an intellectual experiment, based on solid foundations of logic and reason, and the American experience. Marshall was hot blooded, capable of generous enthusiasms as well as of violent outbursts of anger-though it was seldom long before his cooler judgment returned.
>
> I found him at first completely skeptical as to the possibilities in Palestine, and knowing next to nothing about the country and about our work. But he had such a great fund of sympathy and was so warm-hearted, that it compensated for his ignorance of the subject. I remember how, at the end of a long conversation on our prospects, he suddenly burst out in his temperamental way: 'But Dr. Weizmann, you will need half a billion dollars to build up this country'. You'll need much more, Mr. Marshall. That completely disarmed him. He was so baffled that he stared at me for a long time, and I said: 'The money is there, in the pockets of the American Jews. Its your business and my business to get at some of it.' I think that from that moment on he began to understand the magnitude-and the appeal-of the problem.

Marshall and Weizmann shared the same goal: the improvement of the lives of the downtrodden Jews. By 1921 Marshall and Weizmann were slowly coming together.

In the Cleveland Zionist convention of 1921, the leadership group of Brandeis and Judge Julian Mack was defeated in the election of a permanent chairman of the convention. The opposition wanted all Jews of the Diaspora to support the concept of a Zionist Nation, a concept that was anathema to Americans such as Brandeis. With this defeat, Brandeis and his supporters resigned. He made a poignant speech of regret over the changes within the organization, reiterating his support of the "high Zionist ideals." He read off a list of those leaving with him that included several officers and thirty members of the national executive committee. The sounds of weeping could be heard in the hall as (Judge) Mack concluded that 'no action which you have taken, no action that you can take will ever drive me or any of the other gentlemen ... from the ranks of membership in the Zionist Organization of America, and will never lessen by the slightest degree the intensity of their Zionism, their devotion to Palestine and their continuous zealous work.'[7]

Marshall, although frequently angered by opposition and criticism from some Zionists, would not allow that anger to reduce his support for the Jews in Palestine. There were some Zionists interested in dealing with the American non-Zionists, and Weizmann, in spite of opposition from hard-line Zionists continued to want financial support from Marshall's affluent friends. There was even talk that Louis Marshall could be welcomed as a successor to Brandeis.

On February 17, 1924 there was a breakthrough. The non-Zionists convened a Non-Partisan Conference to Consider Palestinian Problems. Both Marshall and Weizmann spoke. Marshall's address included:

> It is now many years since the subject of Palestine has received serious consideration throughout the world. There has never been a time since the Diaspora when Jews have not in their hearts felt a profound love and attachment for the land of their fathers, when they have not felt a tie which bound them to their sacred soil.
>
> It is now more than twenty-five years since the idea took form that something should be done for the purpose of enabling the Jews who desired to live in Palestine, to do so, and to make it one of the great Jewish centers, where there might be cultural development and where there might be a restoration of the economic life of such Jews as desired to have their home there.

Marshall then cited the 1923 Zionist Conference in which the Zionists indicated their willingness to "cooperate" with the non-Zionists in respect to the Jewish Agency created in the Mandate issued to Great Britain as a result of the San

Remo agreement. The Zionists were even willing to surrender one-half of their authority over the agency. Marshall commented:

> We have an opportunity now of saying that we shall have a part ... in that Agency, that it is no more the property of the Zionist Organization. We who have complained about Zionism have now an opportunity to show what we can do to assist the cause of Palestine.
>
> This, in a nutshell, is the matter which is to be decided at this conference. I hope that everybody present will recognize the seriousness of the proposition and will appreciate the fact that after action is taken, if it be in the affirmative, responsibilities will have been assumed, and that we will have to work shoulder to shoulder and side by side with the erstwhile Zionists in attempting to carry out what I consider to be a sacred mission.

Marshall proposed several resolutions, the primary one being:

> Whereas in accordance with the Palestine Mandate issued by the League of Nations, provision has been made for the recognition of an appropriate Jewish Agency, as a public body for the purpose of advising and cooperating with the Administration of Palestine in ... matters as may affect the establishment of a Jewish National Home to secure the cooperation of all Jews who are willing to assist in the establishment of the Jewish National Home.[8]

With this, and two additional resolutions, the union that was once impossible to consider began to come alive. Chaim Weizmann delivered two speeches. They include the following excerpts:

> We who have for almost two generations carried a heavy responsibility view this conference with a deep interest. And may I be permitted, on behalf of the Organization which I have the honor to represent, to express my heartiest thanks to the chairman [Marshall] of this conference, who at all times, in spite of his manifold duties, has shown a deep concern for the problems of Palestine, and at all times has stretched out a helping hand in the performance of our difficult duties.
>
> I shall not dwell on the roads and routes by which these people *(Jews in Europe)* have endeavored to enter Palestine. I think it is correct to say that if there today (was) free movement on the roads of Europe and if those roads were not barricaded by guns, passports, visas, police and contending armies,

there would have been a stream of such people seeking the road to the next port where they would find a ship which would bring them to Palestine.

There is no doubt in the mind of any unbiased observer, be he Jew or non-Jew, be he Zionist or non-Zionist, that there is room in Palestine ... for at least a million and a half people over and above the population which exists at present in the country.

I am in duty and honor bound to emphasize in this conference I do represent masses of Jews scattered all over the world, in every clime, in every station in life thousands and hundreds of thousands of nameless and inarticulate ones who are moved by one sacred sentiment and by one great urge- to build up in Palestine a beautiful community and a country where the Jew and the Jewish soul will give expression to their sentiment of religion, literature, civilization and build up this civilization, not on the back of anybody, but simply as an utterance of that which has lived in us and has made us what we are-an indestructible race. [9]

This betrothal of two forces leading their people was an event that could not have been foretold in 1914, when the several organizations united to give aid solely for the survival of European Jews. Then came more than four years of contention, notably between the American Jewish Committee and the American Zionists, and dissension within the Zionist Organization. When the Jewish delegations came together in France in 1919 they eventually realized that some agreement was paramount for serious consideration of the Jewish people's problems by the mighty and powerful Christian nations. Even the engagement of 1924 between Zionists and non-Zionists would not lead to marriage in the foreseeable future. There were to be episodes of disagreement, disputes, outright enmity, and sharp criticism from each side. The root of the problem was the Zionist members who had striven through difficult times and extensive struggles, to create a successful and united Zionist organization that would create a nation. These Jews could not, or would not, countenance a group that had not supported this Zionist goal and that at times, had spoken out against it. The differences would continue until the wedding ceremony in 1929.

Notes

1 Feingold Pg 155
2 Reznikoff V2 Pg703
3 Ibid Pgs 704-5
4 Ibid Pgs 708 & 710
5 CW Pg 308
6 CW Pgs 308 & 309
7 Urofsky Pgs 293-294
8 "The Pact of Glory"; The high points and optimistic speeches at the conventions, meetings and resulting agreements to go forward, that began in 1923 and 1924 until the final conclusion in 1929 were published in the *"Pact of Glory"* The speeches given and actions agreed upon at the Non-Partisan Conferences from 1924-1928 were a phrase from a speech by Chaim Weizmann. All of the speeches and resolutions were published in a pamphlet after the formation of the enlarged Jewish Agency.
9 The Pact of Glory

Toward the Jewish Agency— Continued

In the early Twenties, the Jews of Russia were in great economic distress. The Russian government formed a Jewish commission that would settle Jews on agricultural land with some assistance that would be available in Russia, but it wasn't enough. The American Joint Distribution Committee [the JDC] came to their aid, forming the American Jewish Joint Agriculture Corporation to solicit funds. Almost $5 million was eventually received. The Zionist Organization protested that such funds should be for Palestine. While the JDC did support projects there, its non-Zionist leaders believed that Zionism was not the sole solution for the problems of the Jews.[1]

Such irritations between the two sides did not affect the friendship of Weizmann and Marshall. They either resolved or ignored these problems as negotiations continued for the convening of the non-Zionist Non-Partisan meetings that began in 1924.

On March 1, 1925 there was another Non-Partisan Conference. It was organized to formulate resolutions that would create a plan for the establishment of an enlarged Jewish Agency. Once duly adopted, Louis Marshall was to appoint persons to a committee to participate in the Agency. On June 27, 1925, he wrote to Dr. Cyrus Adler, stating the necessary procedures:

> ... in accordance with Article IV of the Palestine Mandate [stemming from the Balfour Declaration] issued by the League of Nations, in which Agency equal representation was to be given to non-Zionists and to the Zionist Organization. As Chairman of the Conference, I was directed to appoint an Organization Committee, consisting of persons who were not members of the Zionist organization, for the purpose of bringing about full participation of American Jewry in the Jewish Agency ... I am now designating ... an Organization Committee representative of non-Zionist bodies in the United States ... I shall take the liberty of serving as a member of the Committee ex-officio. The first duty that will devolve upon its members will be

the designation of various non-Zionist organizations which are to be invited to cooperate in the selection of the non-Zionist representatives on the council of the Jewish Agency. It is my firm conviction that no effort should be spared to bring about unity and harmony in the ranks of Israel for the solution of the many problems.

Marshall then listed fourteen organizations affecting Palestine and the future of the Jews in the Holy Land ranging from the American Jewish Historical Society to the Union of Orthodox Rabbis.

At the next Non-Partisan Conference in October, 1925 Marshall presented a resolution that was adopted. He proposed:

> ... in accordance with Article 4 of the Palestine Mandate ... issued by the League of Nations, provision has been made for the recognition of an appropriate Jewish Agency, as a public body for the purpose of advising and cooperating with the Administration of Palestine in such economic, social and other matters as may effect the establishment of a Jewish National Home ... to secure the co-operation of all Jews who are willing to assist in the establishment of the Jewish National Home ... a committee was designated to confer with the Zionist Organization and other bodies for the purpose of effectuating this object (and) ... the principle Jewish communities of Europe ... have taken steps looking to the accomplishment of the same end ...

Those words "Jewish National Home" in Marshall's resolution would not have been thought possible in the years before and after the World War. In Marshall's eyes, the entire American Jewish community should be totally committed to the formation of the Jewish Agency.

Next, the World Zionist Organization would meet to continue to bring about the document that Weizmann would refer to and would be memorialized as the "Pact of Glory."[2]

But, obstacles lay ahead. In the momentous year of 1925 there were agreements as well as disagreements that hindered cooperation. For example, in September in Philadelphia, the Joint Distribution Committee and the Zionists agreed to a combined fundraising campaign to raise $15 million for relief activities in Eastern Europe and a Jewish agrarian settlement in Russia and for building the Jewish National Home in Palestine. But the American Jews also supported building a settlement in Crimean Russia. The Zionists objected because money was again going toward a Russian venture that seemed to have little chance of success, draining money from the building of Palestine.

In October of the same year, at an American Jewish Congress convention Rabbi Stephen S. Wise charged that the JDC had broken its word and sent circulars to organize the campaign appeal for funds. In the circulars the JDC mentioned its projects and ignored those of the Zionists. Marshall attempted to mediate the dispute, but the Zionists set up their own campaign, the United Palestine Appeal.

In December, 1925 General Director Emanuel Neumann's speech at a United Palestine Appeal meeting in Pittsburgh, prompted a letter from Marshall:

> ... A report of the speech delivered by you in Pittsburgh on Sunday ... fills me with astonishment. It was reported in the Jewish Daily Bulletin, and it includes ...
>
> 'Our rich, our powerful, our capitalists, our captains of industry and leaders of finance, have not helped, but sometimes hindered. The sabotage practiced against Palestine by our wealthy people constitutes a blot on the fair name of American Israel. The future historian will find it hard to understand and still harder to justify this obstinate callous indifference to a great historic opportunity, which constitutes ... the last hope of salvation for multitudes of our fellow Jews.'
>
> I deem it my duty to protest against your remarks. I insist that there is no justification for this wholesale attack upon men who have in the past given material proof of their sympathy with all good causes, looking to the improvement of the condition of the Jews in every part of the world. It is they who have contributed largely to the funds administered by the Joint Distribution Committee. Out of those funds upwards of Seven Million Dollars were appropriated for and used in Palestine prior to the creation of Keren Hayesod [the financial arm of the Zionist Organization]. It is they who have contributed largely to the creation of the fund with which The Hebrew University is to be maintained. I deny most emphatically that those whom you referred to have practiced sabotage against Palestine ... It is evident that you do not understand them and that you believe you can dragoon them by denunciation to do their bidding instead of approaching them courteously in such a way as to appeal to their minds and their hearts. I am convinced that the men you are attempting to read out of the ranks of Jewry have of late begun to recognize the merit of certain aspects of Palestine development and that by means of tact and disposition to respect the right of every man to have his views respected, they could have been persuaded to become substantial contributors to the work of rebuilding Palestine. But you have

resorted to the worst method that could possibly be devised to accomplish such a result. Any self-respecting man will naturally resent such intolerance of speech ... they would retort in your words that they cannot justify the 'obstinate callous indifference' manifested by you and some of your associates to the sad plight of the 'multitudes of our fellow Jews' in Eastern Europe whom they have helped in the past....

Let me advise you that if you were setting about deliberately to wreck the plans that are in the making to create a general interest for Palestine, you could not have improved upon your Pittsburgh speech.[3]

In this period almost any act, not clearly agreed upon, could provoke either the Zionists or the non-Zionists. At the center was the Zionist concern that the non-Zionists were continuing to campaign for money for Eastern European Jews and programs. From Marshall's perspective accusations like Neumann's were inconsiderate, unfaithful, untrue, insulting and hurtful. In May 1928, Marshall wrote a long letter to Dr. Weizmann discussing and relating the difficulties of the past months. He told of discussions with individuals in which there was no animosity and there was agreement about plans, campaigns and actions to be followed. Yet, these agreements were either seldom adhered to or ignored as if they had never been.

A typical incident, when the two sides agreed on a tentative plan for resolving the fund raising issues, is related by Marshall in a May 1926 letter to Weizmann: "I was asked, whether I would meet with Mr. Lipsky, Dr. Wise and three other leaders of the Zionist group. I stated that I was greatly pleased to meet them and such a meeting took place at my house."

That meeting, prior to a convention in Baltimore of the United Palestine Appeal, led to agreement between the JDC and the Zionists on budget arrangements and to an "amicable understanding." Marshall's letter explained what happened:

> I attended the Baltimore convention with the idea that it would be followed by a cessation of controversy, but when Dr. Wise, the Chairman arose and employed the usual commonplaces concerning peace with honor and proceeded to launch forth into a tirade against the gentlemen with whom I was affiliated, I felt constrained to say that I regarded the speech as having an underlying body of persistent hostility. I could feel throughout the audience that I might as well have addressed my remarks to the four walls. I subsequently learned that the managers of that meeting had conferred all

night and had directed Dr. Wise as to what he should and what he did not say. I was told by Mr. Lipsky that I should not take him seriously and that nobody connected with the organization took him seriously. I replied that I did and that I was not to be satisfied with any such methods of procedure ... from that time on there was unceasing warfare against the United Jewish Campaign from one end of the country to the other. The Zionist press outdid itself.[4]

Despite this and other similar episodes, Marshall continued to communicate with Weizmann in a conciliatory mode, displaying his affection and confidence in the Zionist leader and the May 1926 agreement survived the animosity of factions on both sides. In January 1927, Weizmann wrote in the *Jewish Daily Bulletin* commending the JDC for the progress because of the sincere interest in Palestine. He concluded: "Our most imperative need just now is for 'Sholom'— peace among all the forces of American Jewry, in order to achieve such unity as will advance the higher interests of all-Israel here and everywhere."

Still another irritation arose in 1927. The Zionists had dispatched three commissions of experts to study the economic state of Palestine, only to result in disagreement and anger from their labor group. Then "the non-Zionist leadership insisted that the formation of the enlarged Jewish Agency was conditional on the formation of a commission of experts that would examine the economic achievement of the settlement in Palestine." Meanwhile, two commissions headed by Lord Melchett of England that included world experts in agriculture, industry and other areas toured Palestine and, upon return, delivered a report that was critical of the "social experiments." A storm within the Zionist leaders erupted, but after sharp debate in Berlin in 1928, there was compromise. It appears that the only reason for the dispute was the non-Zionist insistence that the commissions be formed.

Marshall sailed for London on June 2, 1928. He wrote to his son Robert in May that: ... "I have reluctantly consented to go to London for the purpose of conferring with Sir Alfred Mond, Dr. Weizmann [and others] in preparing the final report of the [Palestine Survey] Commission."[5]

On June 18 the members of the Commission submitted "a unanimous report recommending what should and should not be done and approving the principle of an enlarged Jewish Agency."[6]

On June 19, 1928, from London, Marshall wrote to his children:

> The Commission has unanimously agreed upon the terms of the report and the accompanying conclusions and recommendations. It is practically all in type and will cover 200 pages. I am satisfied with what has been accomplished and so are the members of the Commission and Weizmann. I wrote a chapter relating to the obligations resting on the Government which has evoked much commendation and which I hope will open the door for better cooperation on the part of the Government. I have only words of praise for all concerned in this difficult piece of work ... Felix Warburg & Dr. Frankel [a member of the commission] have been indefatigable and [Maurice] Hexter has worn himself into frazzle. He returns on Saturday and will take with him my papers for delivery at the office. This will save me the annoyance of lugging them about.
>
> Yesterday afternoon I had a pleasant chat with James de Rothschild who called on me. This evening the Weizmanns will give a big dinner where a number of "big wigs" are to attend ... toward the end of the week. [I] proceed to Paris where I have a number of important conferences in view with respect to Eastern European problems. And then—I am happy to say on July 13 I shall be homeward bound. This hob-nobbing with Royalty grows tiresome.
>
> The hotel is decorated and beflowered in order to welcome Miss Earhart, the aerial ambassadress of the national Women's Party, who is to stop here. Great excitement prevails among the personnel.
>
> I am yearning for Knollwood after this hullabaloo—satisfactory though the outcome has been ... after my arrival I shall have to arrange for re-convening the Non-Zionist Conference for the purpose of completing the details of the launching of the new agency, so far as we are concerned. What the Zionists will do will be uncertain. There will be howls and denunciations, rebellions and revolts—perhaps chaos and pandemonium rolled into one and criticisms and philosophical disquisitions by the cord. If there is no safety valve the boiler may burst, but whatever may happen I [am] convinced that we have done the right thing & that unless the Commission's recommendations are adopted and the reconstitution of the Agency takes place, Jewish Palestine will be fini.[7]

On August 21, 1928, in a letter to Weizmann Marshall discussed the distribution of the report of Joint Palestine Survey Commission to the non-Zionists and to the Anglo-Jewish and Yiddish newspapers and to each participant in their conferences. "I urged careful perusal of the report in order that when the conference shall reconvene every person present may be thoroughly familiar with the action of the Commission. I have no doubt that there will be satisfactory attendance of men representing the leading non-Zionist organizations ..." He then spoke of the reaction to the report by the Zionists at a meeting in Pittsburgh:

> I should not conceal my anxiety, occasioned first by the almost cataclysmic outbursts of vituperation and hatred manifested at the Pittsburgh Convention, and the fact that charges and counter-charges were rife and have been the subject of severe criticism on the part of fair-minded and sympathetic men and women. It is not much to say that what occurred has not redounded to the advantage of the Zionist Organization, and has had the effect of cooling the enthusiasm for the upbuilding of Palestine among a considerable of those whose interest could otherwise have been enlisted, and I hope may yet be enlisted, in favor of the Jewish Agency. What has occurred will render our work much more difficult than it otherwise would have been.... When we completed our work in London I felt exhilarated, because it seemed to me that a way had been found whereby Palestine could be redeemed and unity and harmony would prevail in the ranks of Israel. I regret to say that I now feel profoundly discouraged. Nevertheless I intend to do my utmost toward presenting this subject at the reconvened Non-Zionist Conference, in order to persuade those who will be there assembled to overlook even these depressing factors. A statement from you at the Non-Partisan Conference would prove beneficial and might dissipate any hesitancy that has been created by the circumstances to which I have adverted.

> We are of the opinion here that it is more important now than ever that the reports of the experts should be printed, so that those present at the meeting may be able to consider them ... Whatever may betide these reports ... it is quite likely that in the future better counsels may prevail and somehow good may follow after all of the storms which have been aroused by a disclosure of the truth.[8]

In spite of the antipathy of some Zionists, and criticism from the press, the Non-Partisan Conference of 1928 was convened.

On the day preceding the Conference, October 19, *The Jewish Chronicle, the Organ of British Jewry,* opposed to the participation by the non-Zionists, denounced the proposed arrangements in an editorial:

> A meeting of non-Zionists and anti-Zionists is to assemble in New York, the object being further to promote the scheme of an extended Jewish Agency in connection with the Zionist movement. The meeting has been called by Mr. Louis Marshall, in cooperation with Dr. Weizmann who has proceeded to America in order to be present in pursuance of his purpose of, by its means, raiding American money—bags, which is his chief interest in the endeavor. Mr. Marshall professes to see in the mandate, six years after its ratification a call to Jewry, which he feels bound, albeit belatedly, to answer. In the circular convening the meeting, he alludes to the proposed Jewish Agency as in accordance with the Mandate. But this is not true. The Mandate provides that the Zionist Organisation, which for the time was appointed as the "appropriate Jewish Agency," shall take steps to secure the cooperation of all Jews who are willing to assist in the establishment of the Jewish National Home for those are the words that are used in the Balfour Declaration upon which the Mandate is founded. But Mr. Marshall and his friends declare that they are not in favour of but are opposed to this Jewish National scheme. Mr. Marshall has explicitly stated that he is not a Zionist in the national sense, the sense in which the term is used in the Mandate, but only so far that he is willing to help in the reconstruction of Palestine and the settlements there under the aegis of philanthropy of a number of Jewish colonists.
>
> We hope, therefore, that the first business to which the meeting will devote itself, will be to clear up this point and to define beyond any possibility of misunderstanding ... their true position in the matter. For, once that is realised by them, they must, as honorable men, perceive that they cannot conscientiously or consistently, take part in the Agency contemplated by the Mandate assuming the Agency scheme crystallizes into actuality, we shall have the strange spectacle of a Jewish organisation working in Palestine in total disaccord with the letter and the spirit of the Mandate.
>
> We are happy to see the very strenuous opposition against Mr. Marshall's plans among American Jews. We cannot believe that any who care an iota for true Zionism will follow the lead of Mr. Marshall whose support of Zionism has been at most the persistent opposition he has offered to it, instead of the leadership of veterans in the Zionist movement in its cause such as, to men-

tion only one name, Dr. Stephen S. Wise. And with him are, happily, some of the best known and most respected of American Zionists.

On October 20 and 21, 1928 a Non-Partisan Conference was convened in New York City. Marshall spoke on the subject of "The Jewish Agency Defined":

> Primarily the Jewish Agency is to act in an advisory capacity to the Palestinian Government that it should see to it that those who came to Palestine should have opportunities that there should be land acquired upon which they might live and help to build up the country. And so the Jewish Agency evolved into a very important activity of the Jewish people in connection with the rebuilding of the home of our fathers in such a manner as to make it an object of pride to every right-thinking Jew. It is expressed in the Mandate that all Jews who desired to associate themselves with this work were expected to cooperate. And the British Government has indicated that this is its desire, as it should be.

Dr. Weizmann's address:

> Today I simply feel that we are united, and that we have taken upon ourselves a heavy but sacred burden which, with the forces available in Jewry in particular, I am certain we shall carry to a successful conclusion. I think it proper for us to remember … those who have made Palestine a living organism,—those who, with spade and axe and superhuman effort, have converted rocks and swamps into something which is today as near a garden as possible; those who have given all their idealism and intelligence to the cause. It is they who are the real creators of this movement.

> … if nationalism means a political relationship of Palestine to the Jews in other lands, if the Jewish National Homeland is to deprive the Jews without its borders of the station they have attained after such bitter struggles, then I am no nationalist, and no sensible Zionist is a nationalist. If, however, nationalism means the creating of a material basis in Palestine upon which we can build the structure of a Jewish civilization, then we are nationalists.

> *We have entered into a pact for the glory of a great ideal and a great country. That is the common denominator which unites us all.*

> … The Balfour Declaration was not given to Zionists alone. It was given to all of Israel, and all of Israel must receive it with clean hands and clean hearts. Then we may hope to make out of Palestine something that will

redound to the credit of all of you, and that will help you to carry on Jewish tradition.

Other speakers at the Conference included Horace Stern of the United States and Lord Melchett the chief representative from England. Mr. Stern said: "The World Has given Us an Opportunity":

> It has given it to the Jews. It has not distinguished between Dr. Weizmann and the most bitter anti-Zionist. It was given to the Jews. And the world will judge the result by what the Jews do with that opportunity, and we must not fail. One cannot fail to see that the gates of the world are slowly and steadily closing on the Jews. Possibly the time will come when Palestine will be the only country which will offer a refuge to the Jews.

> Because of the mere fact that some persons believe that [the] colony will result ultimately in a Jewish State, and want it to, it does not seem to me that, because I have a different theory of the ultimate destiny of the Jews—that I, or any other Jew, should withhold aid from this cause.

> … any committee that is appointed here should be big enough and broad enough to build up a real organization and to effect a permanent and integral and large organization of the Jews of the United States, Zionists or non-Zionists, and provide for a means of getting annually and as needed the large sums which alone will rehabilitate Palestine.

Lord Melchett, nee Sir Alfred Mond, the President of the British Zionist Foundation, was a long time supporter of the Enlarged Jewish Agency. His father was Ludwig Mond, who was a brilliant young chemist at the University of Heidelberg and left Germany at 23 because of anti-Semitism. In England, he started as a chemist, and went on to become a leading British industrialist. His son Alfred, also an industrialist, held several important British government positions during the World War, and in 1928 he rose to the peerage as the first Lord Melchett. His wife was not Jewish, and his son and daughter were Christians, yet in 1917, he became interested in Judaism and the Jewish people. His children converted to Judaism, and were active in Jewish affairs. He was a leader in the study of Palestine by the Joint Palestine Survey Committee. He spoke on behalf of Palestine, made large contributions to Zionist causes, and bought land for himself in Palestine. Lord Melchett spoke optimistically of the need for unity, making several positive pronouncements that sought to solidify the agreement between the parties:

> If we did not always endeavor to invent differences, a great many of our differences would disappear. I remember Mr. Lloyd George saying one day to me, 'I cannot understand your people. Here we have given them the great opportunity for which they pray every day, to return to Palestine. The whole world is watching to see if they can do for themselves what they have done for so many other countries. And yet they seem so reluctant and terrified at entering into the heritage which has been placed before them. What is the matter with them?'
>
> ... distinctions between Zionists and non-Zionists do not exist except in the figment of people's minds. I assure you that they do not exist among people outside. The world is judging the whole of Jewry for what we make of Palestine.
>
> To help in the rebuilding of Eretz Israel is a privilege. I have received in my life to date more distinctions than my humble services have merited, but there is none which I feel to be a greater one than to have had the privilege of helping to build up Eretz Israel.

After the Conference, Marshall wrote to his son Robert:

> ... on last Saturday evening the sessions of the Non-Zionist Conference began and lasted until 11 o'clock and were resumed on Sunday morning and continued until late in the afternoon. It was on a very elevated plane and every speech that was made was a good speech and a feeling of harmony and unity prevailed. With the exception of Dr. Weizmann and Harry Sacher, who had come from Palestine, no other Zionist spoke until after the Non-Zionists decided to adopt the report of the Survey Commission and to enter into membership in the Jewish Agency, which is to consist of equal numbers of representatives of the Zionist Organization and of non-Zionists. Henceforth we were no longer Zionists or non-Zionists, but Jews interested in Palestine. For the first time the Jews of this country have approached the much-desired culmination of my hopes of the creation of a united Jewry. Whether there will be a rift in the lute nobody can tell ... [9]

There remained Zionists who would not countenance the participation of Jews who would not be members of the Zionist organizations, and would continue to resist their inclusion in an enlarged Jewish Agency. Marshall bristled at their attacks, and only responded to those that he deemed worthy of a response.

In summer 1929, the Sixteenth Zionist Council was to meet in Zurich to form an enlarged Jewish Agency that would include an equal number of Zionists and non-Zionists on its board

Notes

1 EJ V2 Pgs 828-29
2 The Pact of Glory
3 Adler-Letters V2 Pg 117
4 Reznikoff V2 Pgs 749-750
5 Ibid V2 Pgs 755-756
6 Ibid V2 Pg 1172
7 *The New Palestine* newspaper from a radio report by Marshall April 28, 1929
8 AJA-MC
9 Reznikoff V2 PGs 769-772
10 Ibid Pgs 774

<u>Zionists and Non-Zionists— Coming Together 1929</u>

By summer of 1929 Marshall was comfortable and enthused about the impending journey to Zurich, Switzerland, but ChaimWeizmann, who had become his partner in the venture to give life and support to the Jewish Agency, was having difficulty with some recalcitrant members of the World Zionist Organization.

In late 1928, after his trips to the United States, Weizmann returned to London exhausted, on the verge of collapse, and for weeks he was bedridden. In July, after an invigorating trip to "Eretz Israel", a healthy Weizmann arrived in Zurich for the Sixteenth Zionist Congress. From the opening on July 28 to the end on August 9, Weizmann weathered some stormy sessions. Opponents of the non-Zionists were still dubious about the "Pact of Glory" alliance and proposed amendments to the agreement. The debates lasted to the end of the final session. The agreement to enlarge the Jewish Agency was accepted by a vote of 230 to 30.

In New York, on August 2, Marshall was boarding the SS Majestic, bound for Europe, to attend the meeting that would result in the formation of the enlarged Jewish Agency in Palestine by the Sixteenth Zionist Conference. He was in high spirits. He was a representative, even the leader, of the non-Zionist Jews who were now important to the Zionist Organizations of Europe and America in their quest to establish an effective Jewish Agency. All of the years of meetings, conflicts, fiery oratory, debates, extensive letters, and far reaching travel had finally led to agreement. This union of Jews in Europe with Jews of America, the place where the promise of economic and religious freedom was being fulfilled, offered hope for a similar future for the Jews of Palestine.

Zurich was to be the culmination of almost seven years of negotiations between the non-Zionists and the Zionist Organizations. It began in 1923 when Chaim Weizmann decided that Marshall and Felix Warburg were key to his efforts to find Jewish support that went beyond membership in the Zionist organization.

Some five thousand persons who would participate in the Sixteenth Zionist Congress would approve the agreement for an enlargement of the Jewish Agency board. They would be witness to the signing of documents, which would pledge the support of the American leaders for the Jews who had emigrated to Palestine and needed the support of world-wide Jewry, especially the affluent Jews of America, England, France and other European nations. That support from the non-Zionists was conditional on the enlargement of board of The Jewish Agency of Palestine to include the appropriate number of representatives of the Zionists and the non-Zionists, who together would guide the agency.

Aboard the *Majestic*, Marshall wrote e letter to his friend, merchant and philanthropist, Julius Rosenwald:

> While on board ship I have had plenty of time for rest and meditation as well as for reading and writing. It may enable me the better to grapple with problems which have called me away from my occupation. I trust that I may accomplish my objective, that of bringing about unity among the forces of Israel. In my judgment the time is propitious for such a solution of what has heretofore been regarded by many as an insuperable problem.[1]

In this letter, Marshall asked for support for the education of American Jews, but with hindsight one might sense an ominous undercurrent in two of his statements, "We, who have staggered under a heavy load, are getting older. *We would like to feel before we pass from this earthly scene that the Seminary is provided for.*"

Earlier in the letter he said, "… *Alas! the overwhelming need of the unfortunate Jewish victims of the War necessitated the abandonment of this project (education consolidation) in order that the Jews of Eastern Europe should not be exterminated.*"

"EXTERMINATED" (?) An unusual characterization for Marshall to use in connection with the life of the Jewish People. He often spoke and wrote forcefully, but this was a highly dramatic expression even for Marshall.

Marshall was not totally separated from his family as he sailed to Europe. His son-in-law Jacob Billikopf accompanied him on the ship. Billikopf's wife Ruth and their two children were at the Marshall family's summer home, Knollwood, in Saranac Lake, New York as was Marshall's youngest son George. Marshall's eldest son James and his family were in New York City. His son Robert was somewhere in Alaska in pursuit of his vocation and avocation as an explorer and environmentalist, having graduated from the New York State College of Forestry in Syracuse and from Johns Hopkins University.

On board the *Majestic* was Marshall's friend Maurice Hexter, an important member of the American group traveling to the meeting in Zurich. In his autobiography Hexter chronicled the last-minute hitches in the solution of the "insuperable problem":

> While we were still on the boat to Europe we had a wireless from Weizmann saying he was having great difficulty in getting the Zionists to go along on the fifty-fifty split on the Jewish Agency makeup. Our response, by return wire: It's fifty-fifty or we go home. We got to Paris ... and at the request of Warburg and Marshall I was sent on ahead to Zurich and Weizmann. He said he was getting a lot of resistance from his diehards, who felt the equal split would dilute their influence; that they were selling out for the money which non-Zionists were expected to produce. Weizmann was impressed by the firmness of the non-Zionist contingent and promised to redouble his efforts. He then did a lot of arm twisting via telephone and a few hours later called me to say the fifty-fifty principle was safe. Only then did I phone Paris to say it was all right to go to Zurich and the conference.[2]

At 2:40 a.m. on August 9, 1929 The Sixteenth Zionist Conference, convened in Zurich's Tonhalle (Town Hall), finally approved by a vote of 230 to 30 the "Pact of Glory"[3], enlarging the Jewish Agency to include both Zionists and non-Zionists in its council. Weizmann said, "We Zionists were always convinced that after the attainment of our political goal our function would have to be changed. The Jewish National Home, which already exists, is no longer merely a Zionist affair; it is a Jewish affair ..."[4]

Six hours after the conclusion of the Zionist Congress, the first meeting of the Council of the Jewish Agency opened. It was a huge assembly that filled the hall to capacity with opening addresses in Hebrew, Yiddish, French, German and English from a number of famous people representing England, France, Poland, Germany, and Palestine. The pivotal addresses were from Marshall and Weizmann.[5]

Marshall's theme was, "We are one God. We are one People. We are United":

> This is indeed the most extraordinary assembly that I have ever attended. There are gathered here Jews from four continents, from many countries. And of every kind of opinion that the human mind can possibly avow. We have come together to witness the union of Zionists and non-Zionists for the upbuilding of Palestine.... We may have different conceptions of what should be done and of what should not be done, but of one thing I am

confident, that as a result of the organization of the enlarged Jewish Agency, Palestine will be rebuilt.

> We have got to the point where talk is valuable at times, but where work is valuable always. Men who know one another never hate each other ... Let us not get around the tables and speak, but let us get around the tables and think. The fact that the Zionists and the non-Zionists have agreed does not change the laws of nature. Do not expect miracles. We have great practical problems before us which must be solved in a great, broad, practical, business-like way.[6] We have been united through Dr. Weizmann's statesmanship.

Then it was Weizmann's turn to speak: "We are today in the presence of facts whose compelling force no one can escape, and before which all the differences of opinion, all the party antagonisms which have grown up in Jewry in the course of time appear small." Two of these facts were the British Mandate and what the world expects from the Jews in building Palestine. "A third is the change which has come over the Jewish world since the War. Palestine today appears in a wholly different light."

He concluded:

> We entertain the hope that this joint work will also have a unifying effect and be the starting point for a great new unity in Israel ... on a common love for that Judaism ... which is proving itself ... as the great sovereign life force, which we all wish to serve humbly and faithfully. May what we are creating here redound to the honor of the Jewish name and be a blessing to future generations. In that sense we believe that this day will remain enshrined as an historic date in the annals of Jewish history.[7]

Through five sessions, concluding on August 14, the soon-to-be-members of the Council of the Jewish Agency discussed texts, rules, and forms and methods of operation of the Agency. Weizmann was elected president of the council, and Marshall was elected to be chairman.

On August 14, in a final ceremony, Weizmann and Nahum Sokolow appended their signatures to the agreement for the World Zionist Organization, followed by Marshall and the representatives of Jewish communities in twenty countries, including Palestine appended their signatures.[8]

The New Palestine of New York reported in its August 25, 1929 issue:

> After Weizmann and Marshall had signed, these two Jewish leaders, the first a chemist of high standing, a distinguished leader of a great movement, and

the other a distinguished constitutional lawyer, a man of 73 years (sic), noted for his calm logic, threw aside all pretence of unemotionality and embraced and kissed each other with unashamed tears in their eyes. Other delegates could be seen doing the same, Zionists and non-Zionists indiscriminately celebrated the historic occasion with a lavish display of affection.

Notes

1 Reznikoff VII Pgs 889-894
2 Hexter
3 The Pact of Glory—The document establishing the creation of the enlarged Jewish Agency. From a Weizmann speech in 1928
4 CW Pg 223
5 The American Hebrew August 16, 1929
6 The Pact of Glory
7 Ibid
8 CW Pg 221

The Death of Louis Marshall

Good spirits prevailed among the American non-Zionists after the Agency meetings ended. As Cyrus Adler later wrote to a friend about Marshall, "During the formation of the Jewish Agency meeting he was never more forceful and at the same time suave and diplomatic. It was a marvel to all the Europeans there that a man past seventy could have this wonderful vigor and clear resonant voice. He was very happy over the result." The day after the meeting concluded, Adler continued, "a group of us at a table in the lobby of the hotel sat up telling stories and enjoying stories. That night he was taken ill but we knew nothing about it. Mr. Billikopf, who was in the next room, was awakened by him but they both thought it was an ordinary attack of indigestion and it was not until noon that the doctors were summoned. There were of our party [the non-Zionists] Emanuel Libman of New York and Solomon Solis-Cohen of Philadelphia, two most eminent diagnosticians ..."[1]

Maurice Hexter wrote about the events of that morning:

> ... an unusual delegate got on the elevator of the Baur-au-lac Hotel [in Zurich].
>
> He was Dr. Emanuel Libman one of the world's great diagnosticians *the* consulting physician at Mt. Sinai in New York. A floor below, Louis Marshall and I got on the elevator. Dr. Libman gave Marshall a warm hello and a quick glance. When we reached the lobby Libman pulled me aside. 'I'm afraid I have very bad news for you,' he said. 'What is it?', I asked. 'Louis Marshall will be dead within forty-eight hours.'
>
> From almost anyone else ... such a firm mortal prophecy would have been greeted with incredulity. But Dr. Libman's reputation preceded him. Once in the United States he attended a dinner at which President Harding was a guest. After a fast glimpse of the president, Dr. Libman told a friend that Harding would die within six month. He did.

Hexter continued:

> It was a panicky moment. I promptly phoned a prominent local physician and asked if he could be available on short notice. It was a matter of life and death. He agreed. After breakfast, an hour after Dr. Libman made his dread prophecy, Louis Marshall fell ill and had to be removed to a hospital. [2]

The doctors initially suspected an abscess on the gall-bladder and possible involvement of the pancreas. Four or five days after an operation his temperature "vanished." Marshall asked for Adler to visit him. "I went over, sat at his bedside," Adler wrote. "He grumbled a bit said that it was the first time in his life that he had been bothered with nurses. I told him that his physicians had said that while he had been a very poor lawyer he had been less [than] a good patient, at which he laughed and quoted some of the things his mother used to say to him in like circumstances. I left with a heavy heart, but still with a sort of feeling that his vigorous constitution would somehow pull him through."

Marshall, somewhat improved, was still in the hospital. Adler must have assumed that he could go home. He was on the ship sailing for home when he received a radio message from Dr. Libman saying that Marshall showed "marked improvement." However, two days later there was another message that another operation was necessary.

On September 3, Marshall appeared to be improving. Doctors a suggested that Marshall should extend his stay in Zurich to recuperate, but he would have none of it. He had too much to attend to, particularly the completion of the building to house the merger of Congregation Emanu-El and Temple Beth-El in New York. There were briefs, papers and details to be addressed pertaining to Adirondack resources, the rights of Negroes and Indians and of course, the Jewish Agency.

Though he showed improvement his anxious family sent telegrams.

From James Marshall to Jacob Billikopf: "Advise if father or Dr. Libman wants me. Love from all. James." From George Marshall: "(8/29) with Ruth Knollwood negotiating job will sail if helpful everyone well affection father = george=." Within a few days James sailed for Europe.

On September 5 Cyrus Adler received a telegram from Morris Waldman, the executive secretary of the American Jewish Committee: "Greatly distressed to convey following cable just received Marshall's office Ulceration of stomach due to progressive gangrene pancreas necessitates immediate operation Condition critical." The next day there was another telegram from Waldman to Adler:

"Message received from James Marshall. Rallied since second Operation Pulse improved Still critical Chances better today.

Then, a relapse was reported in the *Syracuse Journal*. On September 9 it reported on its front page, "LOUIS MARSHALL SINKING, BLOOD TRANSFUSION GIVEN IN EFFORT TO SAVE LIFE. 73-Year-Old Patient Fails to Rally Following Serious Relapse Over Week-end." *The Syracuse Herald* carried a similar story, accompanied by a picture of Marshall in his law office with the words, "In Valley of Shadow" and "Hope Fading For Famous Syracusan."

On September 11, 1929 at 3 p.m., Louis Marshall died in Zurich. With him were his son James, his sister Bertha Rosenberg, his wife's sister Beatrice Magnes, and Rabbi H. G. Enelow of Congregation Emanu-El. Zurich was the scene of his last achievement, of his beloved adherence to Judaism, testimony to his belief in America, in its Constitution, in the sacredness of the Torah, and in the sanctity of family.

On September 20 *The American Hebrew* reported:

> The day after his death the Jewish Community of Zurich held a funeral service for Marshall followed by a procession of mourners to the train to Paris. In Paris "the train was met by a group of distinguished European Jews. Among them was Rev. Dr. Joseph Silverman of New York, rabbi emeritus of Congregation Emanu-El, a life long friend of the departed Jewish leader. The Jewish community of Paris requested an opportunity to pay final tribute to Mr. Marshall. However, the members of the family, honored the spirit of their father and brother, who despised display ... begged to be left alone with their dead."[3]

The American Hebrew reported on September 27:

> The ship that brought Mr. Marshall to New York arrived on September 20th, met by a delegation from Congregation Emanu-El, as well as New York Mayor James Walker, Police Commissioner Whalen and various Jewish Organizations, including some of Marshall's close friends, eight patrolmen, members of the Shomrim Society of the Police Department carried [the coffin] to a waiting motor hearse and then borne through the streets between rows of motorcycle police to the newly completed Congregation Emanu-El building that was intended to be first used on the forthcoming Rosh Hashanah, but was hastily completed for Louis Marshall's funeral. The coffin was draped with an American flag when it was carried off the ship, and rose-covered when it was brought into the chapel and then into the sanctuary

by four police lieutenants and two captains, all members of the Shomrim Society. Sixty patrolmen acted as ushers.[4]

In Syracuse, the board of trustees of Temple Society of Concord, Marshall's life-long synagogue, adopted a resolution:

> Mr. Marshall needs no eulogy, as his deeds are his everlasting monument, yet it is but fitting that we, the members of the Society of Concord, should give expression to our deep sorrow and grief at this time. Our loss is a personal one, as he loved his native city and remained a member of our congregation to the end. A few months ago he helped us celebrate our ninetieth anniversary and appeared in the best of health and spirits.
>
> The world has lost an eminent citizen. One guided by a rare sense of justice. Always ready to do battle for the political and religious rights of oppressed minorities. Like the prophets of old he drew his inspiration from the Old Testament and fulfilled to the utmost the teachings of Micah: do justly, love mercy and walk humbly with thy God. His death leaves a void hard to fill.

Marshall's family, many honorary pall bearers, co-workers, friends from New York, and from Syracuse were among the more than 3,000 people in the sanctuary of Congregation Temple Emanu-El, all there by invitation. Outside on Fifth Avenue, some 25,000 people stood in honor of Marshall.

The service contained selections from the Psalms, other readings from the Bible, and a choral rendition of "What is Man" from the Yom Kippur memorial service. There was no eulogy, as requested by the family, presumably in keeping with Mr. Marshall's wishes.

Louis Marshall was laid to rest in Salem Field Cemetery in Brooklyn, beside Florence, his wife.

Marshall's death evoked tributes upon tributes, obituaries in abundance. His life and achievements were meticulously recounted in the press throughout the United States and Europe from the newspapers in Syracuse to *The New York Times*. Of the array of languages lauding him one of the most touching tributes was in Yiddish from *The New York Morning Journal*:

> *Louis Marshall, aless Yid, Filantrope, Jurist und Statsmann.*
>
> A great warm Jewish heart, yesterday in Zurich, far from his home, gave its last beat. The leading personality of American Jewry has gone back to the *avot*, forefathers, rich in accomplishment for his people and fellow human beings, a few days after when, in the city of his last breath, he helped create

the greatest work of our present history, the Jewish Agency, which took upon itself the building up of the Jewish Home in Eretz Ysroel. Even though he referred to himself as a non-Zionist, he worked like the best Zionist. When he let his voice be heard—that his group was ready to help build up our ancestral home, it stirred every Jewish heart widely. He died at a great historic moment, leaving as his legacy the Jewish Agency. [5]

From the editorial in *The Syracuse Post-Standard*:

'The great city is that which has the greatest man or woman.'

So wrote Walt Whitman. And it is with like feeling, at the death of Louis Marshall, that Syracuse gives thought to one of its most notable sons, one who not only was born a Syracusan and spent his boyhood in this city and here worked out the career of his early manhood. But who, tho his course of broader achievement took him elsewhere in his later life, never laid aside his love and loyalty for his old home town, never ceased to come back to it with devotion, and as opportunities continued to come, increasingly gave to it and its interests his earnest and effective service.... Always it was justice which was his goal. Justice to all who were in need of justice. But justice in a special way ... to the people who, like himself, were of Jewish origin. His was an intense Americanism. And to that he coupled an equally intense devotion to, and helpfulness for, his fellow Jews, wherever found ... His was a conspicuous and unshakeable belief in the American constitution. To him it was the most notable and enduring of the structures set up for the government of mankind.

Let it be said of him that he was a man who helped humanity, a man who confronting injustice was unafraid, a man whose hand was ready to lift a load or strike a blow, if a blow was necessary for the lessening of misfortune or oppression a worker in our common life who because he was a worker became a leader, a man who crowded his years with service for the benefit of those about him—*altogether an eminent American citizen whom a multitude will hold in grateful remembrance.*

The last picture (a snapshot) of Louis Marshall taken in Zurich 1929.
(The Universal Jewish Encyclopedia)

Notes

1 Adler V2 Pg 174
2 Hexter Pgs 56-7
3 AH September 20, 1929 Pg 521
4 AH September 27, 1929 Pg 541
5 This is a portion from a long tribute to Louis Marshall in *The New York Morning Journal,* September 12, 1929, translated from Yiddish by my friend the late Dr. Gustave Pearlman.

After Marshall's Death

On September 11, 1929 Congregation Emanu-El of the City of New York at a special meeting of the Board of Trustees made the following resolution:

"Congregation Emanu-El is overwhelmed with grief by the news of the death of its beloved and revered President, LOUIS MARSHALL … By the death of LOUIS MARSHALL, American Israel has lost the most powerful religious influence in the Jewish laity. His memory will be an inspiration and a blessing to the whole household of Israel. His life was a magnificent illustration of the opportunities our beloved country offers to a great soul."[1]

On the same day, the Joint Distribution Committee in New York City passed a resolution that began: "Louis Marshall has been gathered to his fathers. For many years we have leaned upon the great strength that was in him. His voice is stilled. The Tribune of his people is no more, but his memory and inspiration will ever consecrate us to carry on the work to which he gave himself."[2]

While Marshall's sudden illness and death were simultaneous with the deadly rioting in Palestine, it was likely that Marshall had been spared any knowledge of that turmoil. Marshall's leadership and his spirit had served to motivate the non-Zionists' greater support for Palestine. Without a strong leader, that motivation deteriorated.

"While the shock of the August disturbances (in Palestine) still reverberated through the Jewish world, a second blow stunned it at this time. Louis Marshall, elected Chairman of the Agency Council passed away. Had Marshall lived a few more years the glittering promise those days of awe ushered in at the founding of the extended Agency might have been promoted by the non-Zionist elements with somewhat less reluctance than they began to evince. The level of thinking and planning among the group dropped appreciably after Marshall's passing."[3]

His death left others, notably Felix Warburg and Lord Melchett of Britain, who had labored with Marshall to help create the Enlarged Jewish Agency and were now the leaders, faced with the October 1929 economic crash that diverted attention and money from Palestine, as well as assaults to come on the Jews of Germany. They proved to be insurmountable.

After Marshall's Death

For Chaim Weizmann it was a difficult period. He feared that he would lose support from the British Government for its commitments in the Balfour Declaration. The Zionist Organization needed more members, money and political skills, and all required time to come to fruition. As it turned out, despite the number of non-Zionist members of the Jewish Agency's board, the Zionists controlled the Agency.

Julius Rosenwald honored his friend's memory. He responded to the letter that Marshall had written to him while on board the ship sailing for Europe in July, 1929. He gave $500,000 to a newly established Louis Marshall Memorial Fund at the Jewish Theological Seminary.

◆   ◆   ◆

Five years later on September 14, 1934, *The American Hebrew* published "The Louis Marshall Memorial Issue", with the headline on page one: "Louis Marshall Died Five Years Ago". It was replete with memories, tributes and testimonies from more than sixty people, Gentile and Jew. There were many references to the loss of a great leader in that time of trouble from 1929 to 1934:

> Some men loom so large in the life of their generation that their passing seems like the vanishing of a mountain from a familiar vista. Marshall towered over the Jewish life of his day, and there are no compeers to compare with him ...
>
> Would that Marshall were here today, able to bring the powers of his personality to the problems we confront. Certain it is that his efforts and his voice would achieve much where more puny spirits fail.
>
> Marshall was above all the Defender of his People. No other American Jew has ever served so long, so loyally, so valiantly, as he. There surged within his heart in overflowing measure that ancient idealism of Israel ...
>
> *Marshall was the one man in the world the Jews could least afford to lose.*
>
> *Would that his voice might be heard among us today*[4]

In 1939 a number of his friends gathered, acknowledging that in the ten years since his death, the world for the Jews had changed radically. Louis Marshall was missed, yet a biography of his memorable achievements would not be published for almost seventeen years. In 1957, two volumes of his selected papers and addresses, edited by Charles Reznikoff, were published. The title, apt but incomplete, was *Louis Marshall, Champion of Liberty.*

The crowds outside of Temple Emanu-El, New York, that attended the Marshall funeral cortage
(Louis Marshall Memorial Edition, The American Hebrew, September 14, 1934)

Notes

1 AJA-MC
2 AJA-MC
3 CW "Toward the Precipice" chapter by Julian Louis Meltzer Pg 226
4 AH

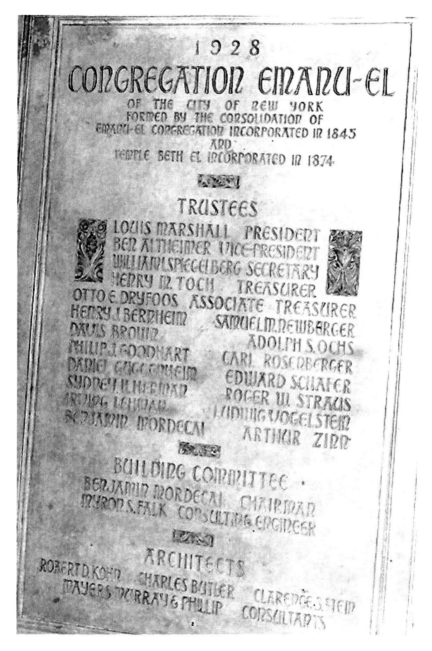

This tablet is in the entrance way of Congregation Emanu-El

Afterword

After spending a day in the American Jewish Archives, my wife and I were wandering in a hallway of Hebrew Union College when a gentleman and a lady stopped to ask if they could be of help. We said no, and after another question, we said that we were doing research on Louis Marshall. We thought that the gentleman was Dr. Alfred Gottschalk, Chancellor Emeritus of the school, and as he walked away he waved an arm, and said,

"Ah, there were giants in those days!"

Louis Marshall would not suffer any insult or discriminatory action toward the Jewish People from Jewish or non-Jewish sources. A fellow Reform Jew once chided him for the time and support that he devoted to the Conservative and Orthodox movements. He responded:

"Nothing Jewish is alien to me!"

Marshall's Family

When Marshall died in 1929 at 72, his children were adults.

James was a noted attorney in New York City, a member of their Board of Education and active in community affairs. In 1920 he married Lenore Guinzburg who was a poet, novelist, essayist, and human affairs activist. She died in 1971. For her work on behalf of poets, in 1975 "The Lenore Marshall Award" for the year's most outstanding book of poetry was established. James and Lenore's two children are Ellen Scholle of White Plains, New York and Jonathan Marshall of Phoenix, Arizona. In 1974 James married Eva Garson. James was 90 when died in 1986.

Ruth Marshall married Jacob Billikopf in 1918. They had two children: David and Florence. At 36 Ruth died of cancer, as her mother Florence did, and as her daughter, also named Florence would at a similar young age. Billikopf was well-known for his social work, labor arbitration and philanthropy, and was apparently a tireless worker for he is frequently mentioned in the World War1 and succeeding activities of Marshall. In 1929 he was in Zurich when Marshall was struck by his terminal illness. In the 1930s he worked intensively to bring Jewish refugees to the Unites States. Interestingly, Marshall usually referred to him as "Billikopf."

Robert Marshall became a prominent wilderness and environmental activist. He received a bachelor's degree from the New York State College of Forestry at Syracuse, a master's degree in forestry from Harvard University, and a doctorate from Johns Hopkins University. His interest in the environment stemmed from his father, and his knowledge and intimacy with the Adirondack Mountains of New York State began with the family's summer residence at Lower Saranac Lake. He became a leading American conservationist and visionary for wilderness preservation throughout America, and there is a testament to him in Montana, a forest named, the "Bob Marshall Wilderness." In 1939, Robert at thirty-eight, died unexpectedly of heart failure. He never married.

George received two Ph.D. degrees in economics, and was greatly interested in conservation. With Bob he became one of the "46ers", those who climbed the 46 major peeks of the Adirondacks. He became an economist, and was a staunch advocate of civil rights. He married Elisabeth Dublin in 1930, and. they had two children, Roger and Nancy Louise. He died in year 2000 at 96.

Marshall's Law Partner

Sam Untermyer played a key role in Marshall's life. They were college classmates and became law partners in New York City when Untermyer invited Louis to join the firm that became Guggenheimer, Untermyer and Marshall. Louis lived with Sam's family when he moved to New York in late 1894. He met Sam's young cousin, Florence Lowenstein, in 1895, and was married to her in May of that year. It may have been difficult for Marshall and Untermyer to practice law as partners. Louis was, as he termed it, a staunch Republican conservative, although he did many "liberal" things that may have disqualified him as a strict "conservative." Sam Untermyer was not only a Democrat; he was a well-known "liberal" until he died in 1940. In 1912, their partnership ended and Sam left the law firm, although the name of the firm was not changed.

When Louis died, Sam's reaction was in several news reports:

"Louis and I have been bosom friends since boyhood for over fifty-two years. We attended law school together. I brought him to New York from Syracuse and he lived with me until his marriage into my family. His love and devotion for the people of our race was beyond compare. No misfortune that befell them in any corner of the earth was too far away to be reached by his outstretched arms. The country has lost one of its most patriotic citizens and greatest constitutional lawyers; the Jews of the world have suffered the irreparable loss of their greatest champion. Words cannot begin to visualize that loss. A great soul has departed."

Henry Ford

Henry Ford survived Marshall and went his way as a great merchant, a loyal American, and alleged friend to his workers. When America entered World War II, his factories went on the war footing, as he made material for the war effort, and the profit from it. At that time, Ford was a friend of Charles Lindbergh, who's anti-Semitism was well known. Near the end of his life, Ford allegedly said that he had nothing against the Jews, that he employed thousands of them. That may have been so, but Henry Ford never wavered in his belief even after the commencement of the World War. In a 1994 article in *American Heritage*, a report of Robert Rosenbluth's ordeal titled "The American Dreyfus," Ford told an acquaintance there really wasn't any war going on: "There hasn't been a shot fired. The whole thing has just been made up by the Jew bankers."

In 1945 the founder of the Ford Motor Company sat with one of Ford's first woman executives, Josephine Gomon, to view newsreels of what the soldiers discovered in a liberated concentration camp. She wrote: "When he saw the piles of corpses and the few walking skeletons, he was then and there taken by one of the several massive strokes he suffered. He never recovered his mind or physical strength."

In 1927 Ford ordered that support of anti-Semitic publications be discontinued. However *The Protocol of the Elders of Zion* lived on, and is still marketed in Europe and Asia. After Ford died on April 7, 1947 at 83, the Ford companies and the Ford family established a policy of good relations with the American Jewish community and with the State of Israel.

Bibliography and Other Sources

Adams
The Incredible Era
Samuel Hopkins Adams
Houghton Mifflin Company
Boston, MA 1939

Adler
I Have Considered the Days
Cyrus Adler
Jewish Publication Society of America
Philadelphia, PA 1941

Adler—Letters
Cyrus Adler Selected Letters
Jewish Publication Society of America
Philadelphia, PA 1985

Adler-Schiff
Jacob H. Schiff: His Life and Letters
Doubleday Page & Co.
New York, NY 1928

AH
American Hebrew and Jewish Tribune
212 Fifth Avenue
New York, NY

AJA-LF
Leo Frank File
American Jewish Archives
Cincinnati, OH

AJA-MC
The Jacob Rader Marcus Center
American Jewish Archives
Louis Marshall Collection
Cincinnati, OH

AJYB	*The American Jewish Year Book 1909-1910, 1911-1912* The Jewish Publication Society of America The American Jewish Committee New York, NY
AJYB V21, AJYB V22	*The American Jewish Year Book 1919, 1920* The Jewish Publication Society of America, Edited for The American Jewish Committee Philadelphia, PA
Bailey	(Re: The Passport Question) *America Faces Russia* Thomas A. Bailey Cornell University Press 1950
Bailey	(Re: Return to Blessed America) *and the Lost Peace* Thomas A. Bailey The Macmillan Company New York, NY 1945
Baldwin	*Henry Ford and the Jews: The Mass production of Hate* Neil Baldwin Public Affairs New York, NY 2001
Black	*The Transfer Agreement* Edwin Black Macmillan Publishing Company New York, NY 1984
CW	*Chaim Weizmann, a Biography By Several Hands* Edited by Myer W. Weisgal and Joel Carmichael Atheneum New York, NY

CW [A]	*Trial and Error The Autobiography of Chaim Weizmann* Schocken Books New York New York, NY 1966
Davies	*The Rosenbluth Case: Federal Justice on Trial* Rosemary Reeves Davies The Iowa State University Press Ames, Iowa, 1970
Davis	*Cyrus Adler At The Peace Conference* Essays in American Jewish History Cincinnati, OH 1958
Dawidowicz	*On Equal Terms* Holt, Rinehart and Winston New York, NY 1982
EJ	Encyclopedia Judaica Jerusalem, Israel 1972
Elbogen	*A Century of Jewish Life* Ismar Elbogen Jewish Publication Society of America Philadelphia, PA 1944
Feingold	*A Time for Searching 1920-1925* Henry L. Feingold Johns Hopkins University Press Baltimore & London
FWP	*Felix M. Warburg Papers* The American Jewish Archives Cincinnati, OH
Golden	*A Little Girl is Dead* Harry Golden The World Publishing Company Cleveland, OH 1965

Hexter	*Life Size* Maurice Hexter Phoenix Publishing West Kennebunkport, ME 1990
House & Seymour	*What Really Happened at Paris* *The Story of the Peace Conference* *1918-1919* Edward Mandell House and Charles Seymour, Ed. Charles Scribner's Sons New York, NY 1921
Janowsky	*The Jews and Minority Rights* Oscar L. Janowsky Columbia University Press New York, NY 1933
Murray	*The Harding Era* Robert K. Murray University of Minnesota Press Minneapolis, MN 55401
Oral History	*James Marshall to Elliott Sanger* The American Jewish Committee New York, NY
Others	Re: The Rosenbluth case: *The Ohio Gang,* Charles L. Mee, Jr., M. Evans & Company, Inc., New York *The First World War,* Martin Gilbert, Henry Holt & Company, New York, 1994 *Over There,* Byron Farwell, W. W. Norton & Co., New York, 1999
Oxford	*The Oxford History of the American People* Samuel Eliot Morison New York—Oxford University Press 1965

The Pact of Glory	A Pamphlet Published By The Allied Jewish Campaign New York, NY 1929
Poles	*The Poles* Stewart Steven Macmillan Publishing Co., Inc., New York, NY 1982
Reznikoff	*Louis Marshall Champion of Liberty* Edited by Charles Reznikoff Jewish Publication Society of America Philadelphia, PA 1957
S.J. Duncan-Clark	*History's Greatest War* S.J. Duncan-Clark Copyright 1920 by E. T. Townsend
Schiff	*Jacob H. Schiff: His Life and Letters* Cyrus Adler Doubleday, Doran & Company, Inc. *New York, NY 1928*
Strauss	*Men and Decisions* Lewis L. Strauss Doubleday & Company, Inc. Garden City, NY 1962
Urofsky	*American Zionism from Herzl to the Holocaust* Melvin L. Urofsky Anchor Press/Doubleday Garden City, NY 1975
Winter & Baggett	*The Great War* Jay Winter & Blaine Baggett Penguin Books USA Inc, New York, NY 1996

Acknowledgments

There are a number of people and institutions that have had a part in this creation. Before I get into acknowledging them, I want to express my sincere gratitude to Thomas A. Murray, Ph.D. who was the complete and invaluable editor of the book. Tom has been a friend, who readily joined with me to correct, revise, and critique the manuscript.

The episode in Jerusalem that I mentioned in the preface came about because of my friendship with Dr. Alan L. Berger. At that time Alan was the head of the Syracuse University Department of Judaic Studies, and his help in this and other instances through the years is greatly appreciated. I am especially grateful to him for arranging the meeting in 1988 with Dr. Moshe Davis. At the present time Alan is the Director of Judaic Studies, the Reddock Eminent Scholar Chair of Holocaust Studies of Florida Atlantic University in Boca Raton, Florida.

Sometime later I did meet Dr. Davis in New York City. In the course of a meeting and lunch he provided insight and encouragement. A bit later he sent me the pamphlet that he wrote about Cyrus Adler at the Versailles Peace Conference which was very useful in the *Versailles* chapter of this book.

The acting archivist of the American Jewish Archives in Cincinnati is Kevin Proffitt. From the time of my arrival at the Archives, he was [and still is] a guide, advisor and friend to me as I plowed through hundreds of items in the Marshall Collection. His staff was remarkably gracious and helpful to me in providing files, copies of material documents, and answering questions. They are a wonderful group, and I cannot thank them enough.

Not long after I began at the Archives, Dr.Gary P. Zola and Dr. Frederic Krome became key members of the Archives, and gave advice and friendship then andwhenever I've asked.

There is another relationship that has been part of this endeavor through the years. Stanley R. Alten, Ph.D. is a professor in the S. I. Newhouse School of Public Communications of Syracuse University, and is a friend and advisor who has guided me, listened to me and given tremendous advice through the years.

Research has taken me to the files of the Klau Library of Hebrew Union College, where I met David Tilles who graciously gave me guidance and advice. I visited the libraries of the Jewish Theological Seminary, Temple Society of Concord, the Onondaga County Library System in Syracuse, the New York City Public Library in Manhattan, and most significantly the Bird Library of Syracuse University and the College of Law library.

Within the Syracuse community there are a number of people who helped me.

A special thanks to Rabbi Daniel A. Jezer who is the rabbi emeritus of Congregation Beth Sholom-Chevra Shas in Dewitt, New York. He gently prodded me to go public with my study of Marshall by speaking at a Shabbat service. Rabbi Sheldon Ezring of Temple Society of Concord in Syracuse, New York arranged for a Friday night service in honor of Louis Marshall where I was invited to speak.

Tracy H. Ferguson, a renowned attorney, took a special interest in my effort. He was a law student in the nineteen-twenties and a member of Temple Society of Concord and he knew Mr. Marshall. When he offered his assistance to me, I told him that I was unable to connect with Congregation Temple Emanu-El in New York City. He said that he would contact a friend who was a board member of Emanu-El. He wrote to Susan M. Newhouse, wife of Donald Newhouse, and she immediately made arrangements to be my host on a tour of the illustrious synagogue. Within a few days we met in the foyer of the temple, and she guided me through everything on every floor. I especially enjoyed their lovely museum, and the very impressive board room where Mr. Marshall's picture is prominently displayed. Mrs. Newhouse was a very gracious host on a memorable day for me.

I greatly appreciated Tracy's role and his great interest. Sadly he became quite ill and passed away before we could have another discussion of Mr. Marshall.

Jeffrey Gorney is a writer and author who made important language and narrative contributions to several chapters.

I made several visits and calls to the library of the American Jewish Committee. They were quite productive thanks to Library Director Cyma Horowitz who was extremely cooperative and helpful. Several photographs from the AJC files were provided by her.

When I met with Dr. Moshe Davis he suggested that I call Maurice Hexter in New York City. I called him and met him at his office in New York. Mr. Hexter was then 99 years old. He told me that he was in Zurich for the Zionist Council to create the Enlarged Jewish Agency, in July and August 1929, and that he worked very closely with Marshall. He said that he was with Marshall on the hotel elevator with Dr. Libman the day after the Council ended. On that morning, when the doctor saw that Marshall was ill, he told Mr. Hexter, in private, that Marshall would die within a few days. As written in the chapter *The Death of Louis Marshall,* he was hospitalized later that day, and in several weeks he passed away. Mr. Hexter's autobiography, *Life Size* includes that episode just as he told it to me.

There are two friends in Syracuse who were not involved in the creation of the book, but have special interest in Louis Marshall. Richard Wilkins is an active participant in Jewish religious and social activities. In 2003 he wrote a letter to our local Anglo-Jewish paper wherein he said that 2006 would be the 150th anniversary of Marshall's birth, and that there should be some recognition of it in the Syracuse community. He was referred to me by a mutual friend who knew of my interest. We met, and set out to interest others. After a while we got together with Alexander Holstein, a leading member of the community. Rather quickly, and aggressively, we formed a committee of ten interested persons who eagerly joined with us. Over the next three years we devised a weekend symposium to take place in November 2006. The committee was wonderfully cooperative with Alex, Dick and I, as we communicated with many of the leading organizations. We were very fortunate to connect with Professor Mark A. Raider who was the Director, Center of Jewish Studies at the University of Albany in New York. He found Jewish history scholars and leaders to participate in lectures and discussions over a weekend. The keynote speaker was Dr. Jonathan Sarna of Brandeis University who joined with friends and colleagues in a delightful series of events.

The Syracuse Jewish Community Center had a special role in the commemoration stemming from 1910 when the Marshall family home was presented to the community. It served as host, contributor, and graciously provided secretarial and administrative help. Funds and much cooperation were provided by Temple Society of Concord, Syracuse University, SUNY School of Environmental Science,

Hillel at Syracuse University, and Syracuse University College of Law. All of the functions and lectures were open to the Syracuse community who attended the events in large numbers, and learned of Marshall's achievements. All in all, it was a suitable tribute to Mr. Marshall's life, and his life-long relationship with the city. Members of the family of Louis and Florence Marshall were invited, and we were delighted to have two grandchildren, two great grandchildren and several cousins attend. They appeared thrilled, grateful, and happily surprised at the warm welcome accorded to them.

James and Lenore Marshall had two children, Jonathan and Ellen. Throughout this endeavor I have spoken and corresponded with, but not met, Jonathan. I have met and corresponded with his sister Mrs. Ellen Scholle. They have been gracious and cooperative. I met Stephen R. Scholle, Ellen's son, in 2006 when we had the commemoration in Syracuse. In September 2007 he invited my wife and I to visit the family's summer home, Knollwood, on Lower Saranac Lake, New York. It was an opportunity to see the large home that the family held so dear for more than one hundred years. I am especially thankful to Stephen for the use of family photographs. That visit was a fitting conclusion to our adventures in this journey through the Marshall family saga.

Herbert Alpert
March, 2008

Index

A

Adler, Cyrus 15, 16, 17, 22, 26, 67, 68, 79, 91, 93, 102, 111, 168, 182, 199, 200, 215, 217, 219, 221, 225

B

Bennett, William S. 33
Botkine, Pierre 20
Brandeis, Justice Louis D. 43, 74, 77, 170, 177, 178, 223

D

Daugherty, Harry 124, 125, 126, 130, 131, 132, 133, 135, 136, 144
Dmowski, Roman 81, 82, 83, 84, 85, 86, 88, 98, 106

E

Elbogen, Ismar 105, 107, 108, 217

F

Ford, Henry vii, 120, 121, 122, 134, 135, 142, 143, 144, 148, 149, 150, 151, 152, 154, 155, 156, 157, 159, 160, 161, 162, 163, 164, 213, 216
Frank, Leo vii, 42, 56, 59, 60, 61, 62, 135, 215
Frank, Lucile 56
Friedman, Rabbi Benjamin 102, 107

G

Goldfogle, Henry 31

Goldstein, Jonah J. 130, 131

H

Harding, Warren G. 120, 121, 124, 125, 126, 136, 149, 199, 218
Herzl, Theodore 171, 172, 173, 219
House, Edward Mandell 218

L

Langhorne, Maurice 139
Lasker, Albert D. 61
Lauterbach, Edward 24
Lehman, Judge Irving 57

M

Marshall, Florence L. 37, 48, 49, 56, 168, 224
Marshall, Jacob ix, 2, 4, 8, 37, 39, 55
Marshall, Zilli Straus ix, 2, 4, 6, 7, 39, 55
Mond, Sir Alfred 186, 191
Morais, Rabbi Sabato 68

P

Pact of Glory 181, 183, 193, 194, 196, 198, 219
Paderewski, Ignace J. 81
Phagan, Mary 57, 59, 64, 65
Pothier, Roland 121, 127

R

Root, Elihu 22, 23, 25
Rosenbluth, Robert O. 121, 127, 128, 129, 130, 133, 138, 142, 144, 213
Ruger, Wallace and Jenney 10

S

Sazonov, M. 33
Schiff, Jacob H. 72, 215, 219
Slaton, John M. 63
Stolz, Benjamin 34
Stolz, Joseph 7, 12, 34, 110
Straus, Nathan 174

T

Thompson, L. L. 136

U

Untermyer, Samuel 10, 13

W

Watson, Tom 60, 61, 63, 65
Weizmann, Chaim x, 77, 153, 164, 174, 176, 179, 181, 194, 207, 216, 217
White, Andrew D. 32
White, Walter 65
Wilson, President Woodrow 68, 69, 74, 78, 80, 96, 97, 100, 101, 106, 112, 113, 114, 115, 117